Jackie Gosby

QBasic
for Beginners

Learning to program using the language included with every DOS 5.0 system

Manfred and Helmut Tornsdorf

Abacus

A Data Becker Book

Copyright © 1992   Abacus
                             5370 52nd Street, SE
                             Grand Rapids, MI 49512

Copyright © 1991, 1992 Data Becker, GmbH
                             Merowingerstrasse 30
                             4000 Duesseldorf, Germany

Edited by: Scott Slaughter, Gene Traas, Robbin Markley

```
Library of Congress Cataloging-in-Publication Data
   QBasic for Beginners / H. Tornsdorf, M. Tornsdorf
       p.   cm.
   Includes index.
   ISBN 1-55755-132-4
     1. BASIC (Computer program language)  I. Tornsdorf, M.
   (Manfred), 1960-    .
   II. Title.
   QA76.73.B3T69     1991                              91-33654
   005.265--dc20                                            CIP

Printed in U.S.A.
10  9  8  7  6  5  4  3  2
```

Table of Contents

1. Introduction To QBasic

QBasic was developed by Microsoft especially for MS-DOS computers.

Since the different PCs usually conform to a standard, called the industrial standard, *QBasic* can be used on any DOS computer. That means that you can write programs, then share them with your friends, and - more importantly - you can also use programs written by other people.

QBasic is a further development of the programming language, GW-BASIC, which was part of earlier versions of MS-DOS for a long time. *QBasic* is much easier to use and more efficient. Beginners will find helpful menus making it much easier to use.

QBasic also uses an intelligent editor, checking each line for proper syntax and providing hints on correcting the error.

The *QBasic* Editor offers an easy and convenient way to enter a program, since it is a full-screen editor similar to a word processor. This makes *QBasic* a lot handier for creating large programs.

Although you can still use line numbers (for reasons of compatibility with other BASIC language programs), they are no longer necessary in *QBasic*. *QBasic* can use programs created with the GW-BASIC language. This makes it easier to switch over to using *QBasic*.

If you want to convert your *QBasic* programs to stand alone programs that don't require the *QBasic* interpreter to run, you can buy Microsoft's QuickBASIC. Then you can transform the completed programs into an EXE program which runs independently. QuickBASIC is more powerful than *QBasic* and is compatible with *QBasic*.

1.1 Your Keyboard and QBasic

Before we begin, we assume you have some basic knowledge of a PC and the capabilities of MS-DOS. If you're not familiar with them, refer to Abacus' *PC and Compatible Computers for Beginners* and *MS-DOS for Beginners*.

These books include tips & tricks on handling diskettes, searching, copying and deleting files, changing in the current drive and operations with the hard drive, etc.

Since *QBasic* is capable of operating on a PC compatible, one subject which might create a problem for you as a beginner is the keyboard. This is because of the different styles and appearances of the keyboard.

1.1.1 Keyboard layout

Some beginner books may describe the different keys that can be used, but on your keyboard it may look slightly different. For example, it may refer to a (Return) key, but on your keyboard it's called the (Enter) key.

If you have a problem identifying a key, refer to the following table. It displays a list of the different key assignments used in this book and how they might appear on your keyboard.

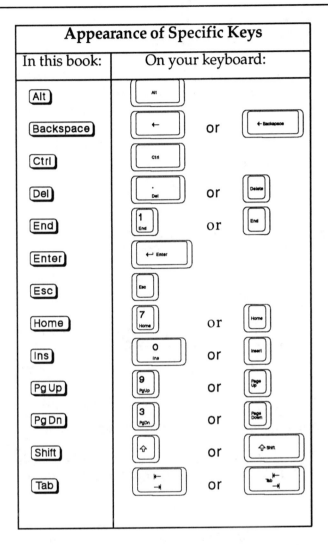

Appearance of Specific Keys	
In this book:	On your keyboard:

If you have trouble locating these keys, or any keys discussed throughout this book, check the manuals supplied with your computer.

1.2 How To Use This Book

Throughout this book you'll notice icons in the left margin. These icons tell you what to do, whether to read, note important information or type something at your computer's keyboard.

The reading icon shows that the following section of the text can be simply read.

The note important information icon points out paragraphs that contain important information.

The program listing icon indicates that the following text is a listing of a computer program.

Commands, options and buttons appear in bolded text

Any words appearing in bolded text (e.g., **Open...**) refer to the commands and options in the *QBasic* menu bar.

QBasic keywords

QBasic keywords appear in uppercase letters (e.g., PRINT). You can type keywords in either uppercase or lowercase.

New terminology

Programs and the first citation of new terms appear in *italics*.

In the program listings, note the ¶ character that appears at the end of the program lines. This character indicates when you are to press the [Enter] key. We're using the ¶ character in the program listings because some of the program lines are too long to fit the format of this book.

2. The QBasic Program

We'll provide information on the *QBasic* program itself in this chapter.

2.1 Starting QBasic

You must first install *QBasic* before you can create your BASIC programs. If you installed all files provided with MS-DOS 5.0 on the hard drive and the DOS directory is in the search path, you can easily start the *QBasic* program.

If *QBasic* is not in a directory defined by your search path, you must make the directory containing *QBasic* the current directory. It's a good idea to put *QBasic* and the programs created with it in a separate directory, such as:

```
\QBASIC
```

Starting from DOS prompt

To start *QBasic* from the system prompt in the command interpreter, type the program name:

```
QBASIC [Enter]
```

Starting from DOS Shell

To start *QBasic* from the DOS Shell, select the **MS-DOS QBasic** program item in the program list area:

5

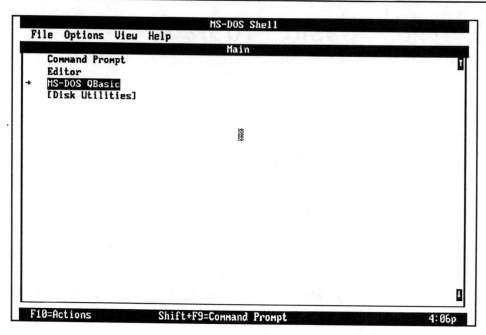

Select "MS-DOS QBasic" in the program list area

The following dialog box will appear:

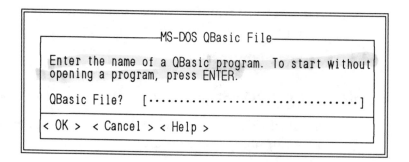

After you have created a *QBasic* program you can type the name of the program in the **QBasic File?** text box and press the Enter key to load the program.

Since we have not created a program, press the Enter key to load *QBasic*.

2.1.1 The QBasic startup screen

In a moment the startup screen of *QBasic* will appear:

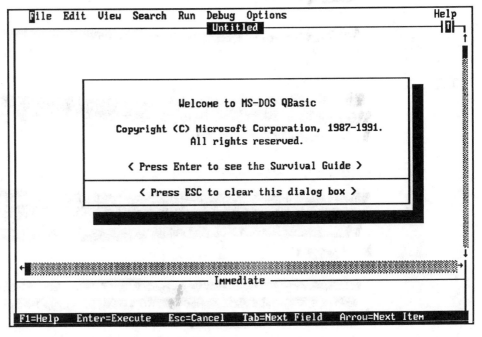

The QBasic startup screen

The *Welcome to MS-DOS QBasic* dialog box appears in the middle of the screen. Press Esc to clear this dialog box from the screen.

2.1.2 The QBasic windows

Notice that the top row of the screen displays the *menu bar*. This horizontal bar displays different *QBasic* menu names. You can use the menus to choose the *QBasic commands*. We'll discuss the individual menus and commands in Section 2.3.

The next line is the *title bar*. It displays the name of the program currently in the memory. If a program has not been loaded yet, the title bar displays "Untitled". This is the default screen you always see when starting *QBasic* without entering any optional parameters.

The View window

The area where you type your program is called the *View window*. It takes up the greatest amount of space on your screen.

You can split the View window into two horizontal sections. This allows you to view or edit two parts of a program simultaneously.

To split the window into two sections, press the Alt + V key combination to select the **View** menu. Then press the P key to select the **Split** command.

Expanding the View window

You can change the size of the active window. Press F6 to move from the top window to the bottom window or the Shift + F6 key combination to move from the bottom window to the top window.

Press the Alt + + key combination to expand the size of the View window one line at a time. Then to reduce the size, press the Alt + − key combination.

You can maximize the size of the View window by pressing the Ctrl + F10 key combination. Press this combination again to return the View window to its normal size.

The Immediate window

Below the View window is the *Immediate window*. You can use this area to enter one line commands directly. The computer executes these commands as soon as you press the Enter key.

Opening the Immediate window

To type a command, you must make the Immediate window the active window by pressing the F6 key. Notice that the cursor is now blinking in the Immediate window. Press the F6 key again to return to the View window.

The Immediate window is a good location to test a certain idea you have for a part of the main program. Use the direction keys to place the cursor anywhere on the first line.

You can enter as many lines as you wish in the Immediate window. However, *QBasic* will only keep the most recent ten lines in memory. After you enter the tenth line, the Immediate window is scrolled up one line.

Since the Immediate window is primarily for testing programs, you cannot directly save program code written in the Immediate window. You must first copy and paste the code to the View window.

Expanding the Immediate window

Since you can normally only see two or three lines of code in the Immediate window, press the [Alt] + [+] key combination to expand the size of the Immediate window.

Press the [Alt] + [-] key combination to reduce the size of the Immediate window.

You can maximize the size of the Immediate window by pressing the [Ctrl] + [F10] key combination. Press this combination again to return the Immediate window to its normal size.

The status bar

At the bottom of the screen is the *status bar*. It displays information about the selected menu. If no menu has been selected, the commands displayed in the status bar can be selected by pressing the appropriate function key or with your mouse.

The lower right corner displays the line and column number of the cursor location. This is handy when working on lengthy programs.

2.1.3 The QBasic scroll bars

The View window is bordered by two *scroll bars*. One scroll bar is on the right side of the View window and the second scroll bar is at the bottom of the scroll bar (above the Immediate window).

These scroll bars are particularly useful in larger programs. Notice the dark rectangle inside the scroll bars. This is the *scroll box*. Its position within the scroll bar indicates which section of the file is currently displayed.

If the scroll box is at the top of the scroll bar, the start of the file is currently displayed. If it is in the middle of the scroll bar, you are seeing the middle portion and if it's at the bottom, the area contains the last part of the file.

You must use a mouse to use the scroll bars to scroll through your program listing. Use the mouse to click on the scroll arrows that appear in the scroll bar.

You can even move the scroll box with the mouse. Place the mouse pointer on the scroll box and press the left mouse button. As you move the mouse pointer, notice how the scroll box moves with the mouse pointer.

The contents of the program are displayed in the View Window as you move the scroll box.

Although the scroll bars are not accessible by the keyboard, you can use the ⬆ or ⬇ direction keys to move through the file one line at a time. Press (PgUp) and (PgDn) to scroll the entire screen contents up or down by one screen.

The horizontal scroll bar on the bottom of the screen works exactly like the vertical bar, except that it moves horizontally. Use the key combinations (Ctrl) + (PgDn) to move right and (Ctrl) + (PgUp) to move left.

2.2 The QBasic Menus

2.2.1 Selecting a menu

Press [Alt] to select the menu bar. Notice that the appearance of the menu bar has changed. You can now press any of the highlighted letter keys to display a particular menu.

It's even easier to select menus with the mouse. Point to the desired command and click with the left mouse button.

If a command has three periods after the command "...", the command is not executed when you press [Enter]. Instead, a dialog box appears where you enter additional information. Pressing [Esc] will cancel a menu selection or input to a dialog box.

Using shortcut keys

You can use the *shortcut keys* to copy and paste text in *QBasic*. Shortcut keys are selected keys or key combinations you can use to choose a specific menu item or command. If a shortcut key is available, it will appear at the right edge of the menu.

For example, when you open the **Edit** menu, notice that four of the commands can be accessed by using shortcut keys:

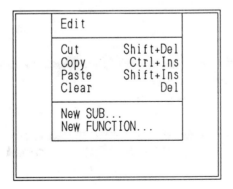

```
 Edit

 Cut       Shift+Del
 Copy       Ctrl+Ins
 Paste     Shift+Ins
 Clear           Del

 New SUB...
 New FUNCTION...
```

One example of a shortcut key combination we'll use often is the the [Shift] + [F5] key combination for the **Start** command in the **Run** menu.

The menu bar displays the titles for each of the menus. These titles are **File, Edit, View, Search, Run, Debug, Options** and **Help**. Various commands are available only at specific times and some commands open dialog boxes for further input.

2.2.2 Using the direction keys

You can use the ⊡ and ⊡ direction keys to open the menus, while the ⊡ and ⊡ direction keys can be used to select a menu. Press one of the direction keys to highlight the desired command and press ⟨Enter⟩ to execute the command.

The direction keys are located in different places on different keyboards. They're usually four separate keys identified by direction arrows. The direction keys may also be located on the numeric keypad.

2.2.3 Using the mouse

You'll find that using a mouse is quick and easy in *QBasic*.

Opening a menu

To open a menu, simply point and click the desired menu name. You can also select individual commands by clicking the left mouse button.

Working with the windows

Click anywhere inside a window to make it active. You can expand or reduce the size of a window by clicking on the title bar and dragging it up or down.

To maximize the size of the window, click on the | ↑ | maximize box in the upper right corner of the window. Alternatively you can double-click anywhere on the title bar.

The following sections discuss how the menus are organized and the functions of each command.

Scrolling text

Move the mouse pointer to the scroll box inside the scroll bar. Press the left mouse button and as you move the mouse pointer, the scroll box moves with the mouse pointer.

2.2.4 Using dialog boxes

Many *QBasic* commands will display a *dialog box*. These commands require additional information to complete a task. You confirm information or answer prompts by responding with some type of input in a dialog box.

Selecting parts of a dialog box

To select the different parts of the dialog box, press the Tab key until the cursor is located at the desired area. You can also use shortcut keys. Press the Alt key and notice how certain letters become highlighted. Press the letter key corresponding to the item of the dialog box you want to select.

Unlike selecting a menu item, you must keep the Alt key held down to use a shortcut key. You can press the Enter key at any point to accept the <OK> button. To clear a dialog box without making any changes, press the Esc key.

2.3 The QBasic Commands

The *QBasic* commands are displayed when you select a menu. In this section we'll introduce the menus, commands and their functions. We'll provide more specific information on the commands in later chapters.

2.3.1 The File menu

Press the [Alt] + [F] key combination to open the **File** menu.

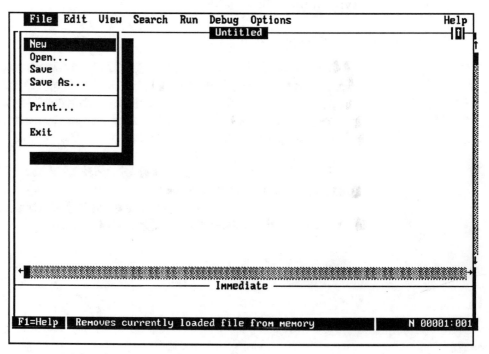

The QBasic File menu

The **File** menu displays the following six commands:

New   Clears the View window and therefore the program listing. Select this command when you want to type or load a new BASIC program.

Open...   Loads an existing program from a diskette or hard drive to QBasic memory. The program contents are then displayed in the View window.

You can also use this command to display all files and directories on your hard drive.

Save   Saves a BASIC program which was previously saved. If you haven't saved the program yet, this command prompts you to enter a program name.

Save As...   Saves a new file or saves an existing file with a new name that you can specify.

- **Print...**   Prints the entire program or a marked block of text on the printer.

Exit   Leaves *QBasic* and returns to the MS-DOS Shell or DOS command line.

 You should always exit *QBasic* before switching off or resetting your computer. If there are still programs in the View window which were not saved, a dialog box appears which asks if these programs should be saved.

Since we have not yet created programs that should be saved, press the ⌈Tab⌋ key to select the **<No>** button and then press ⌈Enter⌋.

If you wanted to return to *QBasic* by cancelling the **Exit** command, select the **<Cancel>** button.

Return to DOS

You'll return to the command area of DOS after quitting *QBasic*, if you started QBasic from DOS.

You can then enter DOS commands to load other applications or switch off your computer.

Return to DOS Shell

If you started *QBasic* from the DOS Shell, you'll return to the DOS Shell screen.

You can then press the ⟨Alt⟩ + ⟨F4⟩ key combination to exit to the command area of DOS or continue to work in the DOS Shell.

2.3.2 The Edit menu

The **Edit** menu contains commands that you can use to move, change or delete program lines. Press the ⟨Alt⟩ + ⟨E⟩ key combination to open the **Edit** menu.

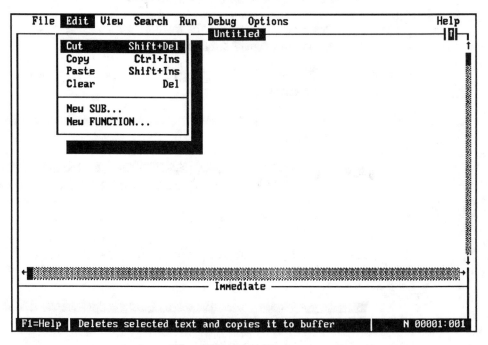

The QBasic Edit menu

The *QBasic* **Edit** menu has the following six commands:

Cut   Deletes a marked block of text from the file and copies the block to the buffer.

Copy   Copies a marked block from the file to the buffer.

Paste   Inserts the contents of the buffer (block of text) at the position of the cursor in the file.

Clear   Deletes a marked block of text. The deleted text is not copied to the buffer.

New SUB...
> Creates a new SUB procedure.

New FUNCTION...
> Creates a new FUNCTION procedure.

2.3.3 The View menu

Press the [Alt] + [V] key combination to open the **View** menu.

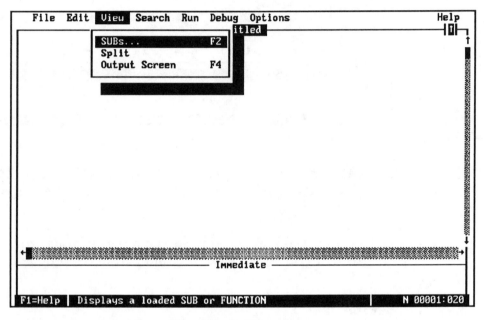

The QBasic View menu

The *QBasic* **View** menu displays the following three commands:

SUBs...   Displays a loaded SUB or FUNCTION.

Split   Divides the View window into two sections to view or edit two parts of a program simultaneously.

Output Screen
> Displays the output screen.

Selecting the **SUBS** command displays a dialog box containing the names of SUB and FUNCTION procedures which may be edited or deleted.

17

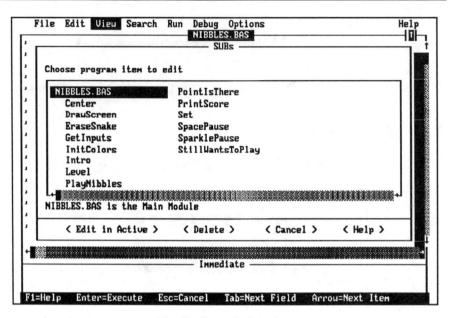

The SUBS dialog box

A subprogram is a separate program (called a subordinate program). *QBasic* withdraws these procedures into a separate part of memory.

However, these procedures remain part of your program and are ready to run along with the main part of the program.

2.3.4 The Search menu

The Search menu allows you to locate and replace specific text strings in your program.

For example, one use of the Find... command may be to move to a later section of the program to locate a specific text string.

Press the Alt + S key combination to open the **Search** menu.

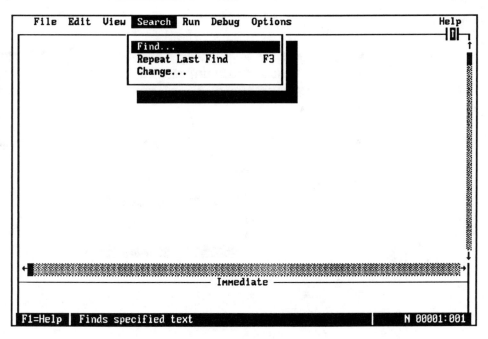

The QBasic Search menu

Find...   Use this command to search for any character string in the file. You can specify whether to search for upper or lowercase letters, search for the target string as a separate word (and not as a part of another word) as well as the target string itself.

Repeat Last Find
         Use this command to repeat the last search.

Change...   Use this command to replace any character string in the document with any other string of characters.

2.3.5   The Run menu

The Run menu displays the commands you'll use to start your program, correct (debug) mistakes while you program and continue program execution from an interrupted point in the program.

Press the [Alt] + [R] key combination to open the **Run** menu.

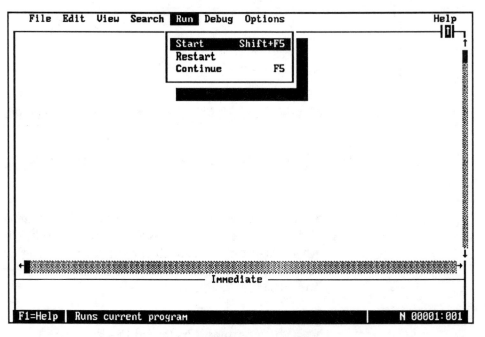

The QBasic Run menu

Start   Runs the program in the active window.

Restart   Resets all variables to zero in order to prepare for single-stepping through a program while debugging. The first executable statement in the program is highlighted.

Continue   Continue execution of a program after it has stopped. **Continue** is often used after a breakpoint. Variables are not cleared. The program continues running with the line immediately following the breakpoint.

2.3.6   The Debug menu

Press the ⌨Alt + ⌨D key combination to open the **Debug** menu.

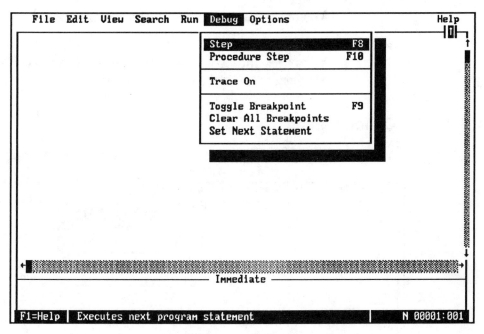

The QBasic Debug menu

Step   Executes next program statement. This command allows you to move through a program one statement at a time while checking for program logic errors.

Procedure Step
            Single steps through a program, but executes procedure calls as a single statement.

Trace On   Highlights each statement in a program as it is executed. This allows you to view the flow of a program.

Toggle Breakpoint
            Use this command to turn breakpoints on and off. Breakpoints are markers in your program. To turn on a breakpoint, move the cursor to highlight the line where you want the breakpoint, then press F9 or choose this command. Your program will run until it reaches this line, then it will stop, allowing printing variables in the

21

Immediate window or single stepping from this point forward.

Clear All Breakpoints
Removes all previously defined breakpoints.

Set Next Statement
Changes the program execution sequence so that the next line executed is the one the cursor is on.

2.3.7 The Options menu

Press the Alt + O key combination to open the **Options** menu.

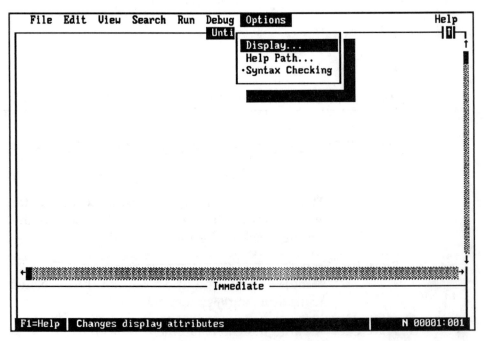

The QBasic Options menu

Display... Use this command to select the color of the screen background and the color of the font (the foreground), to switch the scroll bar on and off and to set the distance between the tabs.

Help Path... Use this command to specify the path for the directory containing the QBASIC.HLP file.

Syntax Checking
This command is a toggle for turning syntax checking on and off. When activated, *QBasic* checks each line entered for syntax errors, formats the line and translates the line to executable form if the syntax is correct.

2.3.8   The Help menu

Press the [Alt] + [H] key combination to open the **Help** menu.

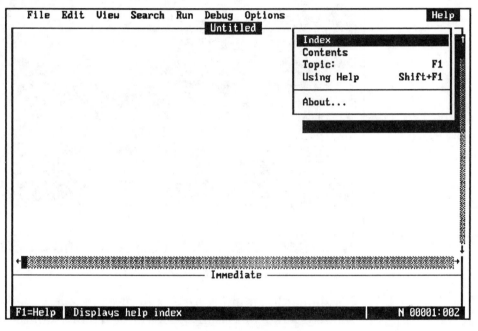

The QBasic Help menu

Index   Displays the Help index.

Contents   Displays **Help** table of contents. This command provides a guide organized according to topics to information in *QBasic* Help.

Topic   Displays information about the *QBasic* keyword the cursor is on.

Using Help   This displays information on getting general help. **Using Help** may be the most important command of *QBasic* to understand. The information provided in the help screens covers virtually every subject about *QBasic* you're likely to encounter.

About...   This displays information about the copyright and version number of *QBasic*.

If you select the **Index** command, the following dialog box will appear:

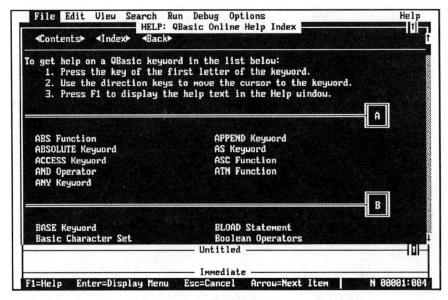

```
 File  Edit  View  Search  Run  Debug  Options                Help
                  HELP: QBasic Online Help Index
  ◄Contents►  ◄Index►  ◄Back►
 To get help on a QBasic keyword in the list below:
    1. Press the key of the first letter of the keyword.
    2. Use the direction keys to move the cursor to the keyword.
    3. Press F1 to display the help text in the Help window.

                                                              ┌───┐
                                                              │ A │
                                                              └───┘
  ABS Function             APPEND Keyword
  ABSOLUTE Keyword         AS Keyword
  ACCESS Keyword           ASC Function
  AND Operator             ATN Function
  ANY Keyword

                                                              ┌───┐
                                                              │ B │
                                                              └───┘
  BASE Keyword             BLOAD Statement
  Basic Character Set      Boolean Operators
 ──────────────────────────── Untitled ─────────────────────

 ──────────────────────────── Immediate ────────────────────
 F1=Help   Enter=Display Menu   Esc=Cancel   Arrow=Next Item │  N 00001:004
```

The QBasic Help index

It's similar to an index for a book. Press the key corresponding to the first letter of the BASIC keyword. For example, press ⓟ to look for help on the PRINT statement. Then use the direction keys to move the cursor to the desired keyword and press the (Enter) key.

You can also receive context-sensitive help at any time. The term "context-sensitive" help refers to the program or application that displays on-screen information relating to the command, statement or function that you selected.

Use the direction keys to move the cursor to the keyword for which you require more information. Then press the (F1) key. This is also the same as selecting the **Topics** command in the **Help** menu.

3. Your First QBasic Program

When *QBasic* is first started, the cursor is located in the upper left corner of the View window. The blinking cursor indicates that *QBasic* is ready to accept your input. This is the location where you can enter *QBasic* statements.

3.1 The PRINT Statement

Let's try using the *QBasic* PRINT statement. Although it sounds like a command to use a printer, the PRINT statement sends output to the screen. *QBasic* uses a different statement to send output to the printer.

To try out this new *QBasic* statement, you should now tell *QBasic* that you want to create a new program. This is done by pressing the Alt + F key combination to open the **File** menu:

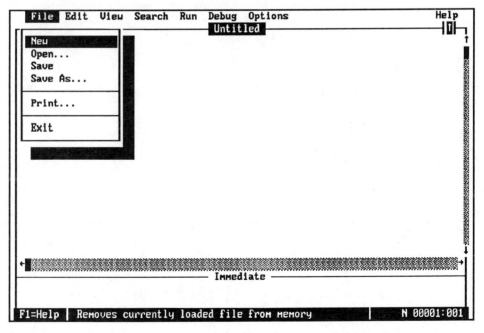

*Selecting the **New** command from the **File** menu*

Then select the **New** command from the **File** menu. Press the Enter key. Now you can create a *QBasic* program. Type the following line:

```
PRINT "Hello, how are you?"
```

Press the Alt + R keys to select the **Run** menu. Then press the Enter key to select the **Start** command.

Notice in the **Run** menu that you can also select the **Start** command with the Shift + F5 key combination. This is an example of a *shortcut key*. By using this key combination, you do not have to first select the **Run** menu. Since the Shift + F5 key combination is a faster method of starting a program, we'll always refer to this shortcut key to start a program.

The *QBasic* screen (View window) is replaced with the following *output screen*:

```
Hello, how are you?




   Press any key to continue
```

You can see that *QBasic* executed your statement and "printed" the word "Hello, how are you?" on the output screen. You have just learned your first *QBasic* statement.

Notice the following line on the output screen:

```
Press any key to continue
```

This message will appear near the bottom of your output screen. It will appear at the conclusion of many *QBasic* programs. The purpose of this message is to inform you that *QBasic* has terminated (ended) the program. You can press any key to return to the View window.

The term "any key" is somewhat misleading because not all keys will work (for example, [Shift]). It's usually easiest to press the [Enter] key to return to the View window.

Once you return to the View window you can switch back to the output screen without restarting the program by pressing the [F4] key. This has the same result as selecting the **Output Screen** command in the **View** menu.

3.1.1 Examples of using PRINT

The following are some examples of how to use the PRINT statement properly:

```
PRINT
```

A PRINT statement by itself (with no *arguments*) will print a blank line.

```
A = 10
PRINT A
```

In this example, PRINT is used to output the value of a variable. The number 10 appears since we previously set A=10.

```
PRINT "A"
```

In this example, the character A appears between quotation marks. This statement will print the character A but not the value of the variable A.

All characters enclosed in the quotation marks are printed exactly as they appear.

PRINT A*B

This example shows you that calculations can also be performed within a PRINT statement. First the product of the variables A*B is evaluated and then it is printed.

If you want the PRINT statement to perform calculations, do not enclose the argument inside quotation marks. Otherwise, QBasic will print the argument and not the result of the calculation. We'll discuss this in more detail later in this chapter.

PRINT A, B

This example illustrates the ability of the PRINT statement to print several variable values from one statement. The comma suppresses the carriage return/linefeed after printing the value of the first variable ("A" in this example).

The comma also positions the cursor to the next *print zone*. *QBasic* divides each line of your output screen into 14 character long tab positions. If a comma is placed between two variables, the second variable is printed at the start of the next tab, at the 15th column on the screen line. If you separate several variables by commas, these variables are printed at the successive TAB positions.

PRINT A; B

This example illustrates the effect of the semicolon. The semicolon suppresses the carriage return, linefeed and the tab function. The characters are printed in succession in the order in which they appear in the PRINT statement. This makes it possible to include descriptive text following the value of a variable.

PRINT "B";20

This example is similar to the previous example. It shows you how to display descriptive text before the value of a variable. In this case, the descriptive text is the name of the variable whose value follows. Again, the semicolon separates the descriptive text from the variable.

```
PRINT "A EQUALS";A
```

This example simply shows you that the descriptive text can be of any arbitrary length. The text can be as detailed as you wish.

3.1.2 Additional comments concerning PRINT

Some additional comments on using the PRINT statement:

The trailing blank space

When printing numbers, note that a position, called the *trailing blank space,* is always reserved for the sign (+/-) of the number. If the number is positive, a space is placed before the number. If the number is negative, a minus sign is placed before the number. The numbers 10 and -10 always occupy the same number of positions.

Text wrap

If your PRINT statement line is longer than 80 characters, *QBasic* will display the first 80 characters on one row and the remaining characters on the following line.

If you typed a PRINT statement line that is longer than 80 characters following another PRINT statement in the same line, *QBasic* would fill the first 80 columns of one row and then continue to the next row.

You'll learn more about the uses of the PRINT statement in later programs.

3.2 Editing Your QBasic Program

The *QBasic* editor offers an easy and convenient way to enter a program, since it is a full-screen editor similar to a word processor. This makes *QBasic* a lot handier for creating large programs.

3.2.1 Editing text

You can type *QBasic* statements just as you would using a text editor.

QBasic offers the following two modes to insert text:

Overtype mode

Each character you type replaces (or overwrites) any character under the cursor. Therefore, you do not have to delete existing text before inserting the new text.

Insert mode

Each character you type appears at the current cursor position. Any characters that are to the right of the cursor are shifted to the right.

You can toggle between these two modes by pressing the [Ins] key or the [Ctrl] + [V] key combination. Notice how the cursor changes to a blinking box.

You can tell which mode you are in by observing the cursor. If the cursor is a rapidly blinking line beneath the characters, *QBasic* is in Insert mode. If the cursor appears as a small blinking box, then *QBasic* is in Overtype mode.

Inserting text

Make certain that you're in the insert mode. Press the [Ins] key if necessary. We want to insert "good friend," after "Hello" in the program from the previous section.

To do this, use the direction keys to place the cursor above the "h" in "how". Type the text you want to insert (in this example "good friend"). Notice how the existing text is shifted to the right. Make certain to insert a space after "friend".

Press the (Shift) + (F5) key combination to start the program. The output screen now appears like this:

```
Hello, how are you?
Hello, good friend, how are you?




   Press any key to continue
```

Overwriting text

Now we want to delete part of the line. Press the (Enter) key to return to the View window. Make certain that you're in the overtype mode. Press (Ins) key or the (Ctrl) + (V) key combination if necessary so that the cursor is a small blinking box.

We want to overwrite the existing text with new text. For example, change the output line "Hello good friend" to "Hello best friend".

To do this, use the direction keys to place the cursor on the letter "g" in "good" and type "best".

After inserting the new text, press the (Shift) + (F5) key combination. The following message appears on the output screen:

```
Hello, how are you?
Hello, good friend, how are you?
Hello, best friend, how are you?




Press any key to continue
```

Press the Enter key to return to the View window. The overtype mode must be switched off by pressing the Ins key again.

3.2.2 Cursor movement

You can *scroll* (move around) the View window by using the four direction keys. You can use other keys to move the cursor through the View window. For example, pressing:

Ctrl + ←	Moves the cursor one word to the left
Ctrl + →	Moves the cursor one word to the right
Ctrl + Enter	Moves to the beginning of the next line
Ctrl + Home	Moves to the top of the program
Ctrl + End	Moves to the end of the program

For a complete list of editing keys, refer to Section 3.2.8.

3.2.3 Copying program lines

Before continuing, we'll need to clear the View window of this program. Press the Alt + F key combination to open the **File** menu and press the Enter key to select the **New** command.

When the following dialog box appears:

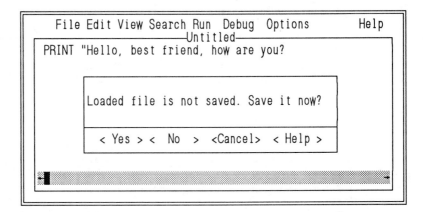

press the <kbd>Tab</kbd> key to select the <No> button and press the <kbd>Enter</kbd> key.

Another similarity to a wordprocessor is *QBasic's* ability to copy several program lines which were identical or similar.

Notice in the following program that four lines are identical:

```
CLS
INPUT chars$
chars$ = chars$ + chars$ + chars$
chars$ = chars$ + chars$ + chars$
chars$ = chars$ + chars$ + chars$
chars$ = chars$ + chars$ + chars$
PRINT chars$
```

Therefore, instead of typing all seven of these lines, type only the first three lines:

```
CLS
INPUT chars$
chars$ = chars$ + chars$ + chars$
```

Then we'll need to select the text we want to copy. Move the cursor back to the beginning of the third line.

Selecting text

Press the <kbd>Shift</kbd> key and press the <kbd>End</kbd> key. Notice that the entire line is highlighted starting at the location of the cursor. This line is called the *selected text*:

```
   File Edit View Search Run  Debug  Options          Help
                          Untitled
 CLS
 INPUT chars$
 chars$ = chars$ + chars$ + chars$
```

Be careful when selecting text. If you accidently press a key when text has been selected, that character will replace that text on the View window. You cannot "undo" or replace the lost text. The best method to "de-select" text is to press the (Esc) key.

Press the (Ctrl) + (Ins) key combination to select the **Copy** command. This command copies the selected line to a temporary buffer called the *Clipboard*. (Alternatively, you could press the (Alt) + (E) to select the **Edit** menu and (C) to select the **Copy** command.)

Use the (↓) direction key to move the cursor to the beginning of the next line:

```
   File Edit View Search Run  Debug  Options          Help
                          Untitled
 CLS
 INPUT chars$
 chars$ = chars$ + chars$ + chars$
```

Press the (Shift) + (Ins) key combination to select the **Paste** command. (Alternatively, you could press the (Alt) + (E) to select the **Edit** menu and (P) to select the **Paste** command.) The line is pasted from the Clipboard to the View window:

```
   File Edit View Search Run  Debug  Options        Help
                    ──Untitled──
 CLS
 INPUT chars$
 chars$ = chars$ + chars$ + chars$
 chars$ = chars$ + chars$ + chars$




 ▮
```

A line copied to the Clipboard remains there until it is replaced by new text. Therefore, the line we copied in the Clipboard can be pasted as often as needed. Use the ⬇ direction key to move the cursor to the beginning of the next line. Press the (Shift) + (Ins) key combination again to add the next line:

```
   File Edit View Search Run  Debug  Options        Help
                    ──Untitled──
 CLS
 INPUT chars$
 chars$ = chars$ + chars$ + chars$
 chars$ = chars$ + chars$ + chars$
 chars$ = chars$ + chars$ + chars$



 ▮
```

Then move the cursor to the next line and press the (Shift) + (Ins) key combination one more time to add the final copy of the line:

```
    File Edit View Search Run  Debug  Options        Help
                         Untitled
  CLS
  INPUT chars$
  chars$ = chars$ + chars$ + chars$
  chars$ = chars$ + chars$ + chars$
  chars$ = chars$ + chars$ + chars$
  chars$ = chars$ + chars$ + chars$
```

Then add the final program line to complete the listing:

```
PRINT chars$
```

```
    File Edit View Search Run  Debug  Options        Help
                         Untitled
  CLS
  INPUT chars$
  chars$ = chars$ + chars$ + chars$
  chars$ = chars$ + chars$ + chars$
  chars$ = chars$ + chars$ + chars$
  chars$ = chars$ + chars$ + chars$
  PRINT chars$
```

Did you notice how much easier and faster it was to copy and paste identical program lines?

In this example, we asked you to type the following line once:

```
chars$ = chars$ + chars$ + chars$
```

However, you could have saved even more time by copying "chars$" once and then pasting it between the plus signs.

You cannot keep adding text in the Clipboard because whatever you place in the Clipboard replaces the previous contents.

If you paste text in an existing line, any characters that are to the right of the inserted text are shifted to the right. You can either press the (Enter) key to add additional lines or press (Enter) at the end of the newly inserted line.

3.2.4 Deleting text

You can delete program lines just as easily as adding program lines.

Using the (Del) key

You can use the (Del) key to insert letters in a program line. For example, if you type "PWINT" instead of "PRINT", use the direction key to move the cursor above the "W". Press the (Del) key. This will move the text to the right of the cursor one character to the left.

Then switch to the insert mode (see Section 3.2.1) and press the correct key (in this example, the (R) key). Then the correct letter is inserted and the text to the right of the cursor is moved one character to the right.

Using the (Backspace) key

If you mistype a word (such as "PRRINT" instead of PRINT) use the direction key to move the cursor above the character immediately to the right of the mistyped letter. Press the (Backspace) key to delete the unnecessary letter.

The (Backspace) key moves the cursor one character to the left. It also moves the character the cursor is on and the remainder of the line one position to the left, erasing the character previously located to the left of the cursor.

Deleting program lines

You have two methods of deleting an entire program line from your program. One method deletes the program lines and moves the following program lines up to replace the deleted lines. The other method deletes the program lines but does not shift the succeeding program lines.

If you want to shift all subsequent program lines up one line, select the line you want to delete. Place the cursor at the beginning of the line. Press the (Shift) key and press the ⊕ key to select the entire line. Notice that the cursor is now blinking in the first row of the next line.

For example, we selected the "PRINT This is a test" line in the following program:

```
   File Edit View Search Run  Debug  Options        Help
                    ─Untitled─
  CLS
  PRINT "This is a test"
  INPUT chars$
  chars$ = chars$ + chars$ + chars$
  chars$ = chars$ + chars$ + chars$
  chars$ = chars$ + chars$ + chars$
  chars$ = chars$ + chars$ + chars$
  PRINT chars$


  ◄█▒▒▒▒▒▒▒▒▒▒▒▒▒▒▒▒▒▒▒▒▒▒▒▒▒▒▒▒▒▒▒▒▒▒▒▒▒▒▒▒▒►
```

Press the (Del) key to delete this line. You could also press the (Alt) + (E) + (T) key combination to select the **Edit** menu and the **Cut** command. The program lines in the View window would then appear like the following:

```
   File Edit View Search Run  Debug  Options        Help
                    ─Untitled─
  CLS
  INPUT chars$
  chars$ = chars$ + chars$ + chars$
  chars$ = chars$ + chars$ + chars$
  chars$ = chars$ + chars$ + chars$
  chars$ = chars$ + chars$ + chars$
  PRINT chars$


  ◄█▒▒▒▒▒▒▒▒▒▒▒▒▒▒▒▒▒▒▒▒▒▒▒▒▒▒▒▒▒▒▒▒▒▒▒▒▒▒▒▒▒►
```

In certain cases you may want to delete a line but not move the text up one line. Select the line you want to delete. Place the cursor at the beginning of the line. Press the (Shift) key and press the (End) key to select the entire line. Notice that the cursor is now blinking next to the last character in this line:

```
     File Edit View Search Run  Debug  Options        Help
                          Untitled
    CLS
    PRINT "This is a test"
    INPUT chars$
    chars$ = chars$ + chars$ + chars$
    chars$ = chars$ + chars$ + chars$
    chars$ = chars$ + chars$ + chars$
    chars$ = chars$ + chars$ + chars$
    PRINT chars$



    ◄█                                                      →
```

Press the (Del) key to delete this line. You could also press the (Alt) + (E) + (T) key combination to select the **Edit** menu and the **Cut** command. The program lines in the View window would then appear like the following:

```
     File Edit View Search Run  Debug  Options        Help
                          Untitled
    CLS

    INPUT chars$
    chars$ = chars$ + chars$ + chars$
    chars$ = chars$ + chars$ + chars$
    chars$ = chars$ + chars$ + chars$
    chars$ = chars$ + chars$ + chars$
    PRINT chars$



    ◄█                                                      →
```

Deleting multiple lines

You can delete multiple lines whenever necessary. Select the lines you want to delete by moving the cursor to the beginning of the first line. Press the (Shift) key and press the (↓) key to select all the

desired lines. For example we want to delete the following three
program lines:

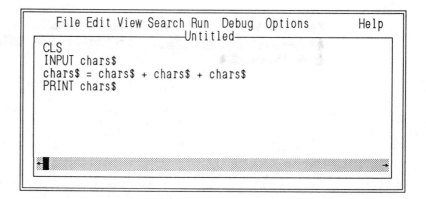

Once the lines are highlighted, press the ⟨Del⟩ key. Now the View
window looks like the following:

```
  File Edit View Search Run  Debug  Options          Help
                    ─Untitled─
  CLS
  INPUT chars$
  chars$ = chars$ + chars$ + chars$
  PRINT chars$



  ▐█░░░░░░░░░░░░░░░░░░░░░░░░░░░░░░░░░░░░░░░░░░░░░░░░░░░░▌
```

Deleting part of a program line

If you want to delete part of the line, follow the same steps as
above. Place the cursor at the location where you want to begin
deleting text. Select the text you want to delete by pressing the
⟨Shift⟩ key and pressing the ⟨→⟩ key until the desired text is
highlighted. You do not need to press the ⟨→⟩ key for each letter;
QBasic will "repeat" the keystroke when you keep the key held
down.

For example, we want to delete "This is a test" in the following
line:

```
      File Edit View Search Run Debug  Options        Help
                          ─Untitled─
 CLS
 PRINT "This is a test"
 INPUT chars$
 chars$ = chars$ + chars$ + chars$
 chars$ = chars$ + chars$ + chars$
 chars$ = chars$ + chars$ + chars$
 chars$ = chars$ + chars$ + chars$
 PRINT chars$


 ◄█▒▒▒▒▒▒▒▒▒▒▒▒▒▒▒▒▒▒▒▒▒▒▒▒▒▒▒▒▒▒▒▒▒▒▒▒▒▒▒►
```

When the text is selected, press the ⌊Del⌋ key to delete the highlighted text.

Be very careful when deleting text. Any text deleted with the ⌊Del⌋ key is not copied into the Clipboard. Therefore, you cannot undo or replace any text that is deleted by the ⌊Del⌋ key.

3.2.5 Additional editing capabilities

Moving program lines

You may need to delete a line from one part of the program and insert that line into another part of a program. Select the line you want to delete by moving the cursor to the start of the line. Then press the ⌊Shift⌋ + ⌊↓⌋ key combination. Then press the ⌊Del⌋ key.

For example, we want to move the selected line in the following program to the end of the program:

```
  File Edit View Search Run  Debug  Options        Help
                       Untitled
 CLS
 REM
 PRINT "Hello Charles"
 PRINT "This is your PC talking"
 PRINT "Isn't it a beautiful day?"
```

Then after pressing the Del key, the program lines below the deleted line are moved up one line:

```
  File Edit View Search Run  Debug  Options        Help
                       Untitled
 CLS
 REM
 PRINT "Hello Charles"
 PRINT "Isn't it a beautiful day?"
```

Then we'll need to move the cursor to the desired line to copy the deleted line from the Clipboard to the new location. Press the Shift + Ins key combination:

```
  File Edit View Search Run  Debug  Options        Help
                       Untitled
 CLS
 REM
 PRINT "Hello Charles"
 PRINT "Isn't it a beautiful day?"
 PRINT "This is your PC talking"
```

Inserting a blank line

If you need to insert a blank line in an existing program, simply move the cursor to the desired line and press the (Enter) key. For example, we want to insert a blank line as the second line in this program. First we need to move the cursor to the desired line:

```
       File Edit View Search Run  Debug  Options        Help
                            ─Untitled─
 CLS
 PRINT "This is a test
 INPUT chars$
 chars$ = chars$ + chars$ + chars$
 chars$ = chars$ + chars$ + chars$
 chars$ = chars$ + chars$ + chars$
 chars$ = chars$ + chars$ + chars$
 PRINT chars$



 ◆■▒▒▒▒▒▒▒▒▒▒▒▒▒▒▒▒▒▒▒▒▒▒▒▒▒▒▒▒▒▒▒▒▒▒▒▒▒▒▒▒▒▒▒▒▒→
```

Then to insert the blank line, we simply press the (Enter) key:

```
       File Edit View Search Run  Debug  Options        Help
                            ─Untitled─
 CLS

 PRINT "This is a test
 INPUT chars$
 chars$ = chars$ + chars$ + chars$
 chars$ = chars$ + chars$ + chars$
 chars$ = chars$ + chars$ + chars$
 chars$ = chars$ + chars$ + chars$
 PRINT chars$
 ◆■▒▒▒▒▒▒▒▒▒▒▒▒▒▒▒▒▒▒▒▒▒▒▒▒▒▒▒▒▒▒▒▒▒▒▒▒▒▒▒▒▒▒▒▒▒→
```

Inserting a new program line

When you need to add a line to an existing program, follow the steps previously discussed to insert a blank line. Move the cursor to the desired line and type the new program line. Notice that this moves the text in the existing line to the right.

When you have typed the new line, press the ⌷Enter⌸ key. The previous line will move down one line.

For example, we want to insert a REM statement in the following program. First we need to move the cursor to the desired line:

```
   File Edit View Search Run  Debug  Options        Help
                         ─Untitled─
  CLS
  PRINT "This is a test
  INPUT chars$
  chars$ = chars$ + chars$ + chars$
  chars$ = chars$ + chars$ + chars$
  chars$ = chars$ + chars$ + chars$
  chars$ = chars$ + chars$ + chars$
  PRINT chars$


  ◄█░░░░░░░░░░░░░░░░░░░░░░░░░░░░░░░░░░░░░░░░░►
```

Then the REM statement is typed at the cursor location and the existing line is shifted to the right:

```
   File Edit View Search Run  Debug  Options        Help
                         ─Untitled─
  CLS
  REM A funny programPRINT "This is a test
  INPUT chars$
  chars$ = chars$ + chars$ + chars$
  chars$ = chars$ + chars$ + chars$
  chars$ = chars$ + chars$ + chars$
  chars$ = chars$ + chars$ + chars$
  PRINT chars$


  ◄█░░░░░░░░░░░░░░░░░░░░░░░░░░░░░░░░░░░░░░░░░►
```

To separate the lines, press the (Enter) key:

```
    File Edit View Search Run  Debug  Options          Help
                        Untitled
   CLS
   REM A funny program
   PRINT "This is a test
   INPUT chars$
   chars$ = chars$ + chars$ + chars$
   chars$ = chars$ + chars$ + chars$
   chars$ = chars$ + chars$ + chars$
   chars$ = chars$ + chars$ + chars$
   PRINT chars$
```

3.2.6 Automatic syntax checking

QBasic checks the syntax of each line of your program after you press the (Enter) key. If *QBasic* cannot understand the line, a "Syntax error" message will appear on the output screen.

The smart editor of *QBasic* will flag certain syntax errors automatically. For example, type the following line:

```
PRINT DRAW
```

As soon as you press the (Enter) key, *QBasic* displays the following dialog box:

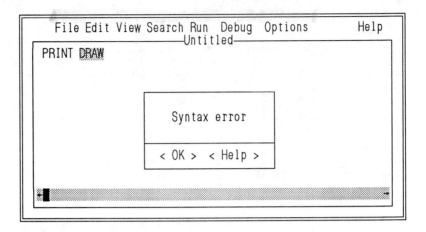

Other mistakes will not be immediately recognized by *QBasic*. For example, replace the following line:

```
PRINT DRAW
```

with this line (use the editing keys we discussed in the previous section):

```
PWINT "This is a test"
```

Press the Enter key. Although this is an obvious error to you, *QBasic* did not display the syntax error dialog box.

However, if you press the Shift + F5 key combination to start this program, the following dialog box appears on the screen informing you of a *syntax error*.

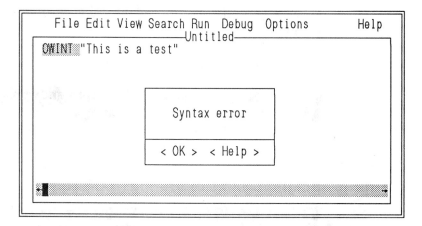

In the example above, typing "OWINT" did not result in a syntax error until we pressed the `Shift` + `F5` key combination. QBasic did not automatically flag it as a syntax error because OWINT was interpreted as a call to a subprogram named OWINT.

You can toggle the automatic syntax checking on and off by selecting the **Syntax Checking** command in the **Options** menu. *QBasic* will still recognize syntax errors with automatic syntax checking off but only when you run the program.

3.2.7 Automatic Text Formatting

As you worked with the `PRINT` statement earlier in this chapter, you may have noticed that *QBasic* is not case-sensitive. *QBasic* recognizes its own statements and functions and converts them to uppercase letters. For example, if you type:

```
Print "Hello, how are you?"
```

as soon as you press the `Enter` key, *QBasic* changes the line to:

```
PRINT "Hello, how are you?"
```

All *QBasic* keywords appear in uppercase letters when you press the `Enter` key. Also, *QBasic* automatically inserts a space before and after all BASIC operators. For example, if you type:

```
Print"Hello, how are you?"
```

as soon as you press the (Enter) key, *QBasic* inserts a space after the keyword:

```
PRINT "Hello, how are you?"
```

If you switch a variable name from uppercase to lowercase, *QBasic* automatically changes all instances of that variable name. For example, if you type the following variable:

```
key$ = "variable test"
PRINT key$
```

and then want to change the name to all uppercase letters, simply change one "key$" and *QBasic* automatically changes the remaining examples to "KEY$".

3.2.8 Summary of editing shortcut keys

In the last part of this section, we'll provide a summary of the keys or key combinations you'll use when editing your *QBasic* programs.

Scrolling the View window

Pressing	Affects the View window by:
(↓)	Moving down one line
(PgDn)	Moving down one page*
(↑)	Moving up one line
(PgUp)	Moving up one page*

Moving cursor

Pressing	Will move the cursor:
(Ctrl) + (Enter)	Beginning of the next line
(↓)	Down one line
(Ctrl) + (End)	End of the program
(End)	Moves to end of line

Ctrl + ←	One word to the left
Ctrl + →	One word to the right
Home	Start of line
Ctrl + Enter	Start of next line
Ctrl + Home	Top of the program
↑	Up one line

Inserting/deleting text

Pressing	Controls the following action:
Shift + Ins	Copies from Clipboard to cursor location
Del	Deletes character below cursor
Backspace	Deletes character to the left
Del	Deletes selected text; Does not copy line to the Clipboard
Tab	Moves text from cursor location to the next tab setting
Ins	Toggles between insert/overtype mode

Selecting text

Pressing	Selects the following:
Shift + Ctrl + Home	All lines from current line to the first line
Shift + Ctrl + End	All lines from current line to the last line
Shift + ←	Character to the left of cursor location
Shift + →	Character to the right of cursor location
Shift + ↑	Entire line above cursor location
Shift + ↓	Entire line below cursor location
Shift + Pg Dn	One page down*
Shift + Pg Up	One page up*
Shift + Ctrl + →	Word to the right of cursor location

Descriptions that are marked with an asterisk (*) must have more than one page of text otherwise the key combination will not work. A "page" refers to the part of the program visible in the active window.

3.3 QBasic and Your First Program

In this section we'll show how you can use *QBasic* to perform math operations and calculations. We'll use these math operations in a *QBasic* program later in this section. The following basic math functions are supported by *QBasic*:

Function	Indicated by	Example
Addition	Plus sign (+)	A + B
Subtraction	Minus sign (–)	A - B
Multiplication	Asterisk (*):	A * B
Division	Slash (/):	A / B

Let's try a few examples of different math operations. Before starting a new program, you must inform *QBasic*, that you want to create a new program. Press the [Alt] + [F] key combination to open the **File** menu and press the [Enter] key to select the **New** command.

If the following dialog box appears, press the [Tab] key to select the <No> button and press the [Enter] key:

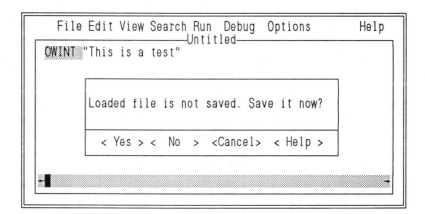

Remember from earlier in this chapter, we mentioned that everything you enter between quotation marks following a PRINT statement is displayed on the screen. Therefore, if you want

QBasic to perform a calculation, you must delete the quotation marks.

For example, if you type the following line:

```
PRINT "3+3 ="
```

QBasic will display "3+3 =" on the output screen when you run this program. However, this is not the answer to the math problem. The program line should now look like the following:

```
PRINT 3 + 3
```

Start this program with the (Shift) + (F5) key combination. You'll see the answer of the math operation on the screen:

```
6




Press any key to continue
```

Your PC is also capable of performing other basic math functions with *QBasic*. Try the following yourself and press (Shift) + (F5) after each line:

```
PRINT 3 - 3
PRINT 4 * 4
```

The first command line will display a 0 and the second command line displays 16 on your output screen.

Next, type the following command line:

```
PRINT 7 ÷ 3
```

To get the ÷ character, press and hold down the (Alt) key and then press the (2), (4), (6) keys on the numeric keypad. Press the (Shift) + (F5) key combination to start the program.

The "Expected: , or ; or end-of-statement" error message normally indicates that *QBasic* did not understand the command line. Instead of the "÷" character you should use the slash "/" to perform division.

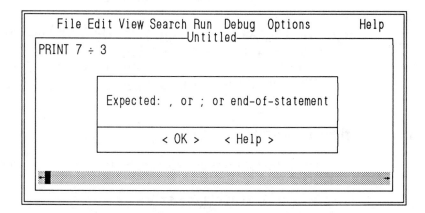

```
   File Edit View Search Run  Debug  Options        Help
                        ─Untitled─
PRINT 7 ÷ 3

       ┌───────────────────────────────────────────┐
       │                                             │
       │   Expected: , or ; or end-of-statement      │
       │                                             │
       │─────────────────────────────────────────────│
       │          < OK >      < Help >               │
       └───────────────────────────────────────────┘

 ■
```

Press the (Enter) key to clear the dialog box. Change the program line to:

```
PRINT 7 / 3
```

After starting the program with the (Shift) + (F5) key combination the result is displayed on the screen:

```
2.333333

   Press any key to continue
```

Notice that the result is rounded off at the seventh position and that a 0 is not displayed before the decimal point. In the next section we'll use various math operations to calculate the gasoline consumption of your automobile.

So far in this chapter, we've used *QBasic* statements to type simple one line programs. However, these simple lines cannot be called programs, since we only created single program lines which were then executed immediately.

Select the **File** menu and press the (Enter) key to select the **New** command. If a dialog box appears in which you're asked if you want to save the current program, use the (Tab) key to select the <**No**> button and press the (Enter) key.

3.3.1 Your first program

Type the following lines (press the (Enter) key after each line):

```
REM GASPRG Chapter 3¶
CLS¶
PRINT "Gasoline consumption"¶
GALLON = 150¶
MILE = 650¶
CONSUMPTION = MILE / GALLON¶
PRINT CONSUMPTION¶
```

Start this program by pressing the (Shift) + (F5) key combination. The following appears on the output screen:

```
Gasoline consumption
4,333333

Press any key to continue
```

3.3.2 The REM statement

Notice that *QBasic* executed the individual lines of the program sequentially. The REM statement lets you place comments in your program at any desired location. These comments can describe the purpose or function of different parts of a program.

The term "REM" is short for REMark. Everything that follows a REM statement in a program line will be ignored by the computer, including other BASIC statements and functions.

You can use a single quotation mark (') in place of REM in a program line. For example, instead of:

```
REM GASPRG
```

you can type:

```
' GASPRG
```

3.3.3 The CLS statement

One of the most useful *QBasic* statements is the CLS statement. This statement clears the screen and places the cursor at the first position in the View window.

In the previous example programs we did not use this statement. You probably noticed that your output screen became "cluttered" with new output from new programs. You can use CLS to clear away unwanted screen clutter on the output display.

QBasic stored the values for GALLON and MILE in order to calculate the consumption in an additional program line.

After you have seen the calculation of the consumption on the output screen, you can return to the program screen by pressing any key. Note that the *QBasic* program you created was not lost; it remains on the screen.

In the next section we want to show you how to change, load and save the programs you've created.

3.3.4 The WIDTH statement

The WIDTH statement is used in a number of different ways, but most important to us is its use in formatting screen output.

QBasic normally defaults to a screen width of 80 characters. It's possible to change this value to 40, which means each character becomes twice as wide. This is not an effect you will want to use in all situations.

However, if you consider the readability of a larger print program, using a 40 column screen would be a definite plus. To change the output screen width to 40 columns, type the following command:

```
WIDTH 40
```

and press the (Shift) + (F5) key combination. Experiment with this mode by entering a few print statements:

```
CLS
WIDTH 40
PRINT "This is a test."
PRINT "This is a 40 column output screen."
```

When you are done, type the following line:

```
WIDTH 80
```

and press the (Shift) + (F5) key combination to return to the 80 column mode.

The WIDTH statement only affects the output screen. It has no affect on the View window. You can only use values of either 40 or 80; any other values would result in an "Illegal function call" error.

Most of our example programs are written in 80 columns, but if you like the effect, or want to experiment a little, try rewriting some of the routines for 40 columns.

3.4 Saving and Loading Your Programs

Before we continue, you should save the program in the View window to your hard drive or to a diskette.

Select the **File** menu with the (Alt) + (F) key combination. Notice that the **File** menu contains two commands that you can use to save your programs:

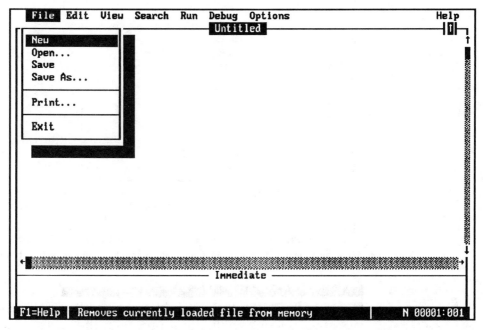

File menu displays two commands to save your programs

The two commands which we'll discuss in this chapter are **Save** and **Save As...**.

3.4.1 Saving new programs

You must select the **Save As...** command when you are:

- Saving a program for the first time.

- Using a new name for an existing program. If you use a new name, the previous file will remain unchanged.

Since we have not yet saved this program, press the Ⓐ key to select the **Save As...** command. The following dialog box appears:

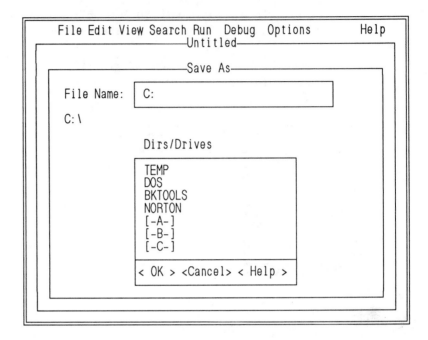

This dialog box is where you can enter the program name. For this example, type GASPRG.BAS in the **File Name:** text box.

 When assigning filenames for the programs (as in all DOS files) only names with up to eight characters can be used. If you assigned a longer name to a program, the excess characters are used as the file extension. Any remaining characters are deleted.

Switching drives

 Press the ⟨Tab⟩ key to move to the **Dirs/Drives** box. Use the ⟨↓⟩ direction key to select another drive and press the ⟨Enter⟩ key. For example, if you want to save a program to drive A:, select **[-A-]** in the **Dirs/Drives** box.

Then the **Save As...** dialog box will appear similar to the following:

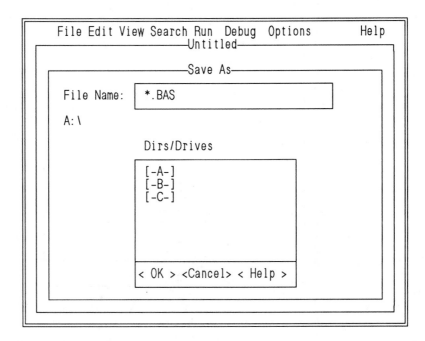

```
File Edit View Search Run  Debug  Options          Help
                         Untitled
                          Save As
  File Name:  *.BAS

  A:\

                     Dirs/Drives

                 [-A-]
                 [-B-]
                 [-C-]




                 < OK > <Cancel> < Help >
```

Now you can type the name of the program in the **File Name:** text box. Then press the (Enter) key to save the program.

Including a path

You can also include the path to the directory in which this program should be saved. To save the program, for example, in the directory PROGRAM (if this directory exists on your C: hard drive), you must type the following in the **File Name:** text box:

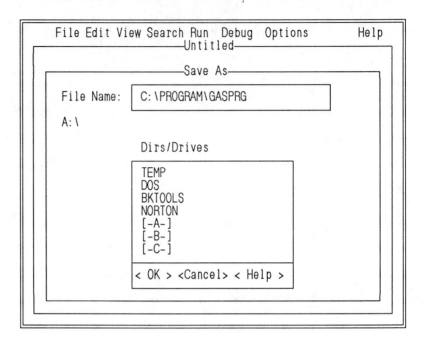

Press the Enter key to save the program in the designated directory.

Accidently replacing a program

Don't worry about accidently replacing or deleting a previous program. The following dialog box will appear if a program has the same name:

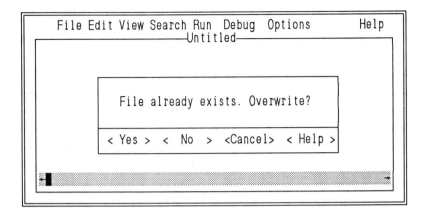

```
      File Edit View Search Run  Debug  Options          Help
                          ─Untitled─

              ┌──────────────────────────────────────┐
              │                                        │
              │   File already exists. Overwrite?      │
              │                                        │
              ├────────────────────────────────────────┤
              │  < Yes >  <  No  >  <Cancel>  < Help >  │
              └────────────────────────────────────────┘


```

Select the **<Yes>** button only if you want to completely replace the existing program with the program currently in the View window. Otherwise, select the **<No>** button to type a new program name in the **Save As...** dialog box.

After you have typed the name, press the [Enter] key. The program is now saved under the name GASPRG.BAS in the current directory of the hard drive or diskette.

Although we added the .BAS extension, you do not need to include the extension. The .BAS file extension is automatically added by *QBasic*. All *QBasic* programs use this file extension.

3.4.2 Saving program changes

Let's return to our example program to calculate gasoline consumption. In our example, the gasoline consumption was rather high because of the values we supplied. How can you calculate the real gasoline consumption of your car?

To calculate the real gasoline consumption, you would have to change the values in the GASPRG.BAS program. For example, assume you drove 300 miles and purchased 18 gallons of gasoline.

Since the program is still in the View window, use the direction keys to move the cursor to the following line:

```
GALLON = 150
```

Move the cursor behind GALLON = and change the 150 to 18:

```
GALLON = 18
```

Then change the following line:

```
MILE = 650
```

Move the cursor behind MILE = and change the 650 to 300:

```
MILE = 300
```

The changed program can be started as usual with the (Shift) + (F5) key combination. The following appears on the output screen:

```
Gasoline consumption
16.66667

Press any key to continue
```

3.4.3 The Save command

If you wanted to save this program under the name GASPRG.BAS, it's very simple using *QBasic*. You could still use the **Save As...** command but it's faster to use the **Save** command.

Select the **File** menu with the (Alt) + (F) key combination. Either press the (S) key or use the direction keys to select the **Save** command and press the (Enter) key. Now the changes to the program are saved under the name appearing in the title bar.

You can select the **Save** command even if the program in the View window was not previously saved. The **Save As...** dialog box will appear (see Section 3.4.2).

Also, if you do select the **Save As...** command to save an existing program, notice that the current program name already appears in the **File Name:** text box. Therefore all you need to do is press the (Enter) key.

3.4.4 Loading programs

Loading a program is similar to saving a program because you'll have the help of a menu. Select the **File** menu with the [Alt] + [F] key combination and then press the [O] key. Alternatively, use the direction keys to select the **Open...** command in the **File** menu and press the [Enter] key.

This opens the following dialog box:

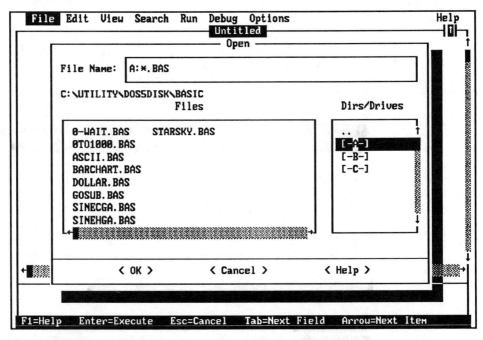

Selecting Open... from the File menu displays this dialog box

Notice the list of programs in the **Files** box. Type the name of the desired program (and path, if necessary) in the **File Name:** text box. You do not need to add the .BAS file extension.

Switching drives

Press the [Tab] key to move to the **Dirs/Drives** box. Use the [↓] direction key to select another drive. If you press the [Enter] key, you'll see in the **Files** box all *QBasic* files in the current directory with the .BAS extension. Follow the steps previously mentioned to load the desired program.

Switching directories

You can move to the next highest directory by moving the cursor to the two periods ".." and pressing (Enter). To go to the next lowest directory, move the cursor to the directory name (which is always in uppercase letters) and press (Enter).

These directories also display the *QBasic* files. Use the direction keys to select the desired program from the **Files** box. Press (Enter) or click with the left mouse button to load the program.

You can use this method to search your hard drive or diskette for programs, since *QBasic* always displays all available files with the .BAS filename extension.

Loading other files

If the program you want to load does not have the .BAS extension, use a * wildcard in the **File Name**: text box:

```
File Name:    *.*
```

to display all files in the current directory.

Press (Tab) (or use the mouse) to move to the **Files** box. Use the direction keys (or the mouse) to select the desired file. The program is automatically placed in the **File Name**: text box.

3.5 Adding Flexibility To Your Programs

Let's return to the gasoline consumption program (GASPRG.BAS) from Section 3.3. We mentioned that you could enter the new and current values into the program after every fuel purchase.

However, after a short time you'll discover that it's tiresome to reload the program each time you want to enter the new values. We'll show you in this section how to avoid this problem.

First we must delete the current program from the program screen and tell *QBasic* that you want to create a new program. Select the **File** menu with the Alt + F keys. Then press Enter to select the **New** command.

If a prompt appears, asking whether you want to save the program, use the Tab key to select the <No> button and press the Enter key.

3.5.1 The INPUT statement

Next ,type the following program lines:

```
CLS
INPUT GALLON
```

Start this program line with the Shift + F5 key combination. Notice that the cursor is blinking to the right of a question mark:

```
? _
```

The blinking cursor indicates that it's waiting for an input at this location.

Type the number "50" and press [Enter]. Notice that the number "50" has replaced the blinking cursor:

```
? 50


   Press any key to continue
```

Press any key to return to the View window area. Press the [↓] direction key to move the cursor to next new line. Type the following:

```
PRINT GALLON
```

If you start this program with the [Shift] + [F5] keys, the question mark appears on the screen. Enter "50" again so that *QBasic* displays the "50" on the screen:

```
? 50
 50

   Press any key to continue
```

Press any key to return to the View window area. Press the [↓] direction key to move the cursor to the next new line. Then add the following two lines to complete the program:

```
INPUT MILE
PRINT MILE
```

When you start the program with [Shift] + [F5], enter 50 following the question mark. The question mark appears a second time but this time representing the value for MILE. Type 1000 for this value. Notice that both numbers are displayed immediately on the screen:

```
? 50
  50
? 1000
  1000


   Press any key to continue
```

We want to include this routine in our GASPRG program.

Load the GASPRG.BAS program by selecting the **File** menu with the [Alt] + [F] keys. Select the **Open...** command and press the [Enter] key or press the [O] key. Follow the same procedures we discussed in the previous section to open GASPRG.BAS.

Since the lines you just typed were a test, we do not want to save them. Therefore, when the prompt appears asking whether you want to save the program, use the [Tab] key to select the **<No>** button and press the [Enter] key.

Then the listing of the GASPRG.BAS program appears in the View window. We'll need to change the following two lines:

```
GALLON = 18
```

change to:

```
INPUT GALLON
```

and change this line:

```
MILE = 300
```

to:

```
INPUT MILE
```

For more information on editing text and switching to the overwrite mode, see Chapter 3.

The modified program should now appear like the following:

```
REM CH3 GASPRG¶
CLS¶
INPUT GALLON¶
INPUT MILE¶
CONSUMPTION = MILE / GALLON¶
PRINT CONSUMPTION¶
```

Start the program by pressing the (Shift) + (F5) key combination. Enter 40 for the first input and 600 for the second input.

Then *QBasic* displays "15" for the gas consumption:

```
Gasoline consumption
? 40
? 600
 15


   Press any key to continue
```

Press (Enter) to return to the View window. You can experiment with other values by starting the program with (Shift) + (F5) and entering different values.

Before continuing, you should save the changes to this program. Since we do not want to save the program as GASPRG.BAS, press the (Alt) + (F) keys to select the **File** menu. Then use the (↓) direction key or press the (A) key to select the **Save As...** command and press the (Enter) key. Type GASPRG1 as the program name in the **File Name:** text box and press the (Enter) key.

The one problem you probably recognized with this program is that the question mark does not explain anything about the value the user should enter. Therefore, we need to make a simple change to the program. Next, we'll discuss how to display a message on the screen to explain the question marks and what the user should input.

3.5.2   Make Your Programs User-Friendly

If you were to ask a friend to start this program, they would be very confused by the meaning of the question marks. Therefore, we'll need to make the GASPRG1 program more user-friendly.

What do we mean by the term *user-friendly*?

A computer program is written to perform certain tasks, like calculate formulas or draw charts. But the user must know exactly how to use the program—what keys to press to recalculate a column of numbers, or change a bar graph's fill pattern. *User-friendly* means that someone who isn't familiar with the program will still be able to use it without a great deal of explanation or training.

For example, in this program, we'll need to insert two PRINT statements into the program to inform the user to enter the gallons consumed and miles traveled. Refer to Chapter 3 for information on how you can insert these two lines in the program.

Insert the following above the INPUT GALLON line:

```
PRINT "Please enter the number of gallons:"
```

Then insert the following line above the INPUT MILE line:

```
PRINT "Please enter the number of miles:"
```

Your complete program should now appear exactly like the following:

```
REM GASPRG¶
CLS¶
PRINT "Gasoline consumption"¶
PRINT "Please enter the number of gallons:"¶
INPUT GALLON¶
PRINT "Please enter the number of miles:"¶
INPUT MILE¶
CONSUMPTION = MILE / GALLON¶
PRINT CONSUMPTION¶
```

Start the program with the [Shift] + [F5] key combination. The following appears on the output screen (using the same values we previously entered):

```
Gasoline consumption
Please enter the number of gallons:
? 40
 Please enter the number of miles
? 600
 15


Press any key to continue
```

The two PRINT statements following the INPUT statement definitely clarify the meaning of the question mark. However, we should also add another PRINT statement to clarify what is meant by 15 on the screen.

Insert the following line above the PRINT CONSUMPTION line:

```
PRINT "The fuel consumption is:"
```

Finally, insert the following line as the last line of the program:

```
PRINT "miles per gallon"
```

The following is how the modified program listing should appear in your View window:

```
REM GASPRG1A¶
CLS¶
PRINT "Gasoline consumption"¶
PRINT "Please enter the number of gallons:"¶
INPUT GALLON¶
PRINT "Please enter the number of miles:"¶
INPUT MILE¶
CONSUMPTION = MILE / GALLON¶
PRINT CONSUMPTION¶
PRINT "miles per gallon"¶
```

Start the program with the [Shift] + [F5] key combination. The following appears on the output screen:

```
Gasoline consumption
Please enter the number of gallons:
? 40
 Please enter the number of miles
? 600
The fuel consumption is:
 15
miles per gallon

Press any key to continue
```

Don't forget to save the program when it's finished. If you want to save this program again under the name GASPRG1.BAS, you must select the **File** menu with the [Alt] + [F] key combination. Then select the **Save** command and press the [Enter] key or press the [S] key. The changes are saved automatically under the name GASPRG1.BAS.

3.6 Printing Your Program

The ability to print data may be very important in your *QBasic* programs. In this section we'll discuss the *QBasic* statements and functions you can use to print program listings, lists, tables and other data.

3.6.1 Printing program listings

To print a program listing you have created press the [Alt] + [F] key combination to select the **File** menu and press the [P] key to select the **Print...** command.

This opens the following dialog box:

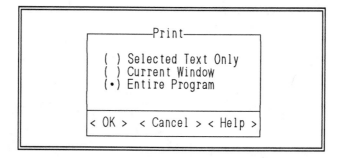

```
┌─────────────────────────────────────────┐
│┌─────────────────────────────────────┐  │
││           ┌─Print─┐                  │  │
││                                      │  │
││   ( ) Selected Text Only             │  │
││   ( ) Current Window                 │  │
││   (•) Entire Program                 │  │
││                                      │  │
│├──────────────────────────────────────┤ │
││  < OK >   < Cancel > < Help >        │  │
│└─────────────────────────────────────┘  │
└─────────────────────────────────────────┘
```

The **Print** command lets you print selected text or text from the current window or the current program.

Before selecting any of the **Print** commands, make certain that your printer is properly connected to LPT1 and is "On Line".

The following options are included in this dialog box:

Selected Text Only

If you want to print only the selected text of the program, use the [↓] direction key to select this option and press the [Enter] key.

Current Window

> Select this option if you want to print the program text in the current window.

Entire Program

> This is the default option (notice the blinking cursor). If you want to print the complete program you created, select the **Print...** command. Use the ⬇ direction key to select the Active Window option. Then press ⏎Enter and *QBasic* will print your program.

3.6.2 The LPRINT statement

If your BASIC program displays a list or table of data, you can use the LPRINT statement to print the output from a program.

This statement has the same purpose as PRINT except it does not display the output from a program on the screen, but on the printer.

Another form of the LPRINT statement is the LPRINT USING statement. We'll discuss that statement in more detail in a later chapter.

Let's change the GASPRG1.BAS from the last section so that the program outputs data to the printer instead of the output screen.

Although the GASPRG1.BAS is a small program, you still need to change every line in the program which contain a PRINT statement. This can become a long process, especially with lengthy programs.

You could use the editing keys we discussed earlier in this chapter. However, a faster method is to use the commands in the **Search** menu. We'll discuss those commands in the next section.

3.7 Searching/Replacing Text

Press the ⎯Alt⎯ + ⎯S⎯ key combination to open the **Search** menu:

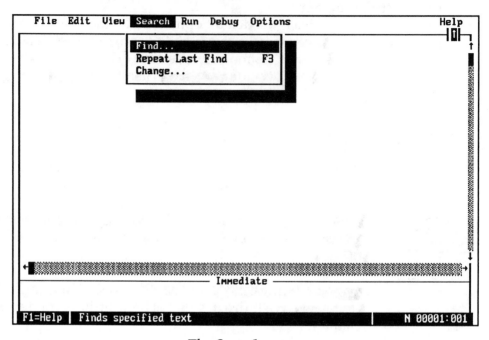

*The **Search** menu*

The commands in the **Search** menu let you locate specific text anywhere in the program. You then have the option of replacing the text with new text.

If you want to locate a specific character, word or even a group of words, select the **Find...** command in the **Search** menu. Press the ⎯Enter⎯ key to open the **Find...** command dialog box.

Type the text that you want *QBasic* to locate in the **Find What:** text box. For example, we want to locate the PRINT statement (make certain to type the text correctly):

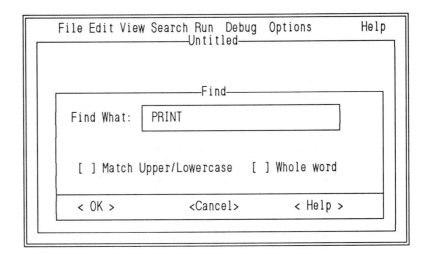

```
    File Edit View Search Run  Debug  Options      Help
                        Untitled

                         Find
    Find What:   PRINT


      [ ] Match Upper/Lowercase   [ ] Whole word

    < OK >          <Cancel>        < Help >
```

You can limit the search by locating specific matches. For example, use the Tab key to move the cursor to the **Match Upper/Lowercase** option. Press the ↑ direction key to switch on this option. An X will appear inside the brackets. Press the ↓ direction key to switch off this option. The X will disappear inside the brackets.

If this option is selected, the search would locate text that matches the specified text exactly. For example, if you were searching for "PRINT", *QBasic* would locate PRINT in the following line:

```
PRINT "This is a wonderful program"
```

but would ignore "print" in this line:

```
INPUT "Please print your name here"; name$
```

The other option is the **Whole Word** option. Use the Tab key to move the cursor to the **Whole Word** option. Press the ↑ direction key to switch on this option. An X will appear inside the brackets. Press the ↓ direction key to switch off this option. The X will disappear inside the brackets.

This option will locate the specified text only when it's surrounded by spaces, punctuation marks or certain other characters.

For example, *QBasic* would locate "PRINT" in the following line:

```
PRINT "This is a wonderful program"
```

However, the letters "PRINT" in the following would be ignored:

```
LPRINT "This is a wonderful program"
```

Press the (Tab) key to move the cursor to the <OK> button and press the (Enter) key. *QBasic* will highlight the first match following the location of the cursor in the View window.

To see if there are additional matches, press the (F3) key. This is the shortcut key for the **Repeat Last Find** command.

3.7.1 Replacing text

The **Search** menu also has one more powerful command that we need to discuss: the **Change...** command.

Press the (Alt) + (S) keys and then the (C) key to open the following screen:

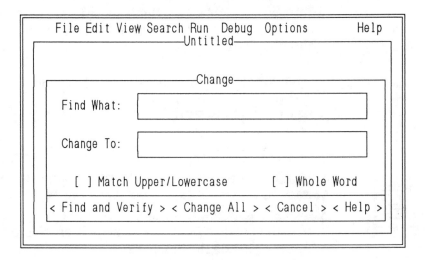

Use the **Change...** command to replace any character string in the document with any other string of characters.

For an example, let's assume that we want to replace PRINT statements with LPRINT statements in the GASPRG.BAS program.

Type the text you want to find in the **Find What:** text box. In our example, this would be PRINT:

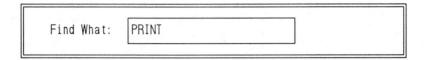

Press the ⌈Tab⌋ key to move the cursor to the **Change To:** text box. In this text box, you'll need to type the replacement text. In our example, this would be LPRINT:

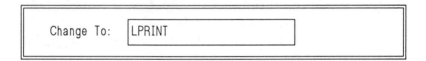

The **Match Upper/Lowercase** and the **Whole Word** options are the same as those for the **Find...** command.

At the bottom of the dialog box are new buttons:

<Find and Verify>

Select this button if you want *QBasic* to locate the search text but to have you verify that you want that text changed. When *QBasic* locates the search text, a new dialog box is displayed:

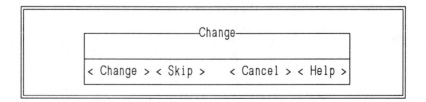

Press the ⌈Tab⌋ key to move the cursor to the **<Change>** button if you want to change the text. Select **<Skip>** if you do not want the highlighted text changed or select **<Cancel>** to cancel the **Change...** command.

<Change All>

Select this button if you want to change all instances of the search text. *QBasic* will <u>not</u> ask you for confirmation before replacing the search text.

Be careful when selecting **<Change All>**. Unless you are absolutely certain you want to replace every instance of the search text, use **<Find and Verify>** instead. You may make incorrect substitutions and you cannot "undo" a change once it is made.

<Cancel>

Select this button if you want to cancel the **Change...** command.

Make certain to have both the **Match Upper/Lowercase** and **Whole Word** switched on. In this example you can select the **<Change All>** option. Then press the [Enter] key.

When *QBasic* has finished making the changes to the program, the following dialog box appears:

Now after the changes have been made, the GASPRG.BAS program should appear as follows:

```
' CH3.7 GASPRG1¶
LPRINT "Gasoline consumption"¶
LPRINT "Please input Gallon"¶
INPUT GALLON¶
LPRINT "Please input mile"¶
INPUT MILE¶
CONSUMPTION = MILE / GALLON¶
LPRINT "The consumption is:"¶
LPRINT CONSUMPTION¶
LPRINT "miles per gallon"¶
```

3.8 Determining Averages

QBasic has one more math capability we need to discuss in this chapter.

For example, after purchasing your Christmas gifts, you want to know the total amount that you have spent. For some time you probably used a pocket calculator which worked quite well. However, too many times you received a different result when recalculating backwards to double-check the answer and you could not find the error.

The error could only be found if you enter everything once or twice more, until the result which appeared most often was considered to be correct. This is much simpler using *QBasic* because you can enter your purchase prices as program lines.

```
CLS¶
EXPENSES = 48.5+ 70.6+ 120+ 60.5+ 78 + 24 + 9.8¶
PRINT EXPENSES¶
```

As soon as you press the [Shift] + [F5] keys, the correct result appears on the screen.

If you discover that one purchase was entered as 70.60 instead of 60.70, simply make the necessary change in the program line and start the program again with [Shift] + [F5]. The correct result appears on the output screen.

If you have more expenses than can fit into one line, simply enter a new line after the expenses being calculated. This second line must also add the result from the previous line:

```
Expenses = Expenses + 80.6 + 50 + 75.5 + 90 + 6.8¶
```

You should also make the program user-friendly so you can understand what is displayed on the output screen. Your complete program should now look similar to the following (remember to press the [Enter] key when you see the ¶ character):

```
' Expenses¶
CLS¶
EXPENSES = 48.5 + 70.6 + 120 + 60.5 + 78 + 24 + 9.8¶
EXPENSES = EXPENSES + 80.60 + 50 + 75.5 + 90 + 6.8¶
PRINT "The total expenses for Christmas were:"¶
PRINT Expenses¶
```

Press the Shift + F5 key combination to start the program. The following appears on the output screen:

```
The total expenses for Christmas were:
714.3




Press any key to continue
```

 The same method can be used to calculate your average monthly telephone bill for the last six months. The only difference is to calculate the sum for the last six months and dividing this result in the next line by 6:

```
' Phoneavg¶
Telephone = 50 + 56.7 + 48 + 58.6 + 70 + 124¶
Average = Telephone / 6¶
PRINT "Total phone expenses for the last 6 months
are:"¶
PRINT Telephone¶
PRINT "The ave5.rage monthly phone bill is:"¶
PRINT Average¶
```

You can experiment with other types of calculations which are important to you and must be performed every day. For example, determine the average amount of the last ten checks you wrote.

4. Variables In QBasic

One of the advantages of every programming language is the fact that it uses variables.

In the case of the BASIC language, a BASIC variable refers to a single object. Depending on how you declare a variable, it can be a type of *numeric variable* or a *string variable*.

4.1 Variable Types

Before discussing how to use variables in *QBasic*, we need to discuss the various types of variables.

Although there are different names for variables, you'll mainly be using four types of variables in *QBasic*. Each of these variable types are designated with a different symbol, called the *type designator*, placed at the end of the variable name.

4.1.1 Numeric variables

Integer variables

This variable type can represent only whole numbers. The type designator is a percent sign appended to the name of the variable (such as A% or C4%).

If this variable type is assigned a non-integer value, only the places before the decimal point are taken into account. A further restriction is placed on the values of variables of this type, in that only values between -32768 and 32767 are allowed.

Single-precision variables

This variable type is one of two floating point variables used to represent decimal numbers. The type designator is an exclamation point placed after the variable name, although this is not absolutely necessary.

Examples of the permitted designations are A! or B2! (A or B2). Single precision numbers are accurate to 6 decimal places. The published range is -1E-38 to 1E+38. The actual range may vary in different versions. Our version allowed a range of -2.938736-39 to 1.701411+38.

Double-precision variables

This variable type is the second type of floating point variables. This is similar to the single-precision real type of variable, with the exception of being accurate to 15 decimal places. Double-precision variables are designated using the number symbol (#). The range is approximately the same as for single-precision.

4.1.2 Character string variables (strings)

This variable type is designated by the dollar sign ($). String variables can store arbitrary strings of characters. No more than 255 characters may be placed in a string variable; otherwise an error message may appear.

4.1.3 Naming variables

You must be careful when selecting a name for a variable. You cannot simply assign random letters to a variable. A program is easier to follow and *debug* (locate and correct errors) when you use meaningful variable names.

The following are suggestions when choosing variable names:

- Variable names can be up to 40 characters in length.

- They should only contain alphanumeric characters (a-z, 0-9) or type declaration characters (!, #, $, % and &).

- *QBasic* keywords cannot be used as variable names. *QBasic* keywords include all BASIC commands, statements, functions and operator names. You can, however, use embedded reserved words. For example, using DRAW as a variable name causes an error, but ZDRAW may be used.

- Variable names cannot have a number as the first character. For example, AMOUNT9 can be used as a variable name, but *QBasic* will not accept 9AMOUNT.

The following table shows examples of incorrect variable names and possible alternatives:

Wrong:	Reason the name is incorrect	Alternative
1NAME$	Name starts with a number	NAME1$
PRINT	PRINT is a reserved keyword	KPRINT
PAY_HOUR$	Do not use the _ character	PAY.HOUR$

4.2 Using Variables

In the previous chapter you may have wondered how *QBasic* understood the words GALLON, MILE and CONSUMPTION. After all, these words are not keywords. We know from Chapter 2 that the computer understands the PRINT and INPUT statements because those statements are part of the *QBasic* language.

4.2.1 BASIC variables

The GASPRG.BAS and GASPRG1.BAS programs in Chapter 2 uses the words GALLON, MILE and CONSUMPTION as *variables*.

BASIC variables play an important part in programming. Selecting the proper name for a variable can make your program listing easier to read and understand. For example, you probably found the variables in the GASPRG program easy to understand. We used self-explanatory variable names like GALLON and MILE.

However, we could have written the program this way:

```
REM CH 3 GASPRG2¶
CLS¶
PRINT "Gasoline consumption"¶
INPUT A¶
INPUT B¶
C = B / A¶
PRINT C¶
```

Do you still understand the program? If you enter and run the program listed above, it displays the same results. An experienced programmer will understand how the program works, but the meaning of the two INPUT statements will remain unclear to the beginner to programming.

Variables can be used exactly like numbers in all mathematical formulas. We used variables for that purpose in the following line from the GASPRG program in Chapter 2:

```
CONSUMPTION = MILE / GALLON
```

Therefore, you should be able to understand the purpose of the variables in the following lines:

```
TIME = 5
DISTANCE = 1000
RATE = DISTANCE / TIME
```

The following line is another example of using a variable:

```
GALLON = GALLON + 20
```

Even using this type of variable is no problem for *QBasic*. Type the following short program:

```
REM CH4a¶
GALLON = 50¶
GALLON = GALLON + 20¶
PRINT GALLON¶
```

Start this program by pressing the [Shift] + [F5] key combination. You'll receive "70" as a result.

In the first line, *QBasic* assigned the value 50 to the GALLON variable. The next line assigns the value (GALLON + 20) to the GALLON variable. Therefore, 50 + 20 = 70.

You could also assign values to variables by using the LET statement. This would appear as follows:

```
LET GALLON = GALLON + 20
```

In the above line, the LET statement informs *QBasic* that the value of GALLON should equal GALLON + 20.

Using the LET statement is optional. The equal sign indicates that *QBasic* should treat this line as a variable assignment. Your programs will work with the LET statement but most programmers use only the equal sign.

4.2.2 String variables

String variables are easy to recognize because they have the character "$" at the end of the variable name. Character strings themselves must be defined in quotation marks, to distinguish them from numbers. 147 is a number, while "147" is a character sequence of three alphanumeric characters. In this case the numbers "1", "4" and "7".

Numeric variables have one main disadvantage: They can only store numbers. You cannot assign your name to such a variable.

For example, make certain that the View window is empty (select the **New** command from the **File** menu if necessary). Type the following program lines:

```
Firstname = Peter¶
PRINT Firstname¶
```

Press the Shift + F5 keys to start this program. You'll notice that only a 0 is displayed on the output screen.

Although "Peter" appears to be a first name to us, *QBasic* assumes it's a numeric variable just like GALLON and CONSUMPTION in the previous examples. *QBasic* assigns the value zero to every variable which does not yet contain a value. Therefore, Peter = 0 in the first line.

How can we tell *QBasic* that we want the word "Peter," not the numeric value of the variable Peter? Think back to our first experiments with the PRINT statement. When you wanted to output data using PRINT, the data was placed between quotation marks. Let's try using quotation marks for the name Peter:

```
Firstname = "Peter"
```

Press the Shift + F5 key combination. You'll receive the following "Type mismatch" error on your output screen:

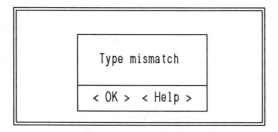

```
        Type mismatch

     < OK >   < Help >
```

Notice that *QBasic* highlights the line in which errors occur. This is part of the smart editor in *QBasic*. The *QBasic* smart editor includes automatic syntax checking that makes it easier to type and edit BASIC programs.

A "Type mismatch" error occurs when the variable is an incorrect type. *QBasic* recognized that we tried to assign a word to a variable which can only accept numbers. Press the (Enter) key to close this window.

Perhaps the "Type mismatch" errors message suggests to you that a certain type of variable exists which can accept words instead of numbers.

Let's try one more possibility. Change the lines so that a dollar sign ($) follows each citation of the variable name:

```
Firstname$ = "Peter"¶
PRINT Firstname$¶
```

Then start the program by pressing the (Shift) + (F5) key combination. The following appears on the screen:

```
Peter

  Press any key to continue
```

The program ran successfully this time because of the dollar sign. This dollar sign informs *QBasic* that a name can be assigned to this variable.

This type of variable is called a *string variable*. String variables can store arbitrary strings of characters. The dollar sign is the *type-declaration character* for string variables. Other types of variables are designated by different type-declaration characters such as % or !.

However, before you attach a "$" behind every variable name in your program, we want to inform you of a small problem. At this point, you may be wondering why you use any variables without the $ type-declaration character.

Load the GASPRG.BAS program with 〔Alt〕 + 〔F〕 from the **File** menu. Select the **Open...** command by pressing the 〔O〕 key. Use the 〔Tab〕 key to move the cursor to the **Files** list box and use the 〔↓〕 direction key, if necessary, to select GASPRG.BAS. When GASPRG.BAS is selected (the name will appear in the **File Name:** text box), press the 〔Enter〕 key.

When the GASPRG program appears in the View window, add a "$" to every variable name:

```
REM ch4b¶
CLS¶
PRINT "Gasoline consumption"¶
GALLON$ = 18 ¶
MILE$ = 300¶
CONSUMPTION$ = MILE$ / GALLON$¶
PRINT CONSUMPTION$¶
```

Start the modified program by pressing the 〔Shift〕 + 〔F5〕 key combination. However, *QBasic* responds with the "Type mismatch" error message again.

Since "GALLON$ = 18" is highlighted, you know that there is a problem with this variable. Press the 〔Enter〕 key to clear the dialog box. Notice the cursor is now blinking at the incorrect variable.

The "Type mismatch" error occurred because a variable with a "$" can only be assigned a value inside quotation marks. Make certain to place all values between quotation marks when using a variable with the "$" type-declaration character:

```
REM CH4c¶
CLS¶
PRINT "Gasoline consumption"¶
GALLON$ = "18"¶
MILE$ = "300"¶
CONSUMPTION$ = MILE$ / GALLON$¶
PRINT CONSUMPTION$¶
```

When you try to start this program with the (Shift) + (F5) key combination, you'll again receive a "Type mismatch" error. This time however, the line "CONSUMPTION$ = MILE$ / GALLON$" is highlighted as the source of the error.

Press the (Enter) key to clear the dialog box. The problem is the "/" division symbol. Normal math operations using string variables is not possible in *QBasic*. Although string variables can accept virtually any values between the two quotation marks, you cannot use string variables for calculations.

Since it does not make sense to use only string variables in the gasoline program, don't save the modified program. Instead, clear it from the View window by selecting **New** in the **File** menu.

If we can't use string variables in the GASPRG.BAS program, what type of program or program line would be appropriate for string variables? The following small program demonstrates the proper use of string variables:

```
REM Ch4Name1¶
CLS¶
PRINT "Please type your first name and press ENTER"¶
INPUT FIRSTNAME$¶
PRINT "Please type your last name and press ENTER"¶
INPUT LASTNAME$¶
PRINT¶
PRINT "Hello ";¶
PRINT FIRSTNAME$;¶
PRINT " ";¶
PRINT LASTNAME$¶
```

This example demonstrates the versatility of string variables. You can type your name in upper or lowercase letters or a combination of both.

Also notice that we placed a semicolon at the end of a few lines. This semicolon changes the PRINT statement. If you add a semicolon following a PRINT statement, *QBasic* displays everything on the same line without starting a new line.

The single PRINT statement moves the next PRINT statement down one line. This leaves a blank line between your last name and "Hello". Now the screen won't appear so cluttered.

Notice the two quotation marks with the space between in the following line from the above program:

```
Completename$ = Firstname$ + " " + Lastname$
```

A " " is considered a string, therefore a character string. However, it consists of only one space. Despite this, it can be assigned without a problem to a string variable. When you combine string variables, *QBasic* simply *concatenates* them (attaches them to one other).

As we mentioned earlier in this section, string variables can accept virtually any character between the quotation marks. If you want proof, type the following short program:

```
REM Ch4CHAR¶
CLS¶
PRINT "Type several random characters"¶
INPUT chars$¶
chars$ = chars$ + chars$ + chars$¶
chars$ = chars$ + chars$ + chars$¶
chars$ = chars$ + chars$ + chars$¶
chars$ = chars$ + chars$ + chars$¶
PRINT chars$¶
```

Start the program by pressing the (Shift) + (F5) keys. Type a single character and press the (Enter) key. The program displays several of the characters across the screen. Press any key to return to *QBasic* and restart the program. Then type several characters and press the (Enter) key. You may even fill the entire screen.

The second line of this program creates three characters out of one. In the next line, these three characters form nine characters and so on. By using this technique, you can multiply a character as many times as desired.

4.3 Variables In Programs

In this section we'll provide more inform ation on the functions and statements discussed in this chapter by using example programs.

4.3.1 Calculating sales tax

We'll start with a simple program to calculate the sales tax. We need this program to display the sales tax and the total cost for every purchase.

Since the sales tax is usually different from one area to another, it must be made a variable in the program. Therefore, we need a total of three variables: price, sales tax and total price.

Remember to use names which can identify the purpose of the variable when creating variable names. Therefore, we'll use the following variable names: SALESTAX, PRICE and TOTALPRICE.

The following is the listing for the SALESTAX program:

```
CLS¶
PRINT "This program will calculate your sales tax"¶
SALESTAX = .04¶
PRINT¶
PRINT "What is the purchase price:";¶
INPUT PRICE¶
TOTALCOST = PRICE + SALESTAX * PRICE¶
PRINT "The total cost is $";¶
PRINT TOTALCOST¶
```

The second line displays the title or purpose of the program. The third line displays the current sales tax. You can change this line to correspond to your local sales tax (04 to 06, for example).

The actual input occurs in the next two lines. The PRINT statement provides an explanation for the following INPUT statement. The PRICE variable prompts the user to enter the amount of the purchase ("purchase price").

The TOTALCOST variable calculates the total cost in the next line. The sales tax is first calculated by multiplying the amount with the tax rate (here 04% or 0.04).

Then the program must add this sales tax to the previous price. This creates the new combined price, which is assigned to the variable of the same name.

Note that your PC knows that multiplication has precedence over addition when executing calculations. Therefore, *QBasic* first calculates "Sales Tax * Price" and adds the result to the price.

Finally, the result is output in the last lines. Notice that we used semicolons at the ends of some lines to keep the output together in a single line.

Save this program under the name SALESTAX.BAS.

4.3.2 Calculating a rebate

Many companies offer rebates to customers purchasing their products. You can easily modify the SALESTAX.BAS program to calculate a rebate you are to receive from a company.

Actually, you only have to enter the rebate which corresponds to the amount of the sales tax and in the line where the calculation occurs, replace the "+" with a "-".

You'll probably want to change the prompts to correspond to the information required by the program. Therefore, the new program lines would look like the following:

```
REM REBATE.BAS¶
CLS¶
PRINT "Rebate Calculation"¶
REBATE = .2¶
PRINT¶
PRINT "What is the cost of the product";¶
INPUT PRICE¶
PRINT¶
NEWPRICE = PRICE - REBATE * PRICE¶
PRINT "Your cost after the rebate is $";¶
PRINT NEWPRICE¶
```

For example, if you purchase merchandise for $6500 with a 20% rebate, the program will determine that your cost is only $5200 for the product.

You can save this program as REBATE.BAS.

4.3.3 Calculating your salary increase

During the last week your boss told you that she's been so impressed with your work that you were offered a salary increase. Although the amount was significant, you received a similar increase last year but very little actual increase remained after the payroll deductions. Therefore, you want to calculate how much of this raise is a net raise.

This program resembles the two previous programs. However, we must calculate several deductions from your gross salary:

• Taxes	• Health insurance
• Pension contribution	• Unemployment insurance
• Personal withholding	

The following is one example of how the program could appear:

```
REM SALARY.BAS¶
CLS¶
INPUT "WHAT IS YOUR NEW ANNUAL SALARY"; GROSS¶
TAX = 20 / 100 * GROSS¶
HEALTHINS = 6.5 / 100 * GROSS¶
PENSION = 4.5 / 100 * GROSS¶
UNEMPLOYMENT = 2 / 100 * GROSS¶
PERSONAL = TAX / 10¶
NET = GROSS - TAX - HEALTHINS - PENSION¶
NET = NET - UNEMPLOYMENT - PERSONAL¶
PRINT "Your annual net pay is now $"; NET¶
```

The first line clears the screen. Then the program prompts you to enter the gross amount of the raise. This amount is stored in the GROSS variable.

Next the individual deductions are calculated. Notice that the calculations appear as "/ 100 * Gross". This format is intentional. The "20" in the third line represents the exact percentage. It's easier to change a value such as 20 instead of using values such as "0.2 * GROSS" or "0.065 * GROSS".

The personal savings plan deduction is not calculated by multiplying GROSS, but as 10% of the TAX. This changes the personal savings plan deduction automatically when another value is used for tax.

The amounts are deducted in the following lines. This produces the net pay.

Make certain to enter the correct values. If you make a mistake when entering a variable name, for example UNEMPLOUMENT instead of UNEMPLOYMENT, you'll receive incorrect results.

If, for example, you earn $20,000.00, the program calculates a net income of $13,000. If your boss offered you a salary increase of $300.00 for learning to program with *QBasic*, you're net income would then be $14,950.

Do not use commas or the dollar sign when typing in dollar figures in examples such as this program. You'll receive a "Redo from start" error message. Type only the number values.

Calculating the difference between your old and new salary is easy to do in *QBasic*.

Press the F6 key to switch to the Immediate window. Type the following program line:

```
PRINT 14950-13000
```

Press the Enter key to see the result of $1950. This is the total net pay increase after the raise. Press any key to return to the Immediate window. Then press the F6 key to switch to the View window.

5. Program Branches

The programs we discussed in the previous chapter were limited to *linear programs*. These are programs which execute the lines consecutively.

An important disadvantage of using linear programs is that the program runs once and then must be restarted in order to get a new result.

In this chapter we'll discuss programs which contain *branches* or *jumps*. A linear program does not have branches of any kind. If there were no statements to perform such program branches, you would be limited to writing only very simple programs in BASIC.

5.1 Unconditional Program Branches

The first and simplest type of a program branch is the GOTO statement. It's called an *unconditional program branch* because it is not tied to any condition—that is, the program performs this branch under all circumstances.

5.1.1 GOTO

In this section we're planning a vacation to a foreign country. You call your local bank to check the current exchange rate. The bank told you that the conversion rate of one dollar is equal to 1.59 FC (FC is the symbol for the foreign country's currency).

However, you want to determine the value in FC of several dollars and not just one dollar. Let's use *QBasic* to write a program to determine the conversion quickly.

This program could appear as follows:

```
REM DOLLAR¶
CLS¶
INPUT "What is the dollar amount"; DOLLAR¶
FOREIGN = DOLLAR * 1.59¶
PRINT "The value in FC is:";¶
PRINT FOREIGN¶
```

Now start the program by pressing the [Shift] + [F5] key combination. Type in a dollar value. Do not include a dollar sign; if you use a dollar sign, the following error message is displayed:

```
What is the dollar amount? $100.00

Redo from start
What is the dollar amount?
```

A "Redo from start" error message is displayed when you enter an incorrect number or type of information to an INPUT statement (the dollar sign in this example). You can, however, include a decimal point to include cents, for example, 121.13 as a dollar amount.

This small program is sufficient if you want to convert a few values. However, it's time-consuming to always press the [Shift] + [F5] key combination to calculate several values. Therefore, let's change the program slightly.

Use the direction keys to position the cursor at the end of the CLS statement. Press the [Enter] key to insert a blank line. Next, insert the following new line:

```
CONTINUE:
```

At the end of the program insert the following line:

```
GOTO CONTINUE
```

Now the program listing should appear like the following:

```
REM DOLLARa¶
CLS¶
CONTINUE:¶
INPUT "What is the dollar amount"; DOLLAR¶
FOREIGN = DOLLAR * 1.59¶
PRINT "The value in FC is:";¶
PRINT FOREIGN¶
GOTO CONTINUE¶
```

Press the [Shift] + [F5] key combination to start the program. Instead of pressing [Shift] + [F5] each time you wanted to compare a dollar value to an FC value, *QBasic* prompts you to enter a new DOLLAR value each time you press the [Enter] key.

This continues until you interrupt the program by pressing the [Ctrl] + [Pause] key combination.

The difference from the preceding program is that your program does not terminate after the last line. Instead, the GOTO statement in the last line instructs *QBasic* to continue at the label following the GOTO.

A *label* (also called the *alphanumeric line label*) is a combination of as many as 40 characters (usually a word) that starts with a letter and ends with a colon. The reason you must use a colon to end a label is so that *QBasic* can identify the name as a label, since it marks the destination of a GOTO statement. In this program example, the word CONTINUE is a label because it is followed by a colon.

When using labels, keep the following in mind:

- Location is very important. The label must be inserted where the execution should continue in the program.

- The name for the label is very important. You should follow the rules and suggestions we discussed in Chapter 3 for naming variables.

In the above example we want to jump to the beginning of the program, following the CLS statement. Therefore, place the label at this location.

Program A in the following illustration shows the structure of a linear program. The program is executed from the first line to the last line in a linear manner.

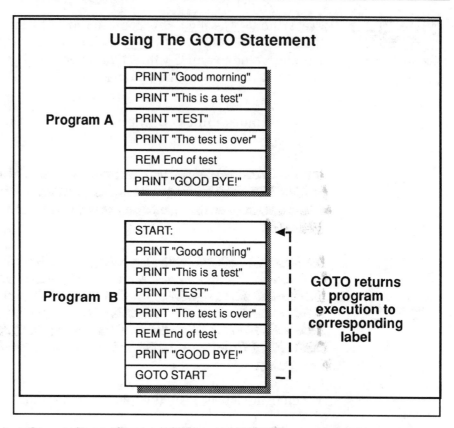

Using The GOTO Statement

Program A
PRINT "Good morning"
PRINT "This is a test"
PRINT "TEST"
PRINT "The test is over"
REM End of test
PRINT "GOOD BYE!"

Program B
START:
PRINT "Good morning"
PRINT "This is a test"
PRINT "TEST"
PRINT "The test is over"
REM End of test
PRINT "GOOD BYE!"
GOTO START

GOTO returns program execution to corresponding label

Comparing a linear program to one using a GOTO statement

Program B displays the same information as Program A. However, the GOTO statement returns the program execution to the START: label in the beginning of the program. The entire program is executed again from the beginning. This type of loop is called an *endless loop*.

This loop is "endless" because the program continues to execute this loop until the user either presses the (Ctrl) + (Pause) key combination or by switches off the computer.

You can create a more user-friendly program if a specified condition would terminate the loop. Then the user could decide to continue or terminate the program. Fortunately, *QBasic* has a statement which can stop the loop inside the program. We'll discuss this statement in the following section.

5.2 Conditional Program Branches

The disadvantage of unconditional program branches is that you can create only "infinite" loops with them. Once the program is started, it can only be stopped by pressing the Ctrl + Pause keys at the same time. This stops the program execution.

One of the strengths of a computer lies in its ability to make logical decisions or comparisons. For example, it can test to see if a variable is greater or less than zero, and then branch within the program, depending on whether the result is true or false. This is an example of a *conditional program branch*.

5.2.1 IF...THEN

The IF...THEN statement is used to stop a loop. It actually consists of two statements which are combined to work together in a program.

When *QBasic* encounters an IF statement, it checks the following condition. If the condition is *true* (fulfilled), it executes the instructions or statements that follow a THEN statement. If the condition after IF is not fulfilled—if it is *false*—the computer continues with the next program line.

Logical operators, strings, variables, comparisons, numbers or their combinations can follow the IF statement.

We make the DOLLAR program more user-friendly by adding the following two lines at the end of the program:

```
INPUT "Do you want to calculate another value (y/n)
"; NEXT$¶

IF NEXT$ = "y" THEN GOTO CONTINUE¶
```

The following is the new listing for the conversion program.

```
CLS¶
CONTINUE:¶
INPUT "What is the dollar amount"; DOLLAR¶
FOREIGN = DOLLAR * 1.59¶
PRINT "The value in FC is:";¶
PRINT FOREIGN¶
INPUT "Do you want to calculate another value (y/n)
"; NEXT$¶
IF NEXT$ = "y" THEN GOTO CONTINUE¶
```

The two lines we added at the end request the user to input either "y" or "n" to calculate another value. The answer to the input is stored in the NEXT$ variable.

Note that since "y" and "n" are characters, you must use a string variable.

We added the IF...THEN statement in the last line to test the condition. If the input was a "y" (IF NEXT$="y") the jump is made to the CONTINUE label (THEN GOTO CONTINUE). Then the program continues to execute.

However, if the input was an "n" (IF NEXT$="n"), then the condition queried with IF is not satisfied and *QBasic* terminates the current line and continues in the next line. Since there is no next line in this program, the program is terminated.

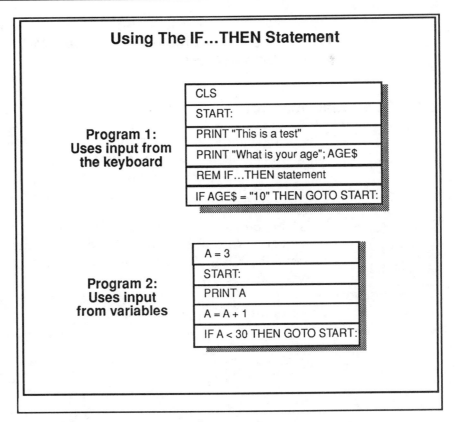

Using The IF...THEN Statement

Program 1:
Uses input from
the keyboard

CLS
START:
PRINT "This is a test"
PRINT "What is your age"; AGE$
REM IF...THEN statement
IF AGE$ = "10" THEN GOTO START:

Program 2:
Uses input
from variables

A = 3
START:
PRINT A
A = A + 1
IF A < 30 THEN GOTO START:

Testing conditions with the IF...THEN statement

The above illustration uses two examples to explain the IF...THEN statement.

In the top example, the keyboard is queried at a certain place. In the next line, the result is tested.

When a certain condition has been satisfied (in this case, the user entering 10 for the age), a jump is made to the beginning of the program. If any other value was entered, the THEN statement is ignored. This means that the program is terminated.

The bottom example uses a variable A = 3, which is incremented by one in a later line.

The IF...THEN statement appears in the last line. It's only valid if the A variable (called the *counter variable*) has not yet reached 30 (called the *end value*).

5.2.2 Relational operators

The program is now more user-friendly and includes new capabilities. The next improvement is to perform the calculations for a series of values without having to input the dollar value again every time.

This can be done easily with the information we discussed previously. We simply start with a dollar value, calculate the FC, increment DOLLAR by 1 and let the program calculate the conversion.

The program will appear as follows:

```
REM DOLLAR2¶
CLS¶
DOLLAR = 1¶
CONTINUE:¶
FC = DOLLAR * 1.59¶
PRINT FC¶
DOLLAR = DOLLAR + 1¶
IF DOLLAR < 20 THEN GOTO CONTINUE¶
```

Instead of the query with INPUT, we increment the current value of DOLLAR by one in the following line:

```
DOLLAR = DOLLAR + 1
```

Since we started at the beginning of the program in the second line with a value of 1 for DOLLAR, it is increased during the first time in this line to 2, during the next execution to 3 and so on.

The last line tests if DOLLAR is still smaller than twenty. If this is the case, the program branches to the label CONTINUE and again calculates the foreign currency value.

However, if DOLLAR has assumed the value of 20, the program is terminated.

Start the program by pressing the (Shift) + (F5) key combination. The following conversion table will appear on the output screen:

```
1.59
3.18
4.77
6.36
7.95
9.54
11.13
12.72
14.31
15.9
17.49
19.08
20.67
22.26
23.85
25.44
27.03
28.62
30.21

Press any key to continue
```

Conversion table using DOLLAR1

Unfortunately, these figures do not mean anything by themselves. We need to clarify this program by adding new statements:

```
REM DOLLAR3¶
CLS¶
DOLLAR = 1¶
CONTINUE:¶
FC = DOLLAR * 1.59¶
PRINT "The amount of $"; DOLLAR;¶
PRINT "equals"; FC; "FC"¶
DOLLAR = DOLLAR + 1¶
IF DOLLAR < 20 THEN GOTO CONTINUE¶
```

Start the program by pressing the (Shift) + (F5) key combination.

```
The amount of $ 1 equals 1.59 FC
The amount of $ 2 equals 3.18 FC
The amount of $ 3 equals 4.77 FC
The amount of $ 4 equals 6.36 FC
The amount of $ 5 equals 7.95 FC
The amount of $ 6 equals 9.54 FC
The amount of $ 7 equals 11.13 FC
The amount of $ 8 equals 12.72 FC
The amount of $ 9 equals 14.31 FC
The amount of $ 10 equals 15.9 FC
The amount of $ 11 equals 17.49 FC
The amount of $ 12 equals 19.08 FC
The amount of $ 13 equals 20.67 FC
The amount of $ 14 equals 22.26 FC
The amount of $ 15 equals 23.85 FC
The amount of $ 16 equals 25.44 FC
The amount of $ 17 equals 27.03 FC
The amount of $ 18 equals 28.62 FC
The amount of $ 19 equals 30.21 FC


Press any key to continue
```

Enhanced conversion table using DOLLAR1

Save this program as DOLLAR3.BAS. Notice that we used two characters or symbols in the above program listing. The equal sign (=) and the less than sign (<). These characters are called *relational operators* because they're used to compare two expressions in order to determine their relationship.

You can use additional characters other than the equal sign (=) and the less than character (<). There are character combinations which indicate tests.

Operator	Definition	Example
=	Equal	A=B
<	Less than	A<B
>	Greater than	A>B
>=	Greater than or equal to	A>=B
<=	Less than or equal to	A<=B
<>	Not equal	A<>B

You can also combine relational operators. For example, in the following line, two conditions must be satisfied simultaneously:

```
IF GAS > 10 AND DIST$ = "TRAFFIC" THEN PRINT
"Consumption high".
```

In this line, a test is made if either one or the other condition was satisfied:

```
IF CONSUMPTION > 10 OR MILE > 500 THEN PRINT "Check
fuel!".
```

By using the `IF...THEN` statement, you have the ability to program *controlled loops*. Controlled means that the loop will not be executed continuously, but will be executed only as long as a specified condition is fulfilled.

5.2.3 FOR...NEXT

In the previous section we created loops using the `IF...THEN` statement. In the conversion program, a counter is used and its value is incremented or decremented (DOLLAR = DOLLAR + 1). The value of the counter is checked at certain points in the program, and the program jumps to another line depending on the result of the test (true or false).

However, using the `IF...THEN` statement to create a loop like this is rather complicated, since the counter and the test are extra programming statements.

One consideration when developing your *QBasic* programs is to avoid entering many lines that can be shortened to one line. This will help prevent errors and will help in debugging (finding errors).

For such cases, *QBasic* provides a special statement which saves us input and makes the program easier to understand.

Open the DOLLAR1 program if it is not the current program. The last time we saved the conversion program, it appeared as:

```
REM DOLLAR3¶
CLS¶
DOLLAR = 1¶
CONTINUE:¶
FC = DOLLAR * 1.59¶
PRINT "The amount of $"; DOLLAR;¶
PRINT "equals"; FC; "FC"¶
DOLLAR = DOLLAR + 1¶
IF DOLLAR < 20 THEN GOTO CONTINUE¶
```

Notice the following three lines:¶

```
DOLLAR = 1¶
...¶
DOLLAR = DOLLAR + 1¶
IF DOLLAR < 20 THEN GOTO CONTINUE¶
```

We can shorten the program by deleting these lines yet achieve the same result by using a FOR...NEXT statement. Add the following lines in place of the above three lines:

```
FOR DOLLAR = 1 TO 19

NEXT DOLLAR
```

The conversion program now appears as follows:

```
REM DOLLAR4¶
CLS¶
FOR DOLLAR = 1 TO 19¶
CONTINUE:¶
FC = DOLLAR * 1.59¶
PRINT "The amount of $"; DOLLAR;¶
PRINT "equals"; FC; "FC"¶
NEXT DOLLAR¶
```

Start the program by pressing the [Shift]+[F5] key combination. You'll see the same information displayed on the output screen as the previous version of the program:

```
The amount of $ 1 equals 1.59 FC
The amount of $ 2 equals 3.18 FC
The amount of $ 3 equals 4.77 FC
The amount of $ 4 equals 6.36 FC
The amount of $ 5 equals 7.95 FC
The amount of $ 6 equals 9.54 FC
The amount of $ 7 equals 11.13 FC
The amount of $ 8 equals 12.72 FC
The amount of $ 9 equals 14.31 FC
The amount of $ 10 equals 15.9 FC
The amount of $ 11 equals 17.49 FC
The amount of $ 12 equals 19.08 FC
The amount of $ 13 equals 20.67 FC
The amount of $ 14 equals 22.26 FC
The amount of $ 15 equals 23.85 FC
The amount of $ 16 equals 25.44 FC
The amount of $ 17 equals 27.03 FC
The amount of $ 18 equals 28.62 FC
The amount of $ 19 equals 30.21 FC


Press any key to continue
```

Notice the following line:

```
FOR DOLLAR = 1 TO 19
```

During the first execution of the conversion program, the DOLLAR variable is set to "1". Then every line that follows is executed until the program encounters the NEXT statement:

```
NEXT DOLLAR
```

Then the DOLLAR variable is incremented by "1" and the program jumps again to the line where the FOR was located. The FOR...NEXT loop is executed until the DOLLAR variable is greater than 19, which is the meaning of "1 TO 19".

The program lines between FOR and NEXT are called a *loop*. Every statement appearing between FOR and NEXT will be repeated as often as the loop is executed.

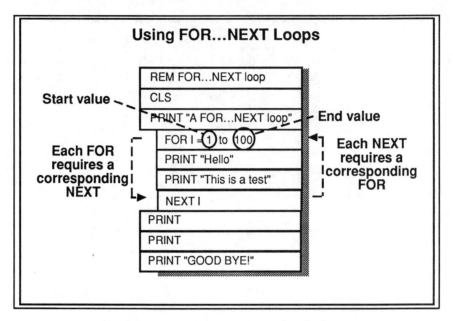

Using FOR ...NEXT in a simple loop

The diagram above shows a simple loop. This loop is started in the following line:

```
FOR I = 1 TO 100 STEP 5
```

The FOR is the actual loop opening statement. The I is the counter variable. Two numbers 1 and 100 are the start and end values.

The loop ends before the statement:

```
NEXT I
```

This indicates that the variable should be incremented at this location. The loop program then starts again at the beginning. It ends when the end-value reaches the value of 100.

Then the complete program after the line NEXT I is executed further.

You must have a NEXT statement correspond with each FOR statement. This includes using the same variable counter name.

For example, the following short program will result in a "FOR without NEXT" error:

```
FOR T = 1 to 10
PRINT "Test"
NEXT R
```

In the program sections of this chapter, we'll use several examples of the FOR...NEXT statement.

5.2.4 WHILE...WEND

The WHILE...WEND statement offers you another option for constructing loops within a program.

The start of the loop is indicated with WHILE and the end with WEND. The logical expression following WHILE is tested before each pass through the loop. As long as the expression is true, the loop is executed up to WEND.

If the condition behind WHILE is no longer fulfilled, the execution of the program continues at the line following the WEND. You terminate a loop with this statement combination quite randomly, as the following example shows:

```
REM WHILWEND¶
CLS¶
RANDOMIZE TIMER¶
WHILE A < 100¶
A = INT(101*RND)¶
Z = Z + 1¶
PRINT A,Z¶
IF A = 100 THEN END¶
WEND¶
```

In this program, the WHILE...WEND loop is executed until the value of A reaches the value 100 by chance. If the statement in the following line is true:

```
IF A = 100 THEN END
```

the statement after the WEND is executed (the program ends).

The counter tells you how many times the loop was executed. We'll use the WHILE...WEND statement in the BARCHART program in Chapter 6.

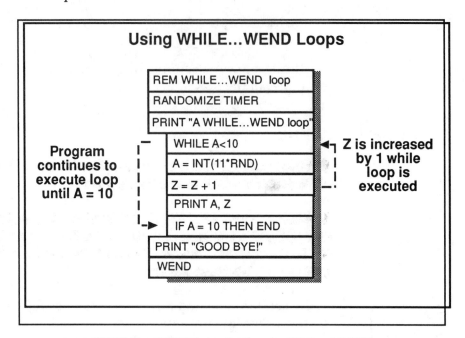

WHILE...WEND is similar to FOR...NEXT

When to use WHILE...WEND

We can make the following general rules for using either the FOR..NEXT or the WHILE...WEND statements:

1. Use the FOR...NEXT loop if you know how many times the loop is to repeat.

2. Use IF...THEN or WHILE...WEND if the number of repetitions of the loop is unknown.

5.2.5 Other statements

QBasic has additional statements for special uses. Since these statements have such specialized uses, we cannot discuss them in much detail in this book.

For more information and correct syntax, look up these statements as you need them in the appropriate **Help** command.

DO...LOOP

Similar to the WHILE...WEND statement, the DO... LOOP statement will repeat a block of statements as long as or until a condition is fulfilled.

SELECT CASE

Run one of several different parts of a program based on the selection of a value.

5.3 Modifying Conditional Program Branches

In an earlier section we discussed a program to calculate the gasoline consumption from the miles travelled and the gallons of fuel purchased.

Since you want to drive on a vacation and cannot take your PC with you (and you cannot borrow a laptop PC), a table would be useful in which you can immediately check your fuel consumption.

A table of this type can be constructed without difficulty using the statements we have already discussed. However, there is one problem. We have two variable values (representing gallons and miles), but in a simple table, only one value can change.

We'll discuss a special trick in a later section to solve this problem. For right now, in the current example we shall simply assume a distance of 300 miles travelled and that you will always buy gasoline after travelling 300 miles.

Now we must consider what values should be contained in this table. We're assuming the following for this example:

- Your car consumes between 6 and 10 gallons every 100 miles.

- The distance you always travel is 300 miles.

Since the destination is 300 miles, the fuel consumption table must range between 18 and 30 gallons.

The beginning of our loop should be as follows:

```
FOR GALLON = 18 TO 30
```

We want to calculate the CONSUMPTION in this loop and then output GALLON and CONSUMPTION on the screen. Then we can terminate the loop with NEXT GALLON.

The following is the program for the fuel consumption table:

```
REM FUELTAB.BAS¶
CLS¶
FOR GALLON = 18 TO 30¶
CONSUMPTION = 300 / GALLON¶
PRINT GALLON, CONSUMPTION¶
NEXT GALLON¶
```

Save the program as FUELTAB.BAS.

Start the program by pressing the [Shift] + [F5] keys. The following table appears on the screen:

```
18          16.66667
19          15.78947
20          15
21          14.28571
22          13.63636
23          13.04348
24          12.5
25          12
26          11.53846
27          11.11111
28          10.71429
29          10.34483
30          10




        Press any key to continue
```

Result of the FUELTAB.BAS program

Although the necessary data is displayed on the screen, we need to make some improvements to this program.

One of the improvements involves starting with other values. As the program is currently written, you must make all the changes in the middle of the program.

If, for example, you want to increase the mileage from 300 to 400, you must change the program line where the calculation is performed:

```
CONSUMPTION = 300 / GALLON
```

If you want to create a table from 18 to 36 gallons, you must change the FOR...NEXT loop:

```
FOR GALLON = 18 TO 30
```

The program becomes easier to understand if variables are defined at the beginning of the program and used instead of simple numbers. You determine exactly what happens in the calculation by looking at the variable name.

To use variables instead of simple numbers has another advantage. Imagine the program becomes three pages long and the number of miles appears ten times in calculations. You would then have to make a change for the mile number in ten locations in the program.

If the following appeared at the beginning of the program:

```
MILE = 300
```

you would only have to change this value once to 400.

The following is an example of the program with these changes:

```
CLS¶
MILE = 300¶
STARTGALLON = 18¶
ENDGALLON = 30¶

FOR GALLON = STARTGALLON TO ENDGALLON¶
CONSUMPTION = MILE / GALLON¶
PRINT GALLON, CONSUMPTION¶
NEXT GALLON¶
```

Although it appears that a line is missing in the middle of this program, the blank line is intentional. It marks the end of the variable definition and the start of the actual program.

However, *QBasic* has a better method of highlighting different sections of a program.

In the previous example, it's much better to use a REM statement instead of the blank line:

```
REM FUELTABa¶
CLS¶
MILE = 300¶
STARTGALLON = 18¶
ENDGALLON = 30¶
REM Start of the actual program¶
FOR GALLON = STARTGALLON TO ENDGALLON¶
CONSUMPTION = MILE / GALLON¶
PRINT GALLON, CONSUMPTION¶
NEXT GALLON¶
```

5.3.1 The STEP keyword

Now we want to discuss another way of using the FOR...NEXT loop. In the following examples, we're assuming that your fuel consumption of your car has improved. Therefore, you no longer need a table between 18 and 30 gallons, but only the values from 24 to 27 gallons.

You can simply set STARTGALLON and ENDGALLON to these values. However, you also determine that GALLON should be incremented by 0.2 and not 1 during every execution of the loop.

This can be done by adding a keyword in the following line:

```
FOR GALLON = STARTGALLON TO ENDGALLON
```

This keyword is called STEP. The following is the listing for the modified program:

```
REM FUELTAB2
CLS¶
MILE = 300¶
STARTGALLON = 24¶
ENDGALLON = 27¶
REM Start of the actual program¶
FOR GALLON = STARTGALLON TO ENDGALLON STEP .2¶
CONSUMPTION = MILE / GALLON¶
PRINT GALLON, CONSUMPTION¶
NEXT GALLON¶
```

Notice the following line from the program listing above:

```
FOR GALLON = STARTGALLON TO ENDGALLON STEP .2
```

We're using .2 following the STEP keyword and not 0.2. Although you can enter "0.2", *QBasic* changes it to .2 automatically.

If no STEP is indicated in the FOR TO line, *QBasic* assumes "+1".

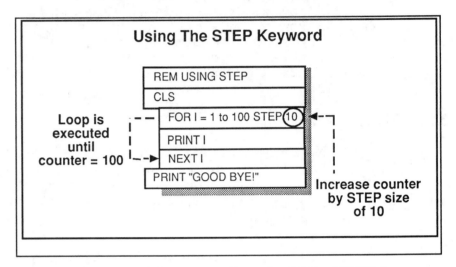

An example of how STEP *affects the FOR...NEXT loop*

You can also write negative numbers after STEP which causes the loop to go from the high to lower values. Of course in this example, STARTGALLON must be larger than ENDGALLON.

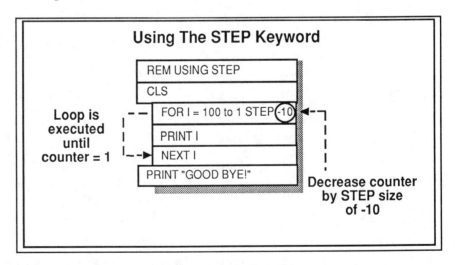

Using a negative size

The following output appears on the screen when you start the program with the [Shift] + [F5] keys:

```
24              12.5
24.2            12.39669
24.4            12.29508
24.6            12.19512
24.8            12.09677
25              12
25.2            11.90476
25.40001        11.81102
25.60001        11.71875
25.80001        11.6279
26.00001        11.53846
26.20001        11.45038
26.40001        11.36363
26.60001        11.27819
26.80001        11.19403




Press any key to continue
```

Result of the FUELTABL program using STEP

Notice that the number of gallons above 25 have unusual values. For example, 25.40001 gallons appear in the table and not 25.4 gallons as you would expect.

QBasic uses *floating point numbers* to calculate variables. Using floating point numbers is more convenient to express very large or very small numbers. While we calculate simply 25.2 + 0.2, *QBasic* uses the values 25.20000 + 0.20000 in its calculations. Since *QBasic* uses floating point numbers in the loop for the calculations, the result is not always exact.

In contrast, the whole numbers without decimal points are called *integers.* An integer must be a whole number in the range from -32,768 to +32,767.

You can add a "%" type designator to instruct *QBasic* that this variable contains only whole numbers. Unfortunately in the following program line from our example:

```
FOR GALLON = STARTGALLON TO ENDGALLON STEP .2
```

we cannot increase the program accuracy by using GALLON% because we also want to use floating point values such as "25.2".

5.3.2 The PRINT USING statement

At this point we can use another statement to help us. Did you notice that *QBasic* often indicated five places following the decimal point?

To determine precisely how many places should be output in front and behind the decimal point, use the PRINT USING statement.

The primary function of PRINT USING is to format data on the screen. For example, switch to the Immediate window by pressing F6 and type the following:

```
CLS : PRINT USING "##.##"; 24.001
```

Press the Shift + 3 key combination to display the pound sign. Then press the Enter key to see the following result:

```
24.00

Press any key to continue
```

Notice that the number of "#" characters before and after the decimal point determines the number of places reserved for numbers in the output.

Let's add the PRINT USING statement in the FUELTAB program:

```
REM GASTAB3
CLS¶
MILE = 300¶
STARTGALLON = 24¶
ENDGALLON = 27¶
REM Start of the actual program¶
```

```
FOR GALLON = STARTGALLON TO ENDGALLON STEP .2¶
CONSUMPTION = MILE / GALLON¶
PRINT USING "##.##    "; GALLON; CONSUMPTION¶
NEXT GALLON¶
```

Press the ⌈Shift⌉ + ⌈F5⌉ keys to start the program.

```
24.00    12.50
24.20    12.40
24.40    12.30
24.60    12.20
24.80    12.10
25.00    12.00
25.20    11.90
25.40    11.81
25.60    11.72
25.80    11.63
26.00    11.54
26.20    11.45
26.40    11.36
26.60    11.28
26.80    11.19




        Press any key to continue
```

PRINT USING improves the appearance of the table

Notice that the amounts in the table now appear in columns. Also the rounding problem in the earlier example has been eliminated. To separate the columns, we added spaces before the second quotation mark in the PRINT USING line.

If you want to print this table, use the LPRINT statement instead of PRINT. This statement redirects the output to the printer.

Simply change the line with the PRINT statement to:

```
LPRINT USING "##.##"; GALLON; CONSUMPTION
```

5.4 Using Random Numbers

Since we've only discussed "serious" problems so far in our programming examples, let's create something more entertaining.

A common *QBasic* program involves the computer producing a random number and the user guessing that number.

The only clue the computer will provide is if the number you select is larger or smaller than its number. If we input the right number, the computer should also reveal the number of guessing attempts.

We need two new statements to generate random numbers for this type of program.

5.4.1 The RND function

To create a random number, use the RND function (abbreviation for "random"). It generates random numbers between 0 and 1. This number can be assigned to a variable with:

```
RANDOMNUMBER = RND
```

A new random number between 0 and 1 is created each time RND is used. Unfortunately, these are not truly random numbers. Instead, they're generated with complicated internal calculations. By using the same start value, this calculation always leads to the same random numbers.

5.4.2 The RANDOMIZE statement

To change the initial value, called the *number seed*, for the calculation (and therefore the random numbers), use the RANDOMIZE statement. This statement changes the sequence of random numbers every time you run the program.

If you enter RANDOMIZE without an expression (or number following the statement), you're asked to enter a number for the random number seed:

```
Random number seed (-32768 TO 32767) ?
```

You may be wondering how to guarantee that new initial values you use are always new values. The easiest way to initialize the random number generator is to use the system clock (or TIMER function).

The value in the built-in clock (timer) in your PC is not random. It returns the number of seconds which have passed since midnight. Since it constantly changes, values using TIMER for the initial value provides different random numbers.

To create true random numbers, we could use the following two lines:

```
RANDOMIZE TIMER
PCNUMBER = RND
```

The COMPUTERNUMBER variable receives values only between 0 and 1. Since guessing numbers such as 0.14956 isn't easy, these numbers should be only whole numbers between 0 and 999.

This can be done by multiplying the random number by 1000 and removing the decimal places.

QBasic does this automatically when we assign a floating point number to an integer variable. Since *QBasic* always rounds a number off to the next highest whole number, we must always use 1000 instead of 999.

The following program is an example of using random numbers.

```
REM RNDTIMER
CLS¶
MAXNUMBER = 999¶
PRINT "I'm thinking of a number between 0 and
";MAXNUMBER;"!"¶
PCNUMBER% = (MAXNUMBER + 1) * RND¶
Guess:¶
INPUT "What is the number"; NUMBER%¶
```

121

```
GUESSNR% = GUESSNR% + 1¶
IF PCNUMBER% > NUMBER% THEN PRINT "My number is
larger!": GOTO Guess¶
IF PCNUMBER% < NUMBER% THEN PRINT "My number is
smaller!": GOTO Guess¶
PRINT "Right!"¶
PRINT "You required "; GUESSNR%;" guesses."¶
```

Press the (Shift) + (F5) keys to start the program.

```
I'm thinking of a number between 0 and 999 !
What is the number? 500
MY NUMBER IS SMALLER!
What is the number? 250
MY NUMBER IS LARGER!
What is the number? 300
MY NUMBER IS LARGER!
What is the number? 350
RIGHT!
You required 4 guesses




        Press any key to continue
```

In the first line, RANDOMIZE TIMER initializes the initial value for
the random numbers so that new numbers are created each time
you start the program.

The next line clears the screen. The largest possible number is
stored in the MAXNUMBER variable. Recall that we mentioned
how much easier it is to change a program in this manner.

The PRINT statement displays the purpose of the program. The
largest possible number in this line is output on the screen. Since
you probably want to use this in your own programs, we should
examine this line closer.

```
PRINT "I am thinking of a number between 0 and
";MAXNUMBER;"!"
```

The `PRINT` statement in this line sends two items on the screen:

- The expression: "I am thinking of a number between 0 and..."

- The content of the MAXNUMBER variable

Notice the semicolons are placed between the two items. A semicolon instructs *QBasic* to print the next value immediately after the first value. In this case, the `PRINT` statement does not start a new line but continues the output on the same line.

We could also have written:

```
PRINT "I am thinking of a number between 0 and 999!"
```

If we later want to set MAXNUMBER to 9999, *QBasic* calculates numbers between 0 and 9999, but the message on the screen claims to let you guess only numbers between 0 and 999.

Therefore, the next line:

```
PCNUMBER% = (MAXNUMBER + 1) * RND
```

creates a whole number between 0 and 999 from the random number.

QBasic recognizes that the PCNUMBER% variable can store only integer numbers through the "%" character. The parentheses surrounding MAXNUMBER + 1 requires that *QBasic* perform this addition function before the multiplication function.

The following line:

```
INPUT "What is the number"; NUMBER%
```

prompts the user to enter a number. This number is stored in NUMBER%.

Since we also count the number of guesses and output this information at the end, we increase the GUESSNR% integer variable in the next line by 1.

We can use a small trick to do this. When a variable is used for the first time, it's assigned the value 0 if no value has been assigned to it. Therefore, GUESSNR% is set in this line from 0 to 1.

The next few lines represent the locations where *QBasic* tests if the number is too large, too small or is the right number.

Notice the following line:

```
IF PCNUMBER% > NUMBER% THEN PRINT "My number is
larger!": GOTO Guess
```

If the number calculated by the computer is larger than the number entered by the user, a corresponding message ("My number is larger!") appears on the screen.

The program also "jumps" to the Guess label where it requests another guess and increases the number of executions. Notice that *QBasic* requires a colon to separate different statements that appear in the same line.

The remainder of the line is executed only when the condition has been satisfied. If the condition is not satisfied, *QBasic* ignores the remainder of the line and continues in the next line.

In the next line a test is performed to determine if the number is smaller than the number entered by the user. A message is output ("My number is larger!") and execution continues at the Guess label to obtain a new input.

What happens if the input matches the random number? *QBasic* outputs a message announcing that the user has successfully guessed the number. Then the program displays the number of guesses required by the user to successfully guess the number.

5.5 Another Example of Random Numbers

In this section, we'll modify the previous program to practice the multiplication tables. The following program uses many of the same statements as the previous program.

We now use the MAXVALUE variable instead of MAXNUMBER to avoid more typing. You can use a shorter name, but make certain that the variable name you use follows the rules we discussed in Section 4.1.

Remember to press the (Enter) key when you see the ¶ character in this program listing.

```
RANDOMIZE TIMER¶
MAXVALUE = 19¶
Calculate:¶
CLS¶
PRINT "*** The big multiplication test ***"¶
PRINT¶
NUMBER1% = (MAXVALUE + 1) * RND¶
NUMBER2% = (MAXVALUE + 1) * RND¶
PRINT "How much is"; NUMBER1%; " * "; NUMBER2%¶
INPUT "Result "; RESULT%¶
PCRESULT% = NUMBER1% * NUMBER2%¶
IF PCRESULT% = RESULT% THEN PRINT "Right": RIGHT% =
RIGHT% + 1: GOTO Continue¶
PRINT "Wrong!!!": WRONG% = WRONG% + 1¶
Continue:¶
INPUT "Want to do another? (y/n)"; IN$¶
IF IN$ = "y" THEN GOTO Calculate¶
PRINT "Right:";RIGHT%, "Wrong:";WRONG%¶
```

You may have to use the direction keys to move (or "scroll") the screen vertically and horizontally in order to view the entire program listing.

On longer programs, you can use the (PgDn) or (PgUp) keys to scroll through the program listing.

In the second line, the MAXVALUE for the random numbers generated, is set to "19", similar to the multiplication table. If you want to practice multiplication, simply enter a "9" here.

The next three lines clear the screen and display the program title. In the following lines two random, whole numbers (%) between 0 and MAXVALUE are generated. Finally, the task assignment is composed again from the fixed text and the variables.

After the query of the result, the computer calculates the (hopefully) correct result and compared with the number which was input. If the two numbers are equal, the proper message is written on the screen, the counter variable RIGHT% is increased by 1 and jumps to the Continue label.

If the user entered an incorrect number, a corresponding message ("Wrong!!!") is displayed. The counter WRONG% variable is then incremented by one. In every case a query occurs if another calculation should be performed.

If the user answers with a "y", a jump is made to the Calculate label at the beginning of the program. Otherwise, the number of the right (RIGHT%) and the wrong (WRONG%) solutions is displayed and the program is terminated.

5.6 Calculated Branch Statements

The calculated jump statements can add flexibility to your programs.

So far in this chapter, we have discussed only jump statements that jump to a specific program line or label. The line numbers or label in the GOTO statement cannot be changed—GOTO Aloop always continues execution at the Aloop: label.

However, it would be convenient if you could enter a value at the start of a program and the program would then branch based on this value. Although this could be achieved with some IF...THEN statements, it would require a jump for each program line, for every comparison.

A simple example will clarify this:

```
REM CALCJUM1.BAS¶
REM JUMP TO CERTAIN LINES¶
PRINT "ENTER A NUMBER BETWEEN 1 AND 4" : PRINT¶
INPUT "WHAT NUMBER";Z¶
IF Z = 1 THEN GOTO TEST1¶
IF Z = 2 THEN GOTO TEST2¶
IF Z = 3 THEN GOTO TEST3¶
IF Z = 4 THEN GOTO TEST4¶
TEST1:¶
   PRINT "You jumped to the TEST1 label!"¶
   GOTO FINISH¶
TEST2:¶
   PRINT "You jumped to the TEST2 label!"¶
   GOTO FINISH¶
TEST3:¶
   PRINT "You jumped to the TEST3 label!"¶
   GOTO FINISH¶
TEST4:¶
   PRINT "You jumped to the TEST4 label!"¶
   GOTO FINISH¶
FINISH:¶
   END¶
```

In this program, a branch is made to the TEST1, TEST2, TEST3 or TEST4 label, depending on the input of a number 1-4.

In such applications, programming these tests with IF . . . THEN is rather complicated and is relatively slow in execution speed.

5.6.1 The ON...GOTO statement

QBasic offers a more flexible solution for such cases. The statement has the following syntax:

```
ON (variable) GOTO (label or line number)
```

This extended GOTO statement with ON allows the program to branch to one or several line numbers or labels following the GOTO. The range of the variables extends from zero to the number of line numbers given. If the variable does not have an integer value, the non-integer portion is ignored. Negative values are also ignored.

If the variable has a value that is larger than the number of line numbers available following the GOTO, the line following the ON . . . GOTO statement is executed.

The following are some simple examples:

Example A:

```
CLS
ON Z GOTO DATA87, DATA88, DATA89, DATA90
PRINT "Sales for the year were:"
    .
    .
    .
```

If the variable Z, in this example, has the value 1, the program jumps to the DATA87 label. If Z runs through the values 2-4 in a loop, the program jumps to the DATA88, DATA89 and DATA90 labels in succession.

The Z variable designates the positions of the individual line numbers that follow the GOTO. If Z assumes values larger or smaller than the number of line numbers behind the GOTO, the program continues with the next statement following the GOTO (the `PRINT` statement in this example). The `GOTO` statement is simply skipped.

Example B:

```
ON Z+3/4 GOTO TEST1, TEST2, TEST3
PRINT
    .
    .
    .
```

You see that an arithmetic expression can be used instead of a variable. The advantage of this `ON...GOTO` statement is that it can replace several `IF...THEN` statements. This saves programming time, as well as memory space.

Our previous short program could have the following form:

```
REM CALCJUM2.BAS¶
REM JUMP TO CERTAIN LINES¶
PRINT "ENTER A NUMBER BETWEEN 1 AND 4" : PRINT¶
INPUT "WHAT NUMBER";Z¶
ON Z GOTO TEST1, TEST2, TEST3, TEST4¶
TEST1:¶
   PRINT "You jumped to the TEST1 label!"¶
   GOTO FINISH¶
TEST2:¶
   PRINT "You jumped to the TEST2 label!"¶
   GOTO FINISH¶
TEST3:¶
   PRINT "You jumped to the TEST3 label!"¶
   GOTO FINISH¶
TEST4:¶
   PRINT "You jumped to the TEST4 label!"¶
   GOTO FINISH¶
FINISH:¶
   END¶
```

Although the CALCJUM2 program executes the same as the CALCJUM1 program, we saved three program lines. You may save even more lines with larger programs in which comparisons with `IF...THEN` occur.

The destination line numbers of ON...GOTO represent certain program segments within the program in which special tasks are generally performed. It helps to designate these with "smooth" line numbers. This can be done in steps of one hundred, as in our example program. This improves the readability of the individual program segments.

5.6.2 The ON...ERROR statement

This statement is a special type of the GOTO statement. It's used to automatically manage errors that occur in a program which in turn allows errors to be handled by the program itself.

A typical program line could look like this:

```
ON ERROR GOTO ERRORHANDLER
```

A small error-handling routine can be located as a block of code marked by the line number or label.

But how do we know what error has occurred and where the error is located?

QBasic has two functions, ERR and ERL, that are tested to tell us this information. ERR determines the error code of the error and ERL is the line number in which the error occurred.

The termination of an error-handling routine is designated by the statement:

```
RESUME (label) or  RESUME (line number)
```

The RESUME statement lets you determine the program line at which the program is to continue execution after the error message.

A similar statement is called RESUME NEXT. It causes the execution to continue with the statement following the one that caused the error.

You can also instruct *QBasic* to print error messages from within the program. You must use the following:

```
ON ERROR GOTO 0
```

You can check the ON ERROR function on your computer with the following program:

```
REM ONERROR.BAS¶
CLS¶
ON ERROR GOTO ERRORHANDLER¶
SOUND 34567,9090¶
END¶
ERRORHANDLER:¶
   PRINT ERL, ERR¶
   RESUME NEXT¶
```

Press the [Shift] + [F5] key combination to start this program line. This program line outputs the following:

```
 0   6



Press any key to continue
```

The error number as well as the number of the line containing the error are passed in the two variables ERL and ERR.

After running the program, check the values of these variables by entering the following statement in direct mode:

```
 PRINT ERR,ERL
```

and you'll notice that although the error number has been cleared from the ERR variable, ERL has retained the error line number. This can be useful in error handling routines.

6. Using ASCII Characters

In this chapter we'll discuss the *QBasic* statements you'll use to display a professional bar chart such as the following:

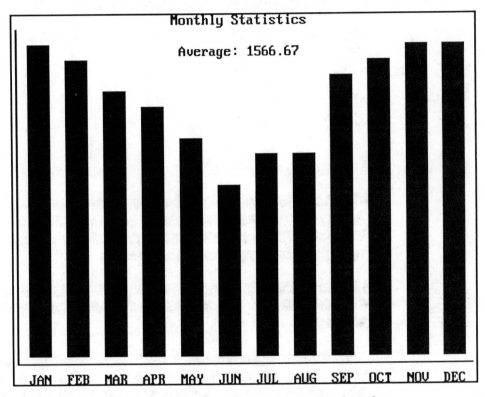

Output from the bar chart program in this chapter

6.1 ASCII Characters

The *QBasic* graphic statements, such as COLOR, PAINT, PALETTE, CIRCLE and others, require that you have one of the following types of graphic adapters installed in your PC:

- CGA (Color Graphics Adapter) is a bit-mapped graphics adapter which can display several colors at the same time.

- EGA (Enhanced Graphics Adapter) color is a high resolution graphics adapter with superior resolution compared to the CGA. This type of graphics adapter is capable of displaying all 16 colors in text mode with a resolution of 640 x 350 pixels.

- VGA (Video Graphics Adapter) is a video display standard which offers a maximum of 256 colors simultaneously and offers better resolution than other adapters.

If you don't have one of the above cards installed in your PC, you can still create graphic programs using *QBasic*. We'll use the ASCII characters which are included in your PC.

We'll discuss special graphics capabilities in more detail in Chapter 9.

6.1.1 What is an ASCII character?

ASCII is an abbreviation for "American Standard Code for Information Interchange". ASCII is a standard computer character set created in 1968 to improve data communication and compatibility between different systems.

The standard ASCII code uses the values from 0 to 127 which consist of 96 uppercase and lowercase letters and 32 control characters.

For example, the character "A" represents the ASCII value 65. If this number is sent to a computer or printer it's always interpreted as the letter "A" (providing the other device is working with ASCII).

It doesn't matter whether you type characters into the computer with the keyboard or send your data across the country with a telephone modem, the receiver translates the value 65 into an "A".

For a complete list of ASCII characters, refer to the Appendices.

In the standard ASCII, the values 65-90 are used for uppercase letters and the values 97-122 for lowercase letters and other characters. The ASCII code of your computer is identical to the standard ASCII code for codes 0-127, which consists of the upper and lowercase letters. Codes 128 through 255 make up an extended ASCII character set.

Most computer manufacturers have decided to use an extended ASCII code so that other characters can be represented as well. Certain characters in *QBasic* do not represent letters but appear like small graphic elements. These characters are accessible directly from your keyboard and include the exclamation point, period, multiplication sign, etc.

In addition, there are some characters which can be created by pressing the Alt key while pressing keys in the numeric keypad. The highest possible number is 255. We'll use some of these ASCII characters in this chapter.

The table below shows an example of different ASCII characters which you can use with *QBasic*. The numbers refer not only to the ASCII number but also to the keys you must press in the numeric keypad:

174	╫	177	▓	197	┼	219	█	249	
175	╜	179	│	205	=	236	∞	251	√
176	░	196	–	206	╬	240	=•	254	▪

For example, to display ASCII character 197 on the output screen, type the following lines:

```
CLS
PRINT "┼"
```

Remember to press the Alt key while pressing the 1 + 9 + 7 from the numeric keypad. Then press the Shift + F5 key combination to start the program. You'll see the ASCII character appear on the output screen:

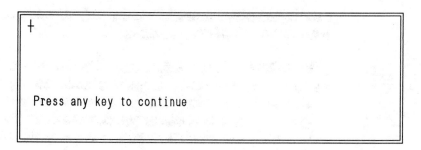

```
+



     Press any key to continue

```

In this chapter, we'll show you how you can use ASCII characters to display different effects on the screen.

Before using ASCII characters to create graphics on the screen, we need to discuss a few new *QBasic* statements. We'll discuss these statements in the following example programs.

6.2 Positioning Text In A Line

The purpose of the first example program we'll discuss in this chapter is to create a screen full of star-like images.

The first step is to create a single star on the screen. Since the "*" (multiplication sign) closely resembles a star, we can display it on the screen using the PRINT statement:

```
REM STARS1¶
CLS¶
FOR I = 1 TO 10¶
PRINT "*"¶
NEXT I¶
```

When you start this program by pressing the ⌜Shift⌝ + ⌜F5⌝ key combination, ten "stars" appear on the left side of the screen:

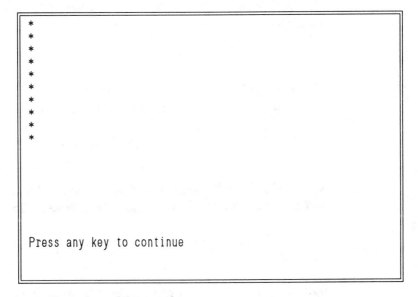

Using PRINT to display ten stars

However, no nighttime sky quite resembles this screen. We need a statement to output a character at a specific location on the screen.

6.2.1 The LOCATE statement

The statement we can use for this purpose is the LOCATE statement. A PRINT statement usually follows LOCATE to output the characters at the location specified by LOCATE.

We also have to inform the LOCATE statement where to place the cursor on the screen. This is done by specifying the row and the column:

```
LOCATE row,column
```

You can enter a number between 1 and 24 as a row and 1 to 80 as the column. For example, the following line would position the cursor at the bottom right corner of the output screen:

```
LOCATE 24,80
```

The following line would position the cursor at the top left corner of the output screen:

```
LOCATE 1,1
```

An even better method of displaying stars in your program is to have them appear in random locations on the screen.

6.2.2 TAB

QBasic has two functions that you can use to output data or characters at specific positions on a screen line.

TAB and SPC are very similar in their uses, but quite different in their effects.

This function and the parameter in parentheses always position the output relative to the start of the line:

```
TAB(column)
```

For example, type the following two program lines:

```
CLS
PRINT TAB(15) "HELLO"
```

Press the Shift + F5 key combination to start this program. You'll see the following on your output screen:

```
            HELLO


Press any key to continue
```

The screen output displays "HELLO" at the 15th position (or column) of the line.

You can use several TAB functions in one program line. If the total for the column exceeds the maximum number of columns in the screen line, the TAB function moves the print position to that column on the next line.

For example, the following program will display "HELLO" on two lines because the column has exceeded the output width:

```
CLS
PRINT TAB(35) "HELLO" : PRINT TAB(55) "HELLO"
```

Press the Shift + F5 key combination to start this program. You'll see the following on your output screen:

```
                    HELLO
                            HELLO

Press any key to continue
```

The TAB function can only be used in PRINT or LPRINT statements.

6.2.3 SPC

We can use the same two program lines above to show you the SPC function. Replace TAB with the SPC function so that the lines look like the following:

```
CLS
PRINT SPC(15) "HELLO"
```

Press the [Shift] + [F5] key combination to start this program. You'll you get the same result on your output screen:

```
          HELLO

Press any key to continue
```

Both the TAB and SPC functions have the same effect when used in this manner. In the next example you will see the difference. Enter the following commands:

```
PRINT TAB(5)"TEST 1" TAB(20)"TEST2"
```

Press the [Shift] + [F5] key combination:

```
  TEST 1          TEST 2

Press any key to continue
```

Notice that "TEST1" appears at the fifth position and "TEST2" appears at the 20th position.

Now change the second TAB to SPC. Your line should then look like this:

```
PRINT TAB(5)"TEST1" SPC(20)"TEST2"
```

Now when you press the [Shift] + [F5] key combination, you'll see the difference in the output on the screen:

```
TEST 1                    TEST 2

Press any key to continue
```

The "TEST2" is not printed at the 20th position from the start of the line, but at the 20th position from the last character of "TEST1".

The SPC function can only be used in PRINT or LPRINT statements.

Therefore, the TAB function always works with the *absolute* position in the screen line and the SPC function with the *relative* position from the last character printed. The values passed to either function may not be larger than 32,767.

6.2.4 Positioning at random locations

To display the stars at random locations, we'll need to use the RND function. The following is the first listing of our graphic program:

```
REM STARS2¶
CLS¶
RANDOMIZE TIMER¶
FOR I% = 1 TO 50¶
X% = (RND * 79) + 1¶
Y% = (RND * 23) + 1¶
LOCATE Y%,X%¶
PRINT "*";¶
NEXT I%¶
```

Press the (Shift) + (F5) key combination to start the program. A screen similar to the following will appear:

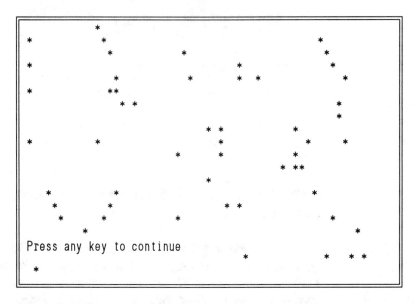

Using LOCATE to display simple graphics

Remember, we're using the RANDOMIZE function in this program. Therefore, your screen will not appear exactly the same every time you start the program.

We've previously discussed most of the statements in this program. However, some statements and functions are used slightly differently in certain parts of the program.

The RANDOMIZE TIMER function in the second row creates a different sequence of random numbers each time a new program is started.

If we did not use RANDOMIZE TIMER, the stars would appear in the same location every time.

The next line starts a FOR...NEXT loop which creates a column (X%) between 1 and 80 and a line (Y%) between 1 and 24. This loop is executed 50 times.

QBasic cannot accept larger values for either X or Y than those specified in the program. These values must equal the dimensions of the screen. If you use other larger values, you would receive an "Illegal function call" error message.

You can delete the "Press any key to continue" prompt which appears at the bottom of the screen by adding the following *screen saver* lines:

```
Blank:
T$ = INKEY$
IF T$ = "" THEN GOTO Blank
```

The program lines would look like this:

```
REM STARS3¶
CLS¶
RANDOMIZE TIMER¶
FOR I% = 1 TO 50¶
X% = (RND * 79) + 1¶
Y% = (RND * 23) + 1¶
LOCATE Y%,X%¶
PRINT "*";¶
NEXT I%¶
Blank:¶
    T$ = INKEY$¶
    IF T$ = "" THEN GOTO Blank¶
```

Although you cannot use larger numbers for X% and Y%, you can experiment with the X% and Y% values by entering smaller values.

Try to reduce the area for the stars by displaying them only in the upper left corner of the screen. For example, replace the X% and Y% values with the following:

```
X% = (RND * 29) + 1
Y% = (RND * 13) + 1
```

To display stars in the top half of the screen, replace the values with the following:

```
X% = (RND * 79) + 1
Y% = 10 + (RND * 12) + 1
```

6.3 Using Random Numbers In QBasic

In this section we'll show you how to use the ASCII characters we discussed in Section 6.1 in a small *QBasic* program to fill, or "paint", the stars at specific locations on the screen.

This program will also show you a second method to create graphics on the screen. In the program in Section 6.2, the position of one star was independent with the position of the preceding star.

In this new program, we want to start at one specific point and continue displaying one star after its predecessor. We'll determine the direction randomly in which the next star will be placed.

The following describes how this program will execute: We place a star at some location on the screen and record its coordinates. Then we randomly place the next star to the left, right, top or bottom. Finally, we'll change the coordinates accordingly and repeat the process with the new star.

The only question which remains is how to randomly determine the direction. Since we have four possible directions, we determine a number at random between 1 and 4 and assign one of the directions to each number.

Be careful when using the LOCATE statement. You can use only coordinates *QBasic* will accept. When you're using LOCATE to place the cursor in a row and column, row can have a value between 1 and 24 and column can have a value between 1 and 80. Refer to the Appendices for more information on LOCATE.

When the coordinates are changed, we must test to make certain they're within the acceptable area of the screen. Otherwise they must be changed to remain in the acceptable area and the drawing must continue at a suitable location. For example:

The X coordinate for the column is stored in X%. At the moment, X% has the value 80 and this places the last star at the right edge of the screen. The new direction is selected as "right" through a random number.

We must now increment the X coordinate by one with "X% = X% + 1". This will make X% contain the value 81 and that is outside the acceptable area. We want to determine that if a star disappears to the right of the screen, it will return on the left side of the screen. In this example program, we need only to set X% to 1.

Now the program listing appears like the following:

```
CLS¶
RANDOMIZE TIMER¶
X% = 40: Y% = 12¶
FOR I% = 1 TO 1000¶
  R% = 4 * RND + 1¶
  IF R% = 1 THEN X% = X% + 1¶
  IF R% = 2 THEN X% = X% - 1¶
  IF R% = 3 THEN Y% = Y% - 1¶
  IF R% = 4 THEN Y% = Y% + 1¶
  IF X% = 0 THEN X% = 79¶
  IF X% = 80 THEN X% = 1¶
  IF Y% = 0  THEN Y% = 24¶
  IF Y% = 24 THEN Y% = 1¶
  LOCATE Y%,X%¶
  PRINT "*";¶
NEXT I%¶
```

Notice that we indented the program lines between the FOR and NEXT lines. Although these spaces do not affect the program, they do make it easier to recognize the loop. This is a good habit to start now. You'll realize the benefit of listing a program this way when entering larger programs.

We've already discussed the first two lines so you should understand their purpose. The following line sets the start coordinates to the center of the screen.

The next line begins a loop, which is repeated 1,000 times. Although this may seem like a high number, the screen will not be completely filled.

A random number between 1 and 4, represented by R%, is used for the direction.

The next four lines provide a change of the coordinates for every possible direction. The X-coordinate is increased by one for a "right" direction and reduced by one for a "left" direction. The same occurs also with the Y-coordinate. Y is increased for "bottom" and reduced for the "top".

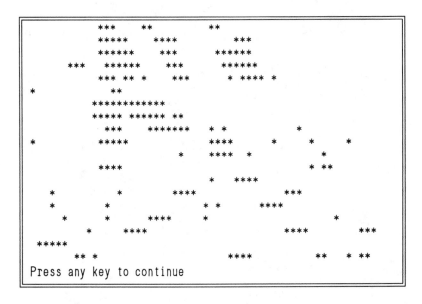

Characters appearing at random screen locations

You'll save time by using the **Copy** command in the **Edit** menu (see Chapter 3).

Although we have now determined the new direction and changed the coordinates accordingly, the test for the acceptable area must still be made.

As explained in a previous example, both coordinates in the following lines are tested to determine if they are too large or too small. Any changes that are necessary to the coordinates are performed in these lines.

Use the LOCATE statement to set the cursor to the new coordinates. The next PRINT statement displays the star at the new position.

The loop ends in the last line. Then the program ends after 1,000 executions.

Save the current program as PAINT.BAS. Then start it by pressing the (Shift) + (F5) key combination.

We want to make two more enhancements to this program. Perhaps you noticed that your PC seems to pause for a short period of time before displaying a new star.

The reason is that new stars are accidentally written into an area which is already full of stars. Our artist (the PC) can work with only image.

A quick way to correct this minor problem is to change the program so that the first 500 stars are drawn with one image (*) and the second 500 stars with the second image (.).

We could simply duplicate the entire program and change the two loops to 500 executions each. However, it's easier to save the characters for the image in a string variable (PENNIB$) and to change this variable after 500 executions (from "*" to "." for example).

The following is how this change appears in the program listing:

```
REM PAINT1.BAS¶
CLS¶
RANDOMIZE TIMER¶
X% = 40: Y% = 10¶
FOR I% = 1 TO 1000¶
  R% = 4 * RND + 1¶
  IF R% = 1 THEN X% = X% + 1¶
  IF R% = 2 THEN X% = X% - 1¶
  IF R% = 3 THEN Y% = Y% - 1¶
  IF R% = 4 THEN Y% = Y% + 1¶
  IF X% = 0 THEN X% = 79¶
  IF X% = 80 THEN X% = 1¶
  IF Y% = 0 THEN Y% = 24¶
```

```
IF Y% = 25 THEN Y% = 1¶
LOCATE Y%,X%¶
IF I% < 500 THEN PENNIB$ = "*"¶
IF I% > 500 THEN PENNIB$ = "."¶
PRINT PENNIB$;¶
NEXT I%¶
Aloop:¶
IF INKEY$ = "" THEN GOTO Aloop¶
CLS¶
```

You can save this program as PAINT1.BAS.

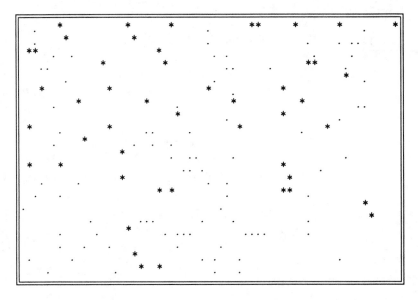

Using two loops to display two images

In the lines entered following the LOCATE statement, the PENNIB$ loop variable is set to one of the two characters. This character is then displayed on the screen.

Also, the last four lines are new to the program. These lines instruct the program to wait for the user to press a key before clearing the screen and displaying the "Press any key to continue" message.

We test INKEY$ to see if it contains the value "". This is the empty string which does not contain any characters. As long as INKEY$ is empty (""), no key was pressed.

The condition in the test line is no longer met after the user presses a key. The program continues to the next line, where the graphic is cleared.

The following procedure:

```
Aloop:
  IF INKEY$ = "" THEN GOTO Aloop
  CLS
```

does not work with every key on the keyboard (for example, Shift). This procedure uses the alphanumeric keys (including the numeric keypad).

6.4 Nested Loops

Now we'll try our first large project. Consider first how to display a bar. We could use a simple program such as the following:

```
REM ch64A.BAS
CLS
FOR I = 1 TO 20
  PRINT "    █" : REM 3 spaces before character
NEXT I
```

This is the first program where we'll use an ASCII character. Note the "█" represents an ASCII character. You can create it by pressing the [Alt] key and pressing the [2] and [1] and [9] keys on the numeric keypad. The "█" character will appear as soon as you release the [Alt] key. You'll need to perform these steps three times in this program line.

Also notice the REM statement following the PRINT line. Remember that a REM statement is used to provide information on different sections of the program. The REM statement in this line is telling you to press the [Spacebar] key three times before entering the "█" character.

Press the [Shift] + [F5] key combination to start the program. Although this program does indeed display a bar on the screen, notice that the bar starts at the top of the screen. A professional bar chart program always displays the bar starting at the bottom of the screen. Therefore, this routine is not suitable for a bar chart program.

However, we can easily change this program by adding the LOCATE statement to start the bar at the bottom of the screen. The LOCATE statement lets us set the cursor position to the bottom of the screen, output a bar character and set the cursor one position higher.

We'll need to use a loop for the individual procedures. Since the lowest position has a large line value (24) and the top position a smaller value (1), we must run the loop "backwards" or decrease the loop counter.

To do this, we can use the STEP keyword. This keyword lets us change the loop counter after every repeat of the FOR...NEXT loop. STEP can represent any value, including negative numbers.

After adding the STEP keyword, the listing of the BAREXAM1.BAS bar chart program now appears as follows:

```
BAREXAM1¶
CLS¶
FOR I = 24 TO 1 STEP -1¶
  LOCATE I, 5¶
  PRINT "█"¶
NEXT I¶
NULL:¶
  CHART$ = INKEY$¶
  IF CHART$ = "" THEN GOTO NULL¶
```

Save this program as BAREXAM2.BAS. Press the (Shift) + (F5) key combination to start the program. Notice that the bar now starts at the bottom of the screen and moves toward the top.

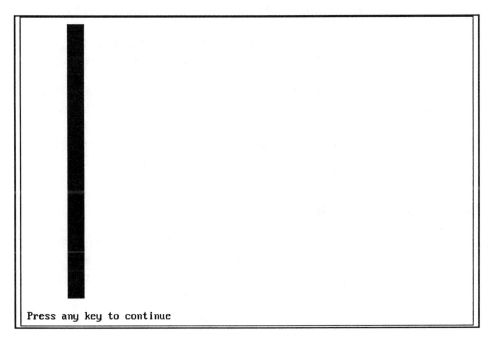

The bar now starts at the bottom of the screen

However, a bar chart usually requires more than one bar. Therefore, we'll need to change the program so that several different bars of varying heights are displayed. This requires various numbers for the height of the individual bars.

These numbers are created by using the RND function. In addition, every new bar must be equal to the right of the previous bar.

The bar chart program must be able to meet each of the following requirements:

1.   Clear the screen and determine random numbers.

2.   Calculate the height from a random number.

3.   Draw line for line up to the desired height.

4.   Move the cursor position the appropriate spaces to the right for the next bar.

5.   Repeat #2 to #4 for each individual bar.

6.   After drawing all parts for all bars, the program must wait for the user to press a key before clearing the screen.

Since two of the above requirements demand multiple statements or functions, we'll need to use a loop in both places.

However, the second loop (3) is located inside the first loop (5). A loop located inside another loop is called a *nested loop*.

6.4.1 Nested loops in detail

We'll use the following short program to examine nested loops in more detail. Type in the program and press the (Shift) + (F5) key combination to start it (remember to press the (Enter) key when you see the ¶ character in this program listing).

```
REM NESTLP1¶
CLS¶
FOR I = 1 TO 9 : REM outer loop begins here,
executes 9 times¶
  FOR J = 1 TO 9 : REM inner loop begins here¶
```

```
    PRINT USING "##   "; J * I;¶
    NEXT J : REM inner loop ends here¶
    PRINT¶
    NEXT I : REM outer loop ends here¶
```

The nested loops in this program, called NESTLP1.BAS, display the following multiplication table on the output screen:

```
1   2   3   4   5   6   7   8   9
2   4   6   8  10  12  14  16  18
3   6   9  12  15  18  21  24  27
4   8  12  16  20  24  28  32  36
5  10  15  20  25  30  35  40  45
6  12  18  24  30  36  42  48  54
7  14  21  28  35  42  49  56  63
8  16  24  32  40  48  56  64  72
9  18  27  36  45  54  63  72  81


Press any key to continue
```

Note the REM statements in the second line and the last line. The outer loop begins in the second line and ends in the last line. The second line is also responsible for executing the outer loop nine times.

The inner loop starts in the third line and ends two lines later. Since each loop is executed nine times, both loops are executed a total of 81 times (9 x 9 times).

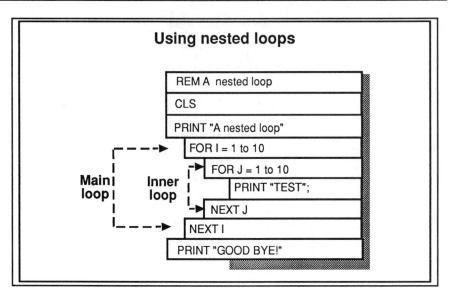

Using nested loops

| REM A nested loop |
| CLS |
| PRINT "A nested loop" |
| FOR I = 1 to 10 |
| FOR J = 1 to 10 |
| PRINT "TEST"; |
| NEXT J |
| NEXT I |
| PRINT "GOOD BYE!" |

Main loop   **Inner loop**

A diagram of a nested loop

Notice in the diagram above that a second loop (called an *inner loop*) was inserted inside the first loop (called *main loop*). The inner loop (J) must have a different variable name for its counter than the outer loop (I). You may not receive an error message if you use the same variable names in both loops, however the program will not execute correctly.

The program first executes the main loop, arrives at the inner loop and executes it ten times. Then the main loop is again executed and a jump is made to its beginning. During the second execution of the main loop, the program lines of the inner loop are again executed ten times and so on.

The result in this example is that every step of the main loop is executed ten times, while every step of the inner loop is executed 10 x 10 times (therefore a hundred times).

If it is not clear to you why we output the results of the multiplication with the PRINT USING statement, then simply replace:

```
PRINT USING "##  "; J * I;
```

with a line using the PRINT statement, such as:

```
PRINT J * I;
```

You can see that the screen appears more disorganized because the numbers are not of equal length. The `PRINT USING "##"` provides two digit spaces for every number, even for single numbers.

The following program, named NESTLP2.BAS, is another example of nested loops:

```
REM NESTLP2.BAS¶
CLS¶
RANDOMIZE TIMER¶
FOR I = 5 TO 50 STEP 5¶
  HEIGHT% = 24 - ((22 * RND) + 1)¶
  FOR J = 23 TO HEIGHT% STEP -1¶
    LOCATE J,I¶
    PRINT "█";¶
  NEXT J¶
NEXT I¶
```

This program will display several bars similar to the following:

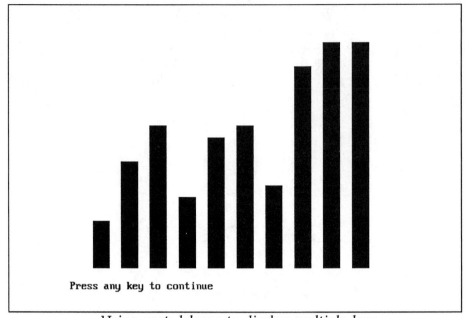

Using nested loops to display multiple bars

The bars on your output screen are probably different than those in the previous picture. Remember that we're using a RANDOMIZE TIMER to generate random numbers. Start the program a second time and you'll see that the bars are not identical to the first output screen.

Since this program uses many familiar statements somewhat differently, we want to explain some of the program lines in more detail. For example, in the third line:

```
FOR I = 5 TO 50 STEP 5
```

the outer loop begins and is executed ten times, although you may not realize it by looking at this program line. By using the STEP keyword, the loop actually operates in incremental steps of five.

We're using the STEP keyword this way because we want to place the bars next to each other. Because of this increment of the runtime variable I, we can insert them into the LOCATE statement directly to set the column position.

In the following line, the height of each bar is calculated. With the formula (22 * RND) + 1, only values between 1 and 23 are created. Since we want to draw from the bottom to the top, we are interested in the position calculated from the bottom. Therefore, we deduct 24 from the result to represent the line at the bottom of the screen.

Since this calculation may be somewhat complicated, let's use an example to make it clear for you. Let's assume the formula (22 * RND) + 1 produces the value 5. The bar should consist of five line levels. We must therefore create from 24 (the bottom) up to 24-5=19 of our line levels.

The inner loop starts in the following line:

```
FOR J = 24 TO HEIGHT% STEP -1
```

Since this loop begins with higher values and moves to smaller values, it requires that we use STEP -1.

The J runtime variable produces the right line for the following LOCATE statement and I contains a displacement of five column positions to the right for every complete bar.

Do not forget the semicolon in the line for the printout of the bar with the PRINT statement. Otherwise *QBasic* will move the column toward the top of the screen each time a new column appears on the bottom line.

Now you have entered only a few lines in a *QBasic* program yet this short program can display straight and evenly spaced bars on the screen. Now we can finally start with our program to create a bar chart.

6.5 Creating Bar Charts

Now we can finally start with our larger bar chart project. In contrast to our previous bar chart programs we also want to supply the graphic with horizontal and vertical lines. These lines are called the *Y-axis* and *X-axis*.

Later we want to show expenses for every month on our bar chart. Therefore, the lower axis should be lettered with the names of the months.

This program requires that we use ASCII characters to draw the X-axis and Y-axis:

The Y-axis will require the "|" ASCII character.

You can create this character by pressing the (Alt) key and pressing (1) + (7) + (9) on the numeric keypad. When you release the (Alt) key, the "|" character appears.

We could use a hyphen for the X-axis but the output screen would not appear professional. Therefore, we can use another ASCII character: the "–" character. Press the (Alt) key and (1) + (9) + (6) on the numeric keypad.

Also, to connect the two axes, we'll use another ASCII character: the "∟" character. Use the same steps as above but press (1) + (9) + (2) on the numeric keypad instead. Remember to press the (Enter) key when you see the ¶ character.

```
REM BARCHAR¶
CLS¶
PRINT TAB(27); "Monthly Statistics"¶
FOR I% = 0 TO 20¶
  PRINT TAB(5); "|"¶
NEXT I%¶
PRINT TAB(5);"∟————————————————————————
————————————————————"¶
PRINT TAB(7); "JAN   FEB   MAR   APR   MAY   JUN   JUL
AUG   SEP   OCT   NOV DEC ";¶
WHILE INKEY$ = "" : WEND¶
CLS¶
```

The spacing in the second PRINT statement is very important. Press the (Spacebar) key five times. Then press the (Alt) key and the ① + ⑨ + ② combination. Then press the (Alt) key and the + ① + ⑨ + ⑥ key combination a total of 60 times.

Don't forget to use the **Copy** and **Paste** commands.

The next PRINT statement is also important. Make certain to press the (Spacebar) key six times before typing "JAN". Add two spaces between each month in this line.

Perhaps you are wondering about the last two lines in this program. They clear the screen at the end of the program when the user presses a key.

Save the program BARCHAR.BAS. We'll be modifying this program throughout the chapter.

The WHILE...WEND statement also appears in this line. A condition is specified following WHILE. As long as this condition is satisfied, the program is executed in a loop which ends at the WEND.

The loop in this program does not include statements because no statements exist between the condition and the WEND. The WEND could just as well have been 20 lines further down in the program and these intervening lines would have been executed until the user pressed a key to satisfy the condition.

Press the (Shift) + (F5) key combination to start the program.

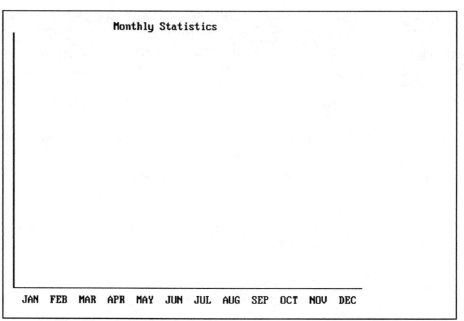

The X-axis and Y-axis displayed on the output screen

When you start this program, only the X-axis, Y-axis and the individual months are displayed. Next, we need to determine the values for the individual months. First, we'll use a simple variable for each month. Then later we'll see how easy it is to process more data in a program.

Insert the following lines into the program between the last PRINT statement and the WHILE...WEND condition:

```
JAN = 1800¶
FEB = 1700¶
MAR = 1900¶
APR = 1800¶
MAY = 1700¶
JUN = 1600¶
JUL = 1600¶
AUG = 1500¶
SEP = 1500¶
OCT = 1600¶
NOV = 1700¶
DEC = 1900¶
```

You can enter other numbers but be careful that the numbers are between 100 and 2000. We're assuming that this is the range for the monthly values later when calculating the bar height. Otherwise, you'll encounter problems when using LOCATE.

As a test, we now want to try to draw the bar for the month of January. For this we use almost the same lines as in the preceding program. Add a few lines directly behind the input of the values for the various months and your program should appear as follows (press the [Enter] key when you see the ¶ character):

```
REM BARCHAR1.BAS
CLS¶
PRINT TAB(27); "Monthly Statistics"¶
FOR I% = 0 TO 20¶
  PRINT TAB(5); "|"¶
NEXT I%¶
PRINT TAB(5);"└──────────────────────────────
──────────────────"¶
PRINT TAB(7); "JAN   FEB   MAR   APR   MAY   JUN   JUL
AUG   SEP   OCT   NOV   DEC";¶
JAN = 1800¶
FEB = 1700¶
MAR = 1900¶
APR = 1800¶
MAY = 1700¶
JUN = 1600¶
JUL = 1600¶
AUG = 1500¶
SEP = 1500¶
OCT = 1600¶
NOV = 1700¶
DEC = 1900¶
BAR% = JAN/100¶
BAR% = 21 - BAR%¶
FOR J% = 21 TO BAR% STEP -1¶
  LOCATE J%,7¶
  PRINT "███";¶
NEXT J%¶
WHILE INKEY$ = "" : WEND¶
CLS¶
```

When you have the program entered, press [Shift] + [F5] to display the bar chart for January. This program should now display the following on your output screen:

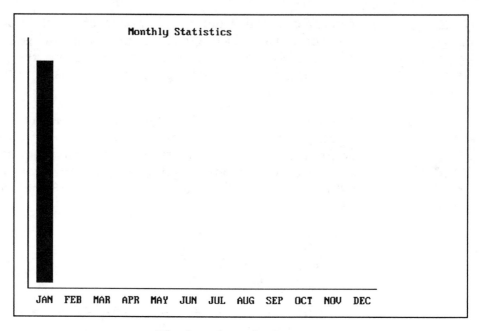

The bar chart for January

Save this program as BARCHAR1.BAS. Now we can start to produce the bars for the remaining months. You must recreate the program lines to define the bars again for each month. This is not only a lot of work, but also makes the program very long.

You may be wondering, why is it that we suddenly have to write a loop to create every bar, while in the previous program we could use a random number in a loop to create the bar height.

In the previous program we could always use the same variable name and use it to create a loop. Now we have twelve different variable names and that makes it difficult.

We'll discuss different *QBasic* statements in a later section that allow us to solve these problems. However, we want to use a simpler method by discussing two new statements which solve this problem.

6.6 Subroutines

The main problem now is not only in drawing the bar twelve times, but always having to use a different variable name. We could build a loop with one variable name and always assign this variable the value of the new month.

However, this idea would not work. The following short program named BADVARS.BAS illustrates the problems involved. It assigns a different value to a variable at the beginning and then jumps to a small output program, which substitutes for our routine for the drawing of a bar chart:

```
REM CH66a.BAS¶
VARIABLE = 10¶
GOTO TESTS ¶
Aloop1:¶
VARIABLE = 20¶
GOTO TESTS ¶
VARIABLE = 30¶
GOTO TESTS ¶
END¶
TESTS:¶
  PRINT "The variable is"; VARIABLE¶
  GOTO Aloop1 ¶
```

The END statement insures that a program is not executed to the last available line, but ends immediately.

The program is executed correctly at first. It outputs the 10 and then sets the VARIABLE to 20. However, after the output of the 20, it jumps back again and outputs the 20 again.

The VARIABLE cannot be set to all values because the return jump from the output always goes to the same line. We require the ability to jump from any place in the program to a frequently used location and then returning to the previous location.

A *subroutine* is a program segment that replaces several often-used, similar program sections. A subroutine is an independent segment of a program, and is usually located at the start or end of the main program.

The jump to the first line of this program section is not made with GOTO, but with GOSUB.

6.6.1 GOSUB...RETURN

GOSUB is an abbreviation for **GO**to **SUB**routine. When the computer encounters the GOSUB statement, it makes note of the line from where it's branching. Then it branches to the line of the subroutine.

The computer continues with program execution until it encounters the return command:

```
RETURN
```

Program execution then returns to and continues with the statements following the GOSUB statement.

If the program encounters the RETURN command without first having received the GOSUB command, the program stops with the "RETURN without GOSUB" error message.

The following short program illustrates the use of the GOSUB and RETURN statements:

```
REM Ch66B.BAS¶
CLS¶
FC = 100¶
GOSUB Calculate¶
FC = 500¶
GOSUB Calculate¶
FC = 10¶
GOSUB Calculate¶
END¶
Calculate:¶
 CLS¶
 PRINT "              Conversion: FC - Dollar "¶
 PRINT¶
 DOLLAR = FC / 1.7¶
 PRINT FC ; " FC are"; DOLLAR ; " Dollars"¶
 PRINT¶
 INPUT "Continue (press ENTER)"; TEST$¶
 RETURN¶
```

The Calculate subroutine begins in the third line with the label and ends in the line with the RETURN. It is executed a total of three times.

The first time it is called is in the third line. Previously FC was set to 100. The subroutine now calculates the amount for DOLLAR and outputs on the screen. After the RETURN from the subroutine, QBasic continues in the fourth line. The same occurs with the 500 and the 10 in the following lines.

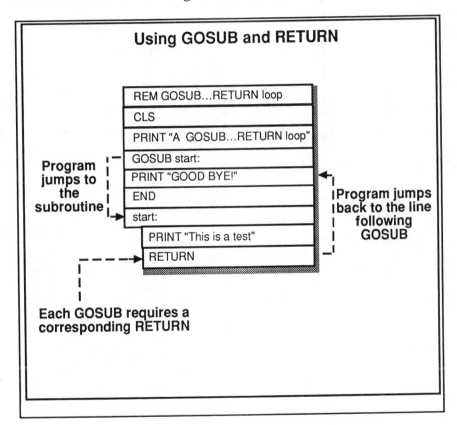

Using GOSUB and subroutines

The previous diagram uses a simple subroutine example to explain the relationship of the actual program (main program) and the subroutine.

The main program is executed to the line in which the GOSUB statement appears. *QBasic* notes this location and jumps to the label Label. The subroutine starting there is executed until the RETURN statement causes the return jump. Then execution of the main program continues after the GOSUB Label statement.

You can jump to the same subroutine in several lines or use different subroutines.

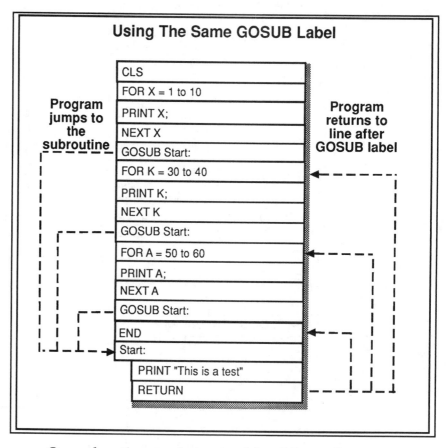

Using The Same GOSUB Label

Program jumps to the subroutine

Program returns to line after GOSUB label

```
CLS
FOR X = 1 to 10
PRINT X;
NEXT X
GOSUB Start:
FOR K = 30 to 40
PRINT K;
NEXT K
GOSUB Start:
FOR A = 50 to 60
PRINT A;
NEXT A
GOSUB Start:
END
Start:
    PRINT "This is a test"
    RETURN
```

One subroutine can be accessed by different lines

It's important to place the END at the end of the main program. If the program was not ended here, it would again execute the subroutine starting at the label and finally discover the RETURN at the end. Since no call of the subroutine with GOSUB had occurred, *QBasic* would display the "RETURN without GOSUB" error message.

6.7 BARCHART Program Listing

Now that you understand these new statements, we can complete the BARCHART program.

We'll use a subroutine for the part of the program which draws the actual bar. We can then call this subroutine once for every month and pass the value for this particular month, as in the program converting FC into DOLLAR.

As a reminder, note the ¶ character that appears at the end of the program lines. This character indicates when you are to press the (Enter) key. Our program now appears as follows:

```
REM BARCHAR2¶
CLS : PRINT TAB(27); "Monthly Statistics"¶
FOR I% = 0 TO 20¶
  PRINT TAB(5); "|"¶
NEXT I%¶
PRINT TAB(5);"└_____
_____"¶
PRINT TAB(7); "JAN    FEB    MAR   APR   MAY   JUN   JUL
AUG   SEP   OCT   NOV   DEC";¶
JAN = 1800¶
FEB = 1700¶
MAR = 1900¶
APR = 1800¶
MAY = 1700¶
JUN = 1600¶
JUL = 1600¶
AUG = 1500¶
SEP = 1500¶
OCT = 1600¶
NOV = 1700¶
DEC = 1900¶
Y = 2¶
BAR% = JAN/100 : Y = Y+5: GOSUB Xdraw¶
BAR% = FEB/100 : Y = Y+5: GOSUB Xdraw¶
BAR% = MAR/100 : Y = Y+5: GOSUB Xdraw¶
BAR% = APR/100 : Y = Y+5: GOSUB Xdraw¶
BAR% = MAY/100 : Y = Y+5: GOSUB Xdraw¶
BAR% = JUN/100 : Y = Y+5: GOSUB Xdraw¶
BAR% = JUL/100 : Y = Y+5: GOSUB Xdraw¶
```

```
BAR% = AUG/100 : Y = Y+5: GOSUB Xdraw¶
BAR% = SEP/100 : Y = Y+5: GOSUB Xdraw¶
BAR% = OCT/100 : Y = Y+5: GOSUB Xdraw¶
BAR% = NOV/100 : Y = Y+5: GOSUB Xdraw¶
BAR% = DEC/100 : Y = Y+5: GOSUB Xdraw¶
WHILE INKEY$ = " " : WEND¶
CLS¶
END¶
Xdraw:¶
  BAR% = 21 - BAR%¶
  FOR J% = 21 TO BAR% STEP -1¶
    LOCATE J%,Y¶
    PRINT "█";¶
  NEXT J%¶
RETURN¶
```

After adding the new lines to the program, press [Shift] + [F5] to display the completed bar chart:

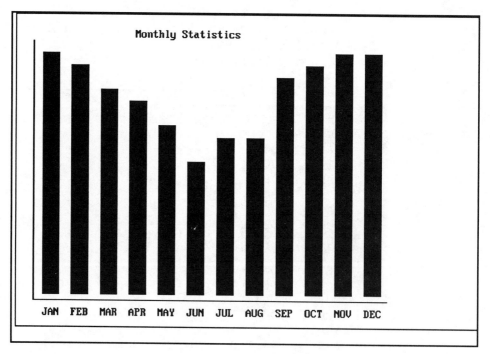

The completed bar chart

Save this program as BARCHAR2.BAS.

Before we finish this section, we need to explain a few lines of the program in more detail.

1.   The lines for the calculation of the height of the bar correspond to those already familiar in the FC conversion program.

2.   The repeated increment Y = Y + 5, should move the bar to the right by increasing the Y position for LOCATE.

3.   These almost identical lines do not have to be retyped every time. You can simply copy them, as you remember. At the end you only have to change what is necessary.

4.   The keyboard query was placed further up front. It no longer is at the end of the complete program, but directly before the end of the main program.

5.   Between the end of the main program and the label of the subroutine, we inserted an END to isolate the following GOSUB subroutine from the remainder of the program.

6.   This subroutine starting at the label PAINT, contains the Y and BAR% variables.

7.   Of course, you can easily assign other values in the program by replacing values in individual months with those you find more interesting.

6.8 Using and Storing Data

If a program requires a large amount of data, numerical values or strings, it is very tedious to have to enter these values each time the program is started.

To avoid these problems, *QBasic* lets you use the READ and DATA statements.

6.8.1 READ and DATA

Type the following short program:

```
REM 6_8_1.BAS¶
CLS¶
READ X¶
PRINT X¶
DATA 50¶
END¶
```

Press the (Shift) + (F5) key combination. The following will appear on your output screen:

```
50


Press any key to continue
```

The first line clears the screen. The numerical variable X is assigned the value 50 with a READ statement in the second line.

If the program encounters the READ statement, it searches for the corresponding DATA line and reads the first value. This value is assigned to the variable that follows the READ.

The contents of the X variable are printed in the third line.

Change the program in the following manner:

```
REM 6_8_1a
CLS
READ X,Y,Z
PRINT X,Y,Z
DATA 10,20,30
END
```

Press the ⎡Shift⎤ + ⎡F5⎤ key combination to display the following on your output screen:

```
10        20        30

Press any key to continue
```

READ first assigned the first value in the DATA line to the X variable. Then it assigned the second value read to the variable Y, and then the third value to the variable Z.

The next value is always read with each READ access to the data in the DATA lines. A pointer is maintained inside the computer that is always advanced each time an item is read. This pointer always points to the next element to be read.

At the start of a program this pointer points to the first element in the DATA line. The next lines should clarify this. The pointer is represented by the ↑ character.

```
DATA 10,20,30
↑
```

When the program encounters a READ, the pointer is incremented by one, and so points to the second element.

```
30 DATA 10,20,30
↑
```

When this element is read, the pointer is again incremented by one. When the pointer reaches the end of a list of DATA instructions, it is <u>not</u> automatically set back to the first element, but points after the last element. If you then try to access the list again with `READ`, the *QBasic* displays an "Out of DATA" error message.

6.8.2 `RESTORE`

What if you want to access the data from the same `DATA` line more than once in a program? In this case, we'll need to use the `RESTORE` statement.

The `RESTORE` statement sets the pointer back to the very first element of `DATA`. This gives you the ability to read the data in the `DATA` lines as often as you like.

Enter the following program to see what happens when the program tries to read more data than is available.

```
REM 6_8_2
CLS
READ A, B, C
PRINT A, B, C
DATA 10,20,30
READ D, E, F
PRINT D, E, F
END
```

After the values 10, 20 and 30 are printed, you'll receive an "Out of DATA" error in the following line:

```
READ D, E, F
```

This line attempted to read the fourth element of `DATA`. However, this element does not exist. To eliminate this error, you can either append three more values in the `DATA` line or reset the pointer with `RESTORE`.

Add the following to the fourth line:

```
RESTORE
```

Now the program lines should look like the following:

```
REM 6_8_2
CLS
READ A,B,C
```

```
RESTORE
PRINT A,B,C
DATA 10,20,30
READ D,E,F
PRINT D,E,F
END
```

Press the [Shift] + [F5] key combination to display the following on your output screen:

```
10      20      30
10      20      30


Press any key to continue
```

The pointer was again set to the first data element with the RESTORE statement. Therefore the numerical variables D, E, and F were assigned the values 10, 20 and 30.

The following line:

```
READ A,B,C
```

causes three values to be read from the DATA line simultaneously.

The values can also be read one at a time as the next example shows.

```
REM 6_8_2A
CLS
FOR I=1 TO 3
READ X
PRINT X
NEXT I
DATA 10,20,30
END
```

In this example, the following lines:

```
READ X
PRINT X
```

are placed in a FOR...NEXT loop that is executed a total of three times. On each pass through the loop, a new value is read from the DATA line, assigned to X and printed.

6.8.3 Using READ and DATA in BARCHAR

One of the problems you'll encounter in the BARCHART program is changing the value for one month or several of the months. For example, what if we want to use the following values:

```
JAN    1400
FEB    1300
MAR    1600
APR    1600
MAY    1900
JUN    1300
JUL    1800
AUG    1600
SEP    1700
OCT    1800
NOV    1900
DEC    1700
```

You'll quickly realize that it's awkward to enter the twelve values representing each month in the BARCHART program since twelve lines must be changed in the program.

To avoid this problem, we can use the READ and DATA statements.

The DATA statement is composed of a list of data items. These items are separated by commas. The type of data that can be placed in a DATA statement can be either numerical or character.

You'll use the READ statement to assign the individual data items in the DATA statements to variables. The variable type that follows the READ must correspond to the type of data contained in the DATA statement. You may not read a string into a numerical variable.

When using the READ and DATA statements, make certain that a DATA value is available for every READ statement. Also, separate all values with a comma. Don't confuse the comma with a decimal point. It's easy to make mistakes using the READ and DATA statements that are difficult to find.

The DATA lines are not required to appear at any specific location within the program. They can be at the beginning, in the middle or at the end. Often programmers place DATA statements at the end of the program, sometimes after the END statement. When the program encounters a READ statement, it automatically searches for the DATA statement.

Perhaps you still remember that we had some difficulties with our bar drawing routine, because of the twelve different variable names for the months. By using the READ and DATA statements, we can use a single variable name.

Instead of storing the twelve values in twelve different variables, we simply store them in program lines which start with the DATA statement. Each time we now use the READ statement, the next value is retrieved from the DATA lines.

The following is a very simple program which uses this method:

```
READ VARIABLE
PRINT VARIABLE
END
DATA 100
```

Although this program is not very useful, it demonstrates the use of the two statements. In the first line, the program uses READ to read the number from the last line which starts with DATA and stores it in VARIABLE.

Remember, when storing several numbers in a DATA line, make certain to separate the characters with commas. We want to demonstrate this with a small program that adds a shopping list.

```
REM SHOPLIST.BAS
REM Shopping list with Read and Data
TOTAL = 0
READ GUESSNR
```

```
FOR I = 1 TO GUESSNR
 READ AMOUNT
 TOTAL = TOTAL + AMOUNT
NEXT I
PRINT "Total Amount: "; USING "####.##"; TOTAL
END
DATA 5, 13.8, 3.9, 4.77, 39.45, 8.99
```

Because the individual values are arranged in an orderly manner on one line, you can quickly check for input errors if the result seems questionable.

Notice that the first value (5) in the DATA line is not an expense. Instead, it indicates the number of available expenses in the DATA line.

We could, of course, set GUESSNR in the program to the right value. This would require that after the input of data we would also change the variable. This can be done directly in the DATA line.

Now we can enhance and simplify the BARCHART program using the READ and DATA statements. To avoid having to input the modified program, we want to explain how to create the new version in the easiest manner.

Load the BARCHART program but immediately save under a new name (for example under BARCHAR3.BAS).

Next delete the lines with the monthly values and those which calculate the individual bar height. This is very simple. Move the cursor to the following line:

```
JAN = 1800
```

This is the first line which should be deleted.

Now move the direction key, while pressing the [Shift] key, until all lines are highlighted up to and including the following line:

```
BAR% = DEC/100 : Y = Y+5: GOSUB Xdraw
```

Now when you press the Del key, all highlighted lines will be deleted.

We only have to input the new lines which were changed. Your program now should appear as follows (remember to press the Enter key when you see the ¶ character):

```
CLS : PRINT TAB(27); "Monthly Statistics"¶
FOR I% = 0 TO 20¶
 PRINT "    |  "¶
NEXT I%¶
PRINT TAB(5);"└_____
_____"¶
PRINT TAB(7); "JAN   FEB   MAR   APR   MAY   JUN   JUL
AUG   SEP   OCT   NOV   DEC";¶
Y = 7¶
FOR I% = 1 TO 12¶
 READ BAR%¶
 BAR% = BAR% / 100¶
 GOSUB Xdraw¶
 Y = Y + 5¶
NEXT I%¶
WHILE INKEY$ = "" : WEND¶
CLS¶
END¶
Xdraw:¶
 BAR% = 22 - BAR%¶
 FOR J% = 22 TO BAR% STEP -1¶
  LOCATE J%,Y¶
  PRINT "█";¶
 NEXT J%¶
RETURN¶
DATA 1900,1800,1600,1500,1300,1000¶
DATA 1200,1200,1700,1800,1900,1900¶
```

Note in the "Y = 7" line. The LOCATE statement is used here to set the initial value for the Y position to 7. Therefore, the first bar will be drawn starting at the 7th column.

The next four lines defines the loop which sequentially reads the values from the two DATA lines, divides them by 100 and then calls the PAINT subroutine. Afterwards the Y position is increased by five.

6.9 Using Arrays In The BARCHART Program

When creating the BARCHART program, we encountered the difficulty of having to store several values in variables. Because several variable names were used, the program could not process these values easily in a loop.

In this section we want to show you how much data can be stored under one name and access this data in a loop. This can be done by using *arrays*.

Because many programmers experience difficulty working with arrays, we debated for a long time if this subject should even be included in a book for beginners. The more complex the arrays, the more difficult it is to work with them. Even advanced programmers have problems with array management.

On the other hand, a beginner can learn how to work with arrays. It's all a matter of practice. We'll begin with very simple examples.

What do we mean by the term "array"?

You probably recall the first version of the BARCHART program, which contained the following lines:

```
JAN = 1800
FEB = 1700
MAR = 1900
APR = 1800
MAY = 1700
JUN = 1600
JUL = 1600
AUG = 1500
SEP = 1500
OCT = 1600
NOV = 1700
DEC = 1900
```

It would be much easier if the twelve different values could be stored in one variable. Then if you needed the value for the third month (MAR), you could tell *QBasic*: I need the third value from the variable.

Since we could use a number to define a month, (i.e., 3), we could use a loop for all twelve months (only symbolic, not written in true *QBasic* statement syntax):

```
FOR I = 1 TO 12
Give me the Monthly Value i of I
Do something with this value
NEXT I
```

To convert this into a functional *QBasic* program, we must first think of a name for the new variable which should contain all twelve values.

Since variable names should be obvious, we'll call it MONTH. Next we must tell *QBasic* that MONTH is not a normal variable (integer, string etc.), but an array.

QBasic now wants to know how many values (or elements) we intend to store in our new variable. This is the purpose of the DIM statement in *QBasic*. It has the following syntax:

```
DIM array name (number of elements)
```

The syntax in this example is:

```
DIM MONTH (12)
```

The MONTH in this syntax is the variable. The number placed in parentheses separated from the actual variable is called the *index*.

The DIM statement is usually located at the beginning of a program. Once an array is dimensioned, it may not be redimensioned again in the program with DIM. Otherwise the computer will display an "Array already dimensioned" error message.

When the DIM statement appears at the beginning of a program, *QBasic* knows from then on that the new MONTH variable is a field and should contain twelve different values.

If we later require the third value from the variable (the field) in the program, we simply write MONTH(3) and *QBasic* gets the right value. If we want, for example, to set the third value to 1800, we can use the following syntax:

```
MONTH(3) = 1800
```

The difficulty in working with a field is that you must always consider what month represents March and write this number into the parentheses of the statement.

For example, if we want to output the months from June to December on the screen, we have to consider what number is June and which is December. Only then can we write:

```
FOR I = 6 TO 12
  PRINT MONTH(I)
NEXT I
```

These three lines are incomplete because we have not yet stored values for the months in the variable. It does explain how a loop can be used to access several variables (or better, the values in one field).

Now we'll use a small program to demonstrate how to use an array. This program creates a field for twelve values, reads these values from the DATA lines and writes selected values on the screen:

```
REM DIMEXAM.BAS¶
CLS¶
DIM MONTH(12)¶
FOR I = 1 TO 12¶
  READ MONTH(I)¶
  PRINT MONTH(I)¶
NEXT I¶
Display:¶
  PRINT "Input a number between 1-12 and press
ENTER"¶
  PRINT "  or press 0 and ENTER to end the program"¶
  INPUT NUMBER¶
  IF NUMBER = 0 THEN END¶
  IF NUMBER < 0 OR NUMBER > 12 THEN GOTO Output¶
  PRINT "The month numbered:"; NUMBER;¶
  PRINT "Has the value:"; MONTH(NUMBER)¶
  PRINT¶
  GOTO Display¶
```

```
DATA   500,  900,1300,1500,1400,1600¶
DATA 1800,1900,1700,1100,  400,  800¶
```

QBasic is instructed in the second line that MONTH is an array with 12 possible values. In the following loop, the 12 values are read from the two DATA lines and displayed on the screen.

In the following lines we get a number between 1 and 12 in the NUMBER variable. Type a "0" to terminate the program or test if the input is in the allowable range.

If this is not the case, the program jumps to a new input of a number. Otherwise *QBasic* would produce an error message. We must agree that MONTH can only contain 12 values.

The PRINT lines output the value for the month. The determining part of the line is: MONTH(NUMBER). The text output in this line is composed of the number input and the value for that month.

The GOTO jump in the next line returns to the input line. At the end of the program are the two DATA lines with the 12 values for the months.

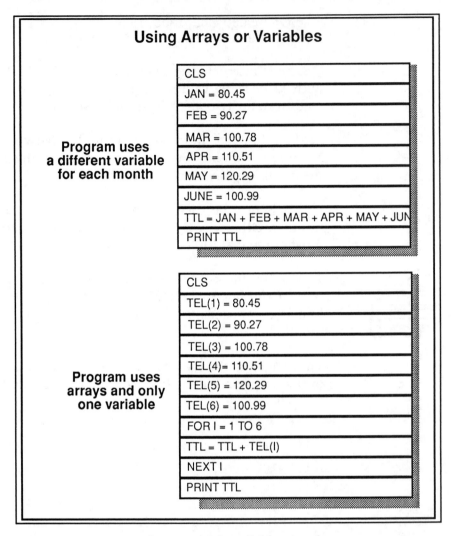

Using Arrays or Variables

Program uses a different variable for each month

```
CLS
JAN = 80.45
FEB = 90.27
MAR = 100.78
APR = 110.51
MAY = 120.29
JUNE = 100.99
TTL = JAN + FEB + MAR + APR + MAY + JUN
PRINT TTL
```

Program uses arrays and only one variable

```
CLS
TEL(1) = 80.45
TEL(2) = 90.27
TEL(3) = 100.78
TEL(4)= 110.51
TEL(5) = 120.29
TEL(6) = 100.99
FOR I = 1 TO 6
TTL = TTL + TEL(I)
NEXT I
PRINT TTL
```

One array can replace several variables in the same program

The previous diagram shows the advantages of array variables. Both programs were created to calculate the monthly cost of the telephone service for the first six months of the year.

In the example at the top, the cost of the phone is assigned to its own variable for the month. This results in using six variables to represent each month. The formula to calculate the total must include all six variable names.

In the bottom example, only one variable (TEL) is used for the expenses of all six months. It contains six partial arrays for the months. This lets you easily change any of the elements.

The total of the expenses can now be easily calculated with a loop which consists of three lines. The variable arrays do not have to be listed separately.

If we had not used an array but stored the twelve values in twelve variables from JAN to DEC, the output from any monthly value could only be determined by using the following lines:

```
IF   INPUT=1   THEN   PRINT"The   month   numbered:";
INPUT;"has the value: ";JAN¶
IF   INPUT=2   THEN   PRINT"The   month   numbered:";
INPUT;"has the value: ";FEB¶
IF   INPUT=3   THEN   PRINT"The   month   numbered:";
INPUT;"has the value: ";MAR¶
...¶
...¶
```

The following facts about arrays should be noted.

1.   A DIM instruction is unnecessary if you need fewer than 11 elements in an array. With an element such as A(4), *QBasic* will execute a DIM A(10) instruction automatically.

2.   Normally, DIM A(10) dimensions 11 elements in the array A(). The indices start with zero and not one. Therefore you must count A(0) in the total as well. The first element may be changed on all arrays from element 0 to element 1 using the OPTION BASE 1 command.

Arrays with the following general syntax of A(X) are called *one-dimensional arrays* because they have only one index. The index can be a variable or a numerical expression.

6.9.1   Adding arrays in the Bar Chart program

In this section we'll add arrays to the BARCHART program. We read the values for the individual months from DATA lines and store them in one field.

The function of the program does not change but you can see the proper use of the new statements in one program. You can then modify or enhance them much easier for your own applications.

```
REM ARRAYS1.BAS¶
DIM MONTH(12)¶
CLS¶
PRINT TAB(27); "Monthly Statistics"¶
FOR I% = 0 TO 20¶
  PRINT TAB(5):"|"¶
NEXT I%¶
PRINT TAB(5);"└─────────────────────
──────────"¶
PRINT TAB(7); "JAN   FEB   MAR   APR   MAY   JUN   JUL
AUG   SEP   OCT   NOV   DEC";¶
Y = 7¶
FOR I% = 1 TO 12¶
  READ MONTH(I%)¶
  BAR% = MONTH(I%) / 100¶
  GOSUB Display¶
  Y = Y + 5¶
NEXT I%¶
WHILE INKEY$ = "": WEND¶
CLS¶
END¶
Display:¶
  BAR% = 21 - BAR%¶
  FOR J% = 21 TO BAR% STEP -1¶
    LOCATE J%, Y¶
    PRINT "█";¶
  NEXT J%¶
RETURN¶
DATA 1900,1800,1600,1500,1300,1000¶
DATA 1200,1200,1700,1800,1900,1900¶
```

You may want to try different enhancements. For example, you can easily calculate the average for all twelve months by inserting the following lines before the WHILE INKEY$ = "" : WEND line:

```
SUM = 0
FOR I% = 1 TO 12
 SUM = SUM + MONTH(I%)
NEXT I%
AVERAGE = SUM / 12
LOCATE 3,26
PRINT "Average: "; USING "####.##"; AVERAGE
```

7. Programming Style

To create a functional program requires more than simply typing *QBasic* statements.

Programming style is the manner in which you construct your program. Before creating a BASIC program, you should first analyze the problem to be solved. This involves making a Program Execution Plan (PEP) or flowchart that lists all the execution steps.

7.1 Program Execution Plan

You'll create a well structured program by using a PEP. If you simply entered a program without a PEP, you may eventually achieve the desired result but it would require extra time and effort. You could easily overlook a routine or command that would improve your program.

7.1.1 Tips on programming style

If you follow these simple rules, you'll create programs that won't be called "spaghetti code", "chaos" or something worse:

- Start with a goal or purpose.

- Use meaningful variables (see Chapter 3 for more information).

- Avoid using GOTO labels.

- Use REM often for documenting program sections.

- Use several lines instead of combining several statements on one line.

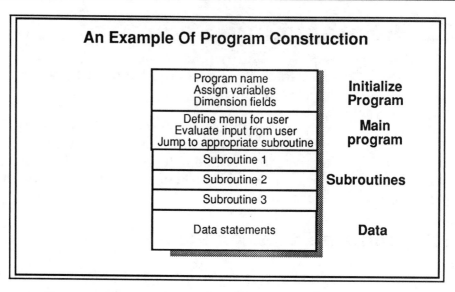

An Example Of Program Construction

Program name Assign variables Dimension fields	**Initialize Program**
Define menu for user Evaluate input from user Jump to appropriate subroutine	**Main program**
Subroutine 1	**Subroutines**
Subroutine 2	
Subroutine 3	
Data statements	**Data**

Proper program construction in a PEP will save time

The previous diagram displays the construction of the program.

In the initialization portion there is some general information, such as instructions on the use of the program and its author.

There must also be some preliminary work performed. This includes mainly the definition of variables and, if necessary, the creation of variable arrays (see Chapter 6 for information on arrays).

In the main program a menu is presented from which the user can make selections. In the second part, the reaction of the user is evaluated. Depending on the choice made by the user, a jump is made to the proper subroutine.

Correspondingly, the main program is followed by different subroutines. At the end is the required data (DATA lines).

7.2 The BANDIT Game

In the remaining sections of this chapter we'll discuss how you can use the ASCII characters from Chapter 6 to create a small computer game.

Another reason we're including this program is to help you develop an effective method of creating, writing and developing a program.

We wrote this game for a friend who owned a PC with a Hercules display card, which was intended mainly for word processing. Most PC games require the CGA, EGA or VGA graphic adapters.

We needed, therefore, to develop a game in *QBasic* which did not require high resolution graphics.

You're probably familiar with slot machines or one armed bandits. In this chapter we'll show you how to create your own version of a one armed bandit using *QBasic*.

7.2.1 Goal of the game

The goal of this game is actually quite simple: match as many symbols in the five windows as possible. These symbols usually represent various amounts of money. The game starts when you deposit 25¢ in the machine. You'll see this amount deducted from the total in the upper right corner.

You'll see symbols flash in the five windows and then stop after a certain amount of time. You must match three symbols in a certain combination to receive credit for the corresponding amount of money. The money still available to you is displayed in one window.

Some slot machines can restart the left wheel while the right wheel remains stopped. If the symbols on the left wheel are not successful, you can restart this wheel.

We gave the BANDIT program the ability to perform this action on its own.

7.2.2 Main screen for BANDIT

The first item we need to consider in the BANDIT program is how the main screen should appear. We'll need to display two boxes to represent the wheels of the slot machine and to represent our available money.

Also we'll need to have a border surrounding these two small boxes. This border should have a different appearance than the other two boxes.

Now, the next step is to determine which ASCII characters can be used to produce the best appearing boxes and border on the screen.

7.2.3 Selecting the correct ASCII characters

Remember from Chapter 4 that you can produce many characters that are not normally visible on the keyboard. These characters are produced by pressing the [Alt] key while pressing the corresponding numbers on the numeric keypad.

The first character we should consider is the border. We want this border to appear differently than the two boxes so we'll need to look in the ASCII table in Appendix F. A double line border would look good so look for a double line border.

This border corresponds to ASCII code 205 (=). However, this code is only for the top and bottom borders; we'll need another ASCII code for the side borders.

In the ASCII table notice that ASCII code 186 (‖) will make a good side border.

Now that the top border and side borders are determined, we'll need to connect the four corners. The ASCII codes for the corners are 187, 188, 200 and 201.

So far we've used the following ASCII codes:

Code	Character	Purpose
186	‖	Side border
187	⅂⅂	Upper right corner
188	⅃	Bottom right corner
200	⅃⅃	Bottom left corner
201	⌈	Upper left corner
205	=	Top/bottom borders

You can test these characters in the View window. Type the following lines, use the [Alt] key and the numeric keypad to enter the ASCII codes (notice that we aren't using normal *QBasic* syntax here):

```
CLS¶
PRINT   "[Alt] + [2][0][1]   [Alt] + [2][0][5]   [Alt] + [1][8][7]"¶
PRINT   "[Alt] + [1][8][6]   [Spacebar]   [Alt] + [1][8][6]"¶
PRINT   "[Alt] + [2][0][0]   [Alt] + [2][0][5]   [Alt] + [1][8][8]"¶
```

Press the [Shift] + [F5] key combination to start the program. You should see the following small box on the output screen:

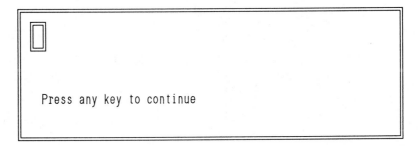

```
Press any key to continue
```

Now we'll need to look through the ASCII table to determine which characters we want to use for the two boxes in the BANDIT program.

We will use the following characters to create the borders and frame for the boxes representing the wheels of the slot machine and our available money:

Code	Char	Purpose
179	|	Side border
191	⌐	Upper right corner
192	∟	Lower left corner
196	–	Bottom/top border
217	⌐	lower right corner
218	∟	Lower left corner

We need a character to use for a wildcard character on the slot machine. We'll use the ASCII code number 232 (Φ).

You can use a sheet of paper to make a preliminary design of how these characters will appear on the screen:

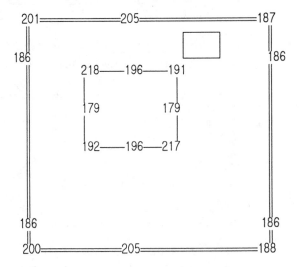

7.2.4 Making the first test

Now that we have an idea (following our PEP) of the appearance of the machine, we can test it on the output screen by using PRINT statements.

When typing this program, don't forget to use the **Copy** and **Paste** commands in the **Edit** menu (see Chapter 3 for more information).

For example, press the (Alt) key and the desired keys from the numeric keypad. Then select the ASCII character and press the (Ctrl) + (Ins) keys to copy it.

We've included some other tips on the next page.

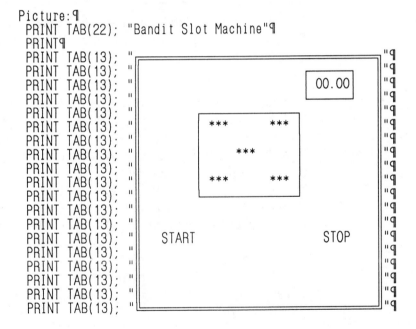

```
Picture:¶
  PRINT TAB(22); "Bandit Slot Machine"¶
  PRINT¶
  PRINT TAB(13);  "                              "¶
  PRINT TAB(13);  "                              "¶
  PRINT TAB(13);  "                              "¶
  PRINT TAB(13);  "                              "¶
  PRINT TAB(13);  "                              "¶
  PRINT TAB(13);  "                              "¶
  PRINT TAB(13);  "                              "¶
  PRINT TAB(13);  "                              "¶
  PRINT TAB(13);  "                              "¶
  PRINT TAB(13);  "                              "¶
  PRINT TAB(13);  "                              "¶
  PRINT TAB(13);  "                              "¶
  PRINT TAB(13);  "                              "¶
  PRINT TAB(13);  "                              "¶
  PRINT TAB(13);  "                              "¶
  PRINT TAB(13);  "                              "¶
  PRINT TAB(13);  "                              "¶
  PRINT TAB(13);  "                              "¶
  PRINT TAB(13);  "                              "¶
```

7.2.5 Suggestions on typing the subroutine

If you're having trouble typing these program lines, we'll give you suggestions that may save you some time.

Follow the picture on the previous page which displays the ASCII codes at their correct positions. This will help you in typing the lines.

Main frame

For the top and bottom borders, press the (Spacebar) a total of 12 times following the PRINT statement. Then press the (Alt) key and the (2) + (0) + (5) key combination a total of 15 times.

Wheel display box

For the top and bottom borders on the wheel box, press (Alt) and the (1) + (9) + (6) key combination a total of 36 times.

Cash box

For the top and bottom borders on the cash box, press the (Alt) key and the (1) + (9) + (6) key combination a total of 7 times.

Use the direction keys to move the cursor to the location in the program line and press (Shift) + (Ins) to paste the character. Press the (Shift) + (Ins) as many times as required to paste the character. By using the **Copy** and **Paste** commands in the **Edit** menu, you'll find it easier than using the (Alt) key and the numeric keypad.

When the lines are completed, you can start the program for a test. Note the label "Picture:" at the beginning of the program. These lines are actually a subroutine which will appear later in the final program.

After reading through this book, you should be able to use the LOCATE statement.

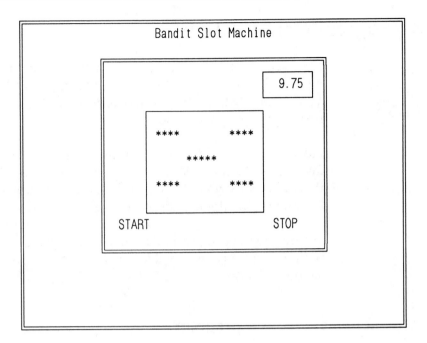

The BANDIT main screen

7.3 Program Construction

 Now we must consider how to construct our program. We could create a linear program. For example, first would be the variable assignments, than the construction of the output screen, the turning of the wheels and so on.

However, because this is a long program, writing in a linear fashion will also make it very difficult to understand. Therefore, it will be constructed differently by using subroutines similar to the one we've already discussed.

We divide the program into a main program and subroutines. The main program is responsible for calling the individual subroutines sequentially.

7.3.1 A schematic of the program

Therefore, the BANDIT.BAS program would require the following parts:

- Dimension arrays

- Assign variables

Main program

We now call a subroutine which determines the required variables at the beginning of the program. This is followed by the main program which must perform the following tasks:

- Display amount of money

- Turn wheels

- Determine winnings

- Wait for a key press and continue with step three

End of the main program

This ends the main program. Now we must define four subroutines to accomplish the following:

• Set variables

• Turn wheels

• Check winnings

• Display winnings and add to wager money

The Spin subroutine to spin the wheels is called several times from the main program. The reason is that after some time individual wheels are stopped, and we determine in a variable if the right or left wheel should be allowed to turn or not.

The part of the main program that calls the Spin subroutine appears as follows:

Spin

• Call Spin to spin the wheels. *Three wheels turn*

• Call Spin. *The left wheel stops but can be restarted*

• Call Spin to spin the wheels. *Left wheel is stopped and the right may be stopped*

• Call Spin to spin the wheels. *Only the middle wheel turns*

7.3.2   Determining basic data

The beginning of the main program initializes basic data needs. This initialization includes dimensioning arrays. BANDIT.BAS dimensions these arrays as follows:

```
DIM ROLL$(9)
DIM WHEEL%(5)
```

We'll need to insert these two lines in the program before constructing the screen display.

These lines define two different arrays. The first is named ROLL$ and it can store nine elements (variables). Notice that this array contains character strings, unlike the arrays which contained numbers in the BARCHART program (see Chapter 5).

Therefore, we have attached a dollar sign to the name. These variables store the characters which will appear on the wheels.

The second array, called WHEEL%(5), is dimensioned in the next line. It can accept five integer (whole number) values. This array is responsible for storing the current position for the five wheels.

Don't panic if you're confused. The purpose and function of these two arrays will become more apparent as we continue to create the program.

7.3.3 Determining variables

Now we want to examine the part of the program which determines the variables. We'll add these lines following the Picture: subroutine.

```
Variables:¶
  ROLL = 9¶
  ROLL$(1) = "  40"¶
  ROLL$(2) = "  80"¶
  ROLL$(3) = "  40"¶
  ROLL$(4) = "  80"¶
  ROLL$(5) = "ΦΦΦ"¶
  WLDCD$ = ROLL$(5)¶
  ROLL$(6) = "  40"¶
  ROLL$(7) = "120"¶
  ROLL$(8) = "  40"¶
  ROLL$(9) = "300"¶
  RANDOMIZE TIMER¶
  FOR I = 1 TO 5¶
    WHEEL%(I) = ROLL * RND + 1¶
  NEXT I¶
RETURN¶
```

The number of the character strings for the wheels is stored in the first line of the variable assignment. This is followed by the assignment of the characters to these character strings.

Don't forget to add the quotation marks so that *QBasic* knows that this is not the number 40, for example, but the characters " ", "4" and "0".

A special character is assigned in these lines as a fifth element for the wheels, which serves as a wildcard. This character is also stored in the WLDCD$ variable to determine later, in a simple manner, if a wildcard is visible on a wheel.

7.3.4 The wheel windows and their distribution

The ROLL$(9) = "300" line completes our definition of the wheel. Since we have determined how one wheel is to appear, we can use it for the two other wheels.

Remember, the slot machine has a total of five wheel windows. We only talk about the left and right wheel, because we want to pretend as if the upper and lower wheel windows belonged to one wheel.

It would be rather dull if all five wheel windows always displayed the same symbol. Therefore, we must use random numbers to determine five different start positions for the individual windows in the next lines. We numbered the wheels as follows:

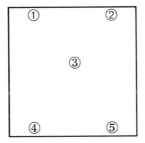

For example, if the following random numbers had been selected:

```
WHEEL%(1) = 3
WHEEL%(2) = 5
WHEEL%(3) = 1
WHEEL%(4) = 7
WHEEL%(5) = 2
```

The symbols in the five windows would appear as follows:

```
40              ΦΦΦ



        40



120             80
```

You may be wondering why some numbers occur more than once. We want certain symbols to occur more frequently than other symbols. (Unfortunately, this is also true for real slot machines, where the lower winnings occur more frequently.)

When we represent our wheels in this manner, it is rather easy for the Spin subroutine to show the turning of the wheels on the output screen. Since the numbers in the array WHEEL%() are simply increased by one, the next symbol is displayed on the screen.

Our subroutine to determine the variables ends in the last line with the required RETURN. After you have input the new lines, please do not start the program.

However, if you were to press the (Shift) + (F5) key combination, an error message would be displayed on executing the subroutine without the right call.

7.3.5 Spin subroutine

The next subroutine is the routine to spin the wheels. It follows immediately behind the variable assignment. It appears as follows (don't forget to press (Enter) when you see the ¶ character):

```
SPIN:¶
 FOR SPIN = 1 TO SPINCOUNT¶
  FOR WAIT% = 1 TO 10000: NEXT WAIT%¶
  IF Left = 0 THEN GOTO Nleft1: REM Do not turn left
wheel¶
  WHEEL%(1) = WHEEL%(1) + 1¶
  IF WHEEL%(1) > ROLL THEN WHEEL%(1) = 1¶
  LOCATE 8, 24¶
  PRINT ROLL$(WHEEL%(1))¶
  Nleft1:¶
    IF Right = 0 THEN GOTO Nright1: REM Do not turn
right wheel¶
    WHEEL%(2) = WHEEL%(2) + 1¶
    IF WHEEL%(2) > ROLL THEN WHEEL%(2) = 1¶
    LOCATE 8, 33¶
    PRINT ROLL$(WHEEL%(2))¶
  Nright1:¶
    WHEEL%(3) = WHEEL%(3) + 1¶
    IF WHEEL%(3) > ROLL THEN WHEEL%(3) = 1¶
    LOCATE 10, 28¶
    PRINT ROLL$(WHEEL%(3))¶
    IF Left = 0 THEN GOTO Nleft2: REM Do not turn
left wheel ¶
    WHEEL%(4) = WHEEL%(4) + 1¶
    IF WHEEL%(4) > ROLL THEN WHEEL%(4) = 1¶
    LOCATE 12, 24¶
    PRINT ROLL$(WHEEL%(4))¶
  Nleft2:¶
    IF Right = 0 THEN GOTO Nright2: REM Do not turn
right wheel ¶
    WHEEL%(5) = WHEEL%(5) + 1¶
    IF WHEEL%(5) > ROLL THEN WHEEL%(5) = 1¶
    LOCATE 12, 33¶
    PRINT ROLL$(WHEEL%(5))¶
  Nright2:¶
    TEST$ = INKEY$¶
    IF INPUT$ = "" THEN GOTO Continue¶
    IF START = 1 THEN START = 0: Left = 1: GOTO
Continue¶
    IF STOP = 1 THEN STOP = 0: Right = 0¶
  Continue:¶
 NEXT SPIN¶
RETURN¶
```

The subroutine accomplishes the spin of the wheels in one loop. The SPINCOUNT variable indicates how often the wheels are turned. This allows the main program to set different spin periods for every call of the subroutine and therefore prevents the player from guessing over time where the wheels would stop. We'll use a random number for this possibility in the main program.

A delay loop is inserted to slow down the program on the computer. The computer is told to execute this loop from 1 to 10000 times without executing other commands.

Your computer only requires a short period of time to execute this loop. However, if this delay loop was missing, the program would execute too fast.

The speed of your computer determines the end value for the loop. Newer and faster PCs (such as those with 80386 or 80486 processors) will execute this loop faster than older PCs. You may have to experiment with different values. If you want the wheels to turn slower, select a smaller value.

The next five lines are responsible for turning the wheel in window #1. These lines are repeated four more times for the other four windows.

Since the different output screen positions and the stopping of the wheels should be considered individually, these lines should not be gathered into a loop.

Two variables determine if the wheels should be turned or stopped:

Variable	Controls wheels in
LEFT	Left two windows
RIGHT	Right two windows

The left wheel is turned if LEFT = 1 but the wheel is stopped if LEFT = 0. The same is true for the RIGHT variable.

Therefore, the five lines begin with a query. If the main program set LEFT to 0, the next four lines are skipped and the wheel is not turned. If LEFT is equal to 1, the following line is executed. In this line the position of the wheel is increased by one. However, nothing changes on the output screen yet.

Now we must be careful that the wheel cannot reach a position beyond nine because there are no symbols available for this. Therefore, we test in the line:

```
IF WHEEL%(1) > ROLL THEN WHEEL%(1) = 1
```

If the position of the wheel (WHEEL%(1)) is the maximum possible, then the position (determined in ROLL with 9) has been exceeded. In this case we simply set the position to one, because even in a real wheel the last symbol would be followed by the first.

The two following lines output the symbol required for the position of the wheel at a certain location on the output screen.

Because the expression:

```
ROLL$(WHEEL%(1))
```

is not very simple to understand, we want to explain it with one example.

Let's assume the position of the wheel in WHEEL%(1) was a 1 and was increased to two. Then ROLL$(2), which represents the symbol " 80", is displayed on the output screen.

The lines that follow are very similar in construction. The next five lines are responsible for the second wheel window on the top right. In the first line a test is performed if RIGHT = 0 and if this is the case, skipping the part of the program for spinning this wheel.

The next four lines turn the middle wheel. The test for a stopped wheel is missing here because if the middle wheel is stopped, all wheels are stopped and the SPIN subroutine does not have to be called.

The following lines up to the line:

```
IF INPUT$ = "" THEN GOTO Continue
```

are a repetition of the previous parts, but for the lower wheel windows, left and right. Also, here the wheels are only turned if the appropriate LEFT variable or RIGHT variable is set to one.

The keyboard is checked in the next line following the spin of the wheels. If a key was pressed, the character is stored in INPUT$. This is required to enable the player to start or stop the wheels by pressing a key.

We'll use the following two variables to start or stop the wheels:

Variable	Controls
START	The left wheel
STOP	The right wheel

If START = 1, the left wheel can be started again, but if STOP = 1, the right wheel can be stopped by pressing a key.

This line tests if the user pressed any key. If this is not the case, INPUT$ does not contain a character, therefore "" and the program jumps directly to the end of the loop.

If, on the other hand, a key was pressed, a test must be made to determine if starting or stopping is allowed. Begin with the line:

```
IF START = 1 THEN START = 0: Left = 1: GOTO Continue
```

If START = 1, the left wheel can be started. First START = 0 prevents another start. The variable LEFT is set to one. This allows the spin for the two left wheel windows. At the end of the line a jump is made to the CONTINUE: label, because the next line should not be executed. Without this jump, the left wheel would be started by pressing a key and the right wheel would be stopped.

In the following line is the same query for stopping the right wheel. If STOP = 1, then STOP = 0 is set and a new stop is prevented. In addition, RIGHT is set to 0 and the two right wheel windows are not turned anymore.

Our loop for spinning the wheel ends in the last line. This loop is executed as often as indicated by the counter SPINCOUNT. After the last execution of the loop the SPIN subroutine ends and returns to the main program.

7.3.6 The main program

Now we must discuss the listing for the main program. The main program should be placed at the beginning of the program. It appears as follows (remember to press the Enter key when you see the ¶ character):

```
REM Main program¶
CLS¶
DIM ROLL$(9)¶
DIM WHEEL%(5)¶
MONEY = 10¶
GOSUB Picture: ' Construct display ¶
GOSUB Variables: ' Set Variables ¶
Start:¶
 SPINCOUNT = 20 + 10 * RND¶
 STOP = 0¶
 START = 0¶
 Left = 1¶
 Right = 1¶
 MONEY = MONEY - .3¶
 IF MONEY < 0 THEN END¶
 LOCATE 5, 39¶
 PRINT USING "###.#"; MONEY¶
 GOSUB SPIN: ' SPIN¶
 Left = 0¶
 SPINCOUNT = 15 + 5 * RND¶
 START = 1¶
 LOCATE 17, 19¶
 PRINT "█"; ' USE ASCII CODE 219¶
 GOSUB SPIN¶
 LOCATE 17, 19¶
 PRINT " ";¶
 START = 0¶
```

```
      Left = 0¶
      Right = 1¶
      SPINCOUNT = 15 + 5 * RND¶
      STOP = 1¶
      LOCATE 17, 43¶
      PRINT  "█";  ' USE ASCII CODE 219¶
      GOSUB SPIN¶
      LOCATE 17, 43¶
      PRINT " ";¶
      STOP = 0¶
      Right = 0¶
      SPINCOUNT = 15 + 5 * RND¶
      GOSUB SPIN¶
       GOSUB WIN:  ' Check  winnings  and  calculate  if
      necessary ¶
      RANDOM% = RND * 4 + 1¶
       IF  WHEEL%(RANDOM%)  <  ROLL  THEN  WHEEL%(RANDOM%)  =
      WHEEL%(RANDOM%) + 1¶
      Blank:¶
       INPUT$ = INKEY$¶
       IF INPUT$ = "" THEN GOTO Blank¶
       IF INPUT$ <> "q" THEN GOTO Start: ' New Execution ¶
      CLS : END¶
```

Notice that we're using ' instead of REM. The single quotation mark can replace the REM keyword. However, do not use the single quotation mark in a DATA line. *QBasic* will interpret the quotation mark as a value.

The CLS statement in the first line clears the output screen. Then the arrays are dimensioned as we discussed earlier. The ROLL$ array stores nine elements (variables).

The WHEEL%(5) array is dimensioned in the next line. It can accept five whole number values. This array is responsible for storing the current position for the five wheels.

In the fourth line the initial amount of money in MONEY is set to 10 dollars.

Each of the next two program lines call a subroutine. The first subroutine calls the screen display picture of the bandit and the second subroutine sets the variables.

The continuously executed main program begins with the START: label. Before the subroutine for spinning the wheels can be called, some variables must be set. This starts in the next line with SPINCOUNT.

The player cannot guess when the left wheel stops because by adding a random value (10 * RND) to the fixed value 20. The duration of the spin will then be different every time.

Through STOP = 0 and START = 0 every influence on the spinning of the wheels is prevented in this phase, when the user presses a key. LEFT = 1 and RIGHT = 1 insure that all three wheels turn.

The available amount of wager is reduced by 25 cents. If this is not possible (MONEY < 0), the program ends.

If the program continues, the cursor is set to the display of the wager money and the current amount is displayed. Since PRINT USING prevents results such as 9.30001, we can display the wager money in the desired format (three places in front and two after the decimal point).

Now the subroutine for spinning the wheels can be called with GOSUB SPIN.

After all three wheels have been turned, the phase comes where the left wheel is stopped, but can be restarted. First we set LEFT to 0. Then we find a random number for the length of the spin phase. In the line "START = 1" we allow the start of the left wheel.

To inform the player that the left wheel can be started, the program displays a start knob under the text START on the output screen. This is done in the next two lines.

Now the SPIN subroutine is called again. If the player wants to use the opportunity for a new start is of no importance at this point in the main program, since the subroutine will perform this function.

The third phase of a play cycle is next. If the left wheel is stopped, the right can be stopped. First we must make the button for the new start disappear. We simply overwrite it with one space in the lines:

```
LOCATE 17, 19
PRINT " ";
```

To make certain, we again set START to 0 and LEFT to 0. With RIGHT = 1 and STOP = 1 the right wheel turns, but can be stopped. We set the number of revolutions with the line:

```
SPINCOUNT = 15 + 5 * RND
```

Also, below the STOP message we output a symbolic button for stopping with the lines:

```
LOCATE 17, 43
PRINT "█";
```

Now the subroutine for spinning the wheels can be called. In the last phase of the play, only the middle wheel should turn. First the Stop button must be overwritten with one space. This is done in the following lines:

```
LOCATE 17, 43
PRINT " ";
```

The variables are then set in such a way, that only the middle wheel is turned and starting and stopping is not possible. In the line GOSUB SPIN, the SPIN subroutine can be called for the last time.

In the line GOSUB Profit a subroutine is called which checks the winnings and increases the wager, if necessary. Since we still must create this subroutine, before the test start, insert the following lines at the end of the program:

```
Profit:¶
RETURN¶
```

This is a very brief subroutine which consists only of the label and the return jump command.

Notice the following lines of the main program:

```
RANDOM% = RND * 4 + 1¶
IF  WHEEL%(RANDOM%)  <  ROLL  THEN  WHEEL%(RANDOM%)  =
WHEEL%(RANDOM%)  +  1¶
```

Don't worry if you cannot immediately understand these lines. They're used to advance one of the five wheels by one position, in a random manner.

The reason for this is that the SPIN subroutine always moves all five wheels the same number of revolutions. This would not create all possible combinations.

Since one of the wheels can be changed by using a random number, all combinations eventually become possible.

Incidentally, we only change the position of the wheel if it is not a 9. If it was 9, we would have to insert another program line to set the wheel to one again.

In the following lines:

```
INPUT$ = INKEY$¶
IF INPUT$ = "" THEN GOTO Blank¶
IF INPUT$ <> "q" THEN GOTO Start: ' new execution
run¶
```

we wait for the player to press a key after every execution run and start again at the beginning of the main program (GOTO Start) - unless the Q key was pressed.

When the player presses the Q key, the output screen is cleared and the program terminated. If you have added the required lines:

```
Profit:¶
RETURN¶
```

at the end of the program, you can start the provisional program as a test. We think you will have a lot of fun, even if, at the moment, it does not contain any winnings.

7.3.7 Subroutine to calculate your winnings

You'll need to determine how much money you've won playing against the BANDIT. The subroutine we use in this program to calculate the winnings actually consists of three sub-programs. This split makes the subroutine easier to read and understand.

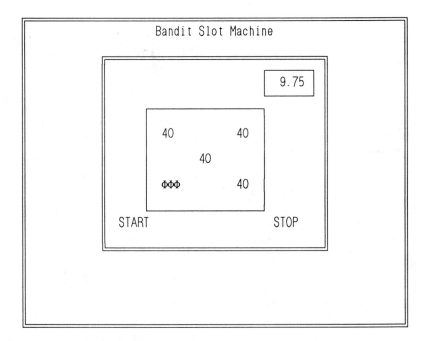

An example of a winning game

Before we print the last program portions, we want to say a few more things about calculating winnings. A win occurs when three contiguous wheels show the same symbol.

The phrase "three contiguous wheel windows" means:

- The three top

- The three left

- The three right

- The three bottom

- The diagonal from top left to right bottom

- The diagonal from top right to left bottom

We have selected these six combinations so that neither wins nor losses will occur too often. You can modify it later according to your own imagination if a profit (or loss) occurs too frequently.

When determining the winnings, we must consider another possibility. Imagine that we first test the three top wheel windows, determined a profit of 40¢, added it to the amount of money wagered and return to the main program.

Unfortunately, the player is not satisfied, because according to the three bottom wheel windows, a profit was due. We must first test all 6 combinations for a possible win and calculate the highest profit. This is done by the following subroutine (press the ⏎Enter⏎ key when you see the ¶ character):

```
WIN:¶
 REM Check Profit ¶
 WIN$ = ""¶
 WIN = 0¶
 MAXWIN = 0¶
 R1$ = ROLL$(WHEEL%(1))¶
 R2$ = ROLL$(WHEEL%(2))¶
 R3$ = ROLL$(WHEEL%(3))¶
 R4$ = ROLL$(WHEEL%(4))¶
 R5$ = ROLL$(WHEEL%(5))¶
 IF R1$ = R2$ AND (R1$ = R3$ OR R3$ = WLDCD$) THEN
WIN$ = R1$: GOSUB Calculate¶
 IF R1$ = R4$ AND (R1$ = R3$ OR R3$ = WLDCD$) THEN
WIN$ = R1$: GOSUB Calculate¶
 IF R4$ = R5$ AND (R4$ = R3$ OR R3$ = WLDCD$) THEN
WIN$ = R4$: GOSUB Calculate¶
```

```
      IF R2$ = R5$ AND (R2$ = R3$ OR R3$ = WLDCD$) THEN
WIN$ = R2$: GOSUB Calculate¶
      IF R1$ = R5$ AND (R1$ = R3$ OR R3$ = WLDCD$) THEN
WIN$ = R1$: GOSUB Calculate¶
      IF R2$ = R4$ AND (R2$ = R3$ OR R3$ = WLDCD$) THEN
WIN$ = R2$: GOSUB Calculate¶
      IF MAXWIN <> 0 THEN WIN = MAXWIN: GOSUB Max: GOTO
Top¶
      IF R3$ = WLDCD$ THEN MONEY = MONEY + .25¶
      Top:¶
RETURN¶
Calculate:¶
      REM There is a Profit, calculate it¶
      LOCATE 15, 27¶
      PRINT "WIN";¶
      WIN = VAL(WIN$) / 100¶
      IF WIN$ = CHR$(1) THEN WIN = 10¶
      IF MAXWIN < WIN THEN MAXWIN = WIN¶
RETURN¶
Max:¶
      FOR COUNT = MONEY TO MONEY + WIN STEP .1¶
        LOCATE 5, 39¶
        PRINT USING "###.##"; COUNT;¶
        FOR WAIT% = 1 TO 10000: NEXT WAIT%¶
      NEXT COUNT¶
      MONEY = MONEY + WIN¶
      LOCATE 5, 39¶
      PRINT USING "###.##"; MONEY¶
      LOCATE 15, 27¶
      PRINT "        ";¶
RETURN¶
```

The WIN subroutine begins with the first line and ends with the first RETURN. It calls the CALCULATE subroutine which calculates the amount of money won from the winning combination. It also insures that the highest win is calculated. The MAX subroutine displays the winnings in a realistic manner on the output screen.

Let us start with the first subroutine. In the first lines three variables are reset. WIN$ later contains the symbol of the wheels which occurs three times and determines the amount won. The WIN variable contains the applicable amount of money and in MAXWIN the largest win is calculated.

Notice the five lines that start with the RX$ variable. These lines have the function of assigning the contents of five variables with a long and complicated name to 5 variables with short names.

This saves us much typing in the following program lines and also prevents the lines from becoming too long. In R1$ to R5$ the character strings are stored again, which are visible in the five wheel fields.

Next the program tests if three identical symbols occur in the six possible combinations. We allow a profit under two conditions (like a real slot machine):

- The three symbols are identical.

- Two symbols are identical and the middle wheel window displays the wildcard.

Let's look at the first line of the test:

```
IF R1$ = R2$ AND (R1$ = R3$ OR R3$ = WLDCD$) THEN
WIN$ = R1$: GOSUB Calculate¶
```

While examining the line, consider the sequence of the numbering:

```
R1$         R2$
      R3$
R4$         R5$
```

The beginning of this line is very simple:

"If the symbol on the top left is identical to the symbol on the top right, ...".

Now let's expand that thought to other areas of the screen:

"If the symbol on the top left is identical to the symbol in the middle (OR the symbol in the middle is a wildcard ....).

The AND between these two parts of the program line insures that the rest of the line behind the THEN is only executed if the first condition AND the second condition are both satisfied simultaneously.

The parentheses has the same effect as in a mathematical formula. It tells *QBasic* that the expression in parentheses should be tested first.

If the three top symbols are equal, or two are equal and the middle wheel shows a wildcard, then the part behind the THEN is executed. WIN$ is set to the symbol which occurred and the second subroutine is called in the CALCULATE line.

It calculates the winnings and compares it with the highest profit up to now. If the current winning is higher, it becomes the new MAXWIN. We shall soon get to this part of the program.

In the following lines, five additional possible winning combinations are tested. When a win has been found, the subroutine with the winning symbol (WIN$) is called.

The following line:

```
IF MAXWIN <> 0 THEN WIN = MAXWIN: GOSUB Max: GOTO
Top
```

tests if any win occurred.

If this is not the case, a third subroutine starting on the MAX line is called. This subroutine adds the win and displays it on the screen. In addition, the following line will be skipped.

This line is used if no win was achieved, but the middle wheel window shows a wildcard. In this case it adds at least 25¢ and therefore adds the subtracted 25¢ again. The main subroutine ends with the first RETURN.

The second subroutine begins at the CALCULATE label and is always called when a winning combination was achieved. Also, in WIN$ is the symbol which occurred several times. The player is successful when the message "WIN" is displayed on the slot machine. This is done with the following lines:

```
LOCATE 15, 27
PRINT "WIN";
```

Notice a new statement in the following line:

```
WIN = VAL(WIN$) / 100
```

The VAL function is used to make a monetary amount from the winning symbol. This function attempts to convert a string of digits into a numeric value. The string " 40" becomes the number 40 and the string "300" a 300. For more information on the VAL function, refer to the next chapter.

In the string numbers are converted from left to right, until no new numbers occur. If the first character of the character string is not a number and not a space, a 0 is produced.

Let us look at some examples:

String expression	Returns this value:
" 40"	40
"120"	120
"12ABC"	12
"**900"	0
" "	0

The number determined with the VAL statement must still be divided by 100, because " 40" is 40 cents. A special case is tested in the following line:

```
IF WIN$ = CHR$(1) THEN WIN = 10
```

If the winning symbol, which occurred three times, is the wildcard, the result is $10 and WIN is set to 10. The following line makes certain that the highest profit which occurred during a game is stored in MAXWIN.

It tests if the current winnings are larger than MAXWIN. In this case the current winnings are stored in MAXWIN, otherwise not. This line is a simple capability to determine the maximum of a series of numbers. You'll need something similar in one of your own programs.

The second subroutine ends with the RETURN. The following third subroutine is only called if there was a win at all. The profit is stored in the variable WIN. We could simply add this profit to the amount of wager and end the subroutine.

Since we are programming a simulated slot machine, we should at least make it as realistic as possible. In these machines the money of the wager is increased "dime" for "dime". This is done with the following loop:

```
FOR COUNT = MONEY TO MONEY + WIN STEP .1¶
  LOCATE 5, 39¶
  PRINT USING "###.##"; COUNT;¶
  FOR WAIT% = 1 TO 10000: NEXT WAIT%¶
NEXT COUNT¶
```

This loop goes from the current amount of money to the new amount (MONEY + WIN) in increments of one dime (10 cents). The intermediate amount (in COUNT) is displayed. The line:

```
FOR WAIT% = 1 TO 10000: NEXT WAIT%
```

again represents a delay loop. This slows down the processing speed of your PC. The next line ends the loop for counting the money.

If the line:

```
MONEY = MONEY + WIN
```

was missing, you would soon be frustrated as a player. The amount of money would be counted after one win, but the action would continue with the old amount.

The available wager money is in the MONEY variable for the program and was not yet increased. This is done in this line.

Finally the new total is again displayed and the message WIN is removed from the output screen by overwriting it with spaces. The third subroutine ends with the last RETURN.

7.3.8   Experiment on your own

You should now save the completed program under an appropriate name, for example:

BANDIT.BAS

and enjoy playing the game.

Perhaps in a moment of good luck, you can achieve a result like the following:

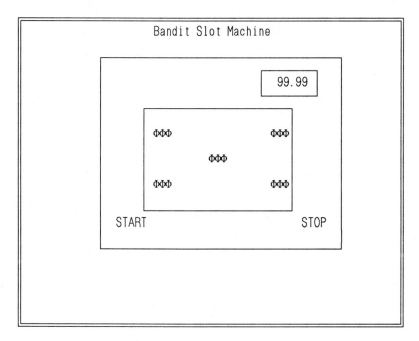

The ultimate jackpot screen in BANDIT.BAS

If you cannot hit this jackpot, maybe you should rely less on your luck and instead modify the program a little, for example:

- Add a subroutine which would force the result shown above if a certain key was pressed.

- Add a subroutine to beep each time you win some money.

- Add a sound subroutine to play music each time you win some money. See Chapter 9 for more information on sound and music.

Besides having some fun, that was really the object of our game.

Before we summarize the *QBasic* statements and functions we've discussed in this chapter, we'll list the entire BANDIT.BAS program for you in the next section.

7.4 The BANDIT Program Listing

We'll list the entire BANDIT.BAS program in this section. If you encountered some errors when typing the program, you can compare your program lines with the following program lines.

Note the ¶ character that appears at the end of the following program lines. This character indicates when you are to press the (Enter) key.

```
CLS¶
DIM ROLL$(9)¶
DIM WHEEL%(5)¶
MONEY = 10¶
GOSUB Picture: REM Display construction¶
GOSUB Variables: REM Set Variables¶
START:¶
 SPINCOUNT = 20 + 10 * RND¶
 ASTOP = 0¶
 START = 0¶
 Left = 1¶
 Right = 1¶
 MONEY = MONEY - .25¶
 IF MONEY < 0 THEN END¶
 LOCATE 5, 39¶
 PRINT USING "###.##"; MONEY¶
 GOSUB SPIN: REM SPIN¶
 Left = 0¶
 SPINCOUNT = 15 + 5 * RND¶
 START = 1¶
 LOCATE 17, 19¶
 PRINT "■";¶
 GOSUB SPIN¶
 LOCATE 17, 19¶
 PRINT " ";¶
 START = 0¶
 Left = 0¶
 Right = 1¶
 SPINCOUNT = 15 + 5 * RND¶
 ASTOP = 1¶
 LOCATE 17, 43¶
 PRINT "■";¶
 GOSUB SPIN¶
 LOCATE 17, 43¶
 PRINT " ";¶
 ASTOP = 0¶
 Right = 0¶
 SPINCOUNT = 15 + 5 * RND¶
 GOSUB SPIN¶
```

```
    GOSUB WIN: REM Check winnings and calculate if necessary¶
    ARANDOM% = RND * 4 + 1¶
     IF  WHEEL%(ARANDOM%)  <  ROLL  THEN  WHEEL%(ARANDOM%)  =
WHEEL%(ARANDOM%) + 1¶
Blank:¶
  TEST$ = INKEY$¶
  IF TEST$ = "" THEN GOTO Blank¶
  IF TEST$ <> "q" THEN GOTO START: REM New execution¶
CLS : END¶
Picture:¶
  PRINT TAB(22); "Bandit Slot Machine"¶
  PRINT¶
  PRINT TAB(13);  "                                          "¶
  PRINT TAB(13);  "                                          "¶
  PRINT TAB(13);  "                             00.00         "¶
  PRINT TAB(13);  "                                          "¶
  PRINT TAB(13);  "                                          "¶
  PRINT TAB(13);  "                  ***      ***            "¶
  PRINT TAB(13);  "                                          "¶
  PRINT TAB(13);  "                     ***                  "¶
  PRINT TAB(13);  "                                          "¶
  PRINT TAB(13);  "                  ***      ***            "¶
  PRINT TAB(13);  "                                          "¶
  PRINT TAB(13);  "                                          "¶
  PRINT TAB(13);  "                                          "¶
  PRINT TAB(13);  "   START                     STOP         "¶
  PRINT TAB(13);  "                                          "¶
  PRINT TAB(13);  "                                          "¶
  PRINT TAB(13);  "                                          "¶
  PRINT TAB(13);  "                                          "¶
  PRINT TAB(13);  "                                          "¶
Variables:  ¶
  ROLL = 9  ¶
  ROLL$(1) = "  40"¶
  ROLL$(2) = "  80"¶
  ROLL$(3) = "  40"¶
  ROLL$(4) = "  80"¶
  ROLL$(5) = "ΦΦΦ"¶
  WLDCD$ = ROLL$(5)¶
  ROLL$(6) = "  40"¶
  ROLL$(7) = "120"¶
  ROLL$(8) = "  40"¶

  ROLL$(9) = "300"¶
  RANDOMIZE TIMER¶
  FOR I = 1 TO 5¶
    WHEEL%(I) = ROLL * RND + 1¶
  NEXT I¶
RETURN¶
SPIN:¶
  FOR SPIN = 1 TO SPINCOUNT¶
    FOR AWAIT% = 1 TO 10000: NEXT AWAIT%
```

```
      IF Left = 0 THEN GOTO Nleft1: REM Left wheel does not
turn¶
  WHEEL%(1) = WHEEL%(1) + 1¶
  IF WHEEL%(1) > ROLL THEN WHEEL%(1) = 1¶
  LOCATE 8, 23¶
  PRINT ROLL$(WHEEL%(1))¶
Nleft1:¶
      IF Right = 0 THEN GOTO Nright1: REM Right wheel does NOT
turn¶
      WHEEL%(2) = WHEEL%(2) + 1¶
      IF WHEEL%(2) > ROLL THEN WHEEL%(2) = 1¶
      LOCATE 8, 33¶
      PRINT ROLL$(WHEEL%(2))¶
Nright1:¶
      WHEEL%(3) = WHEEL%(3) + 1¶
      IF WHEEL%(3) > ROLL THEN WHEEL%(3) = 1¶
      LOCATE 10, 28¶
      PRINT ROLL$(WHEEL%(3))¶
      IF Left = 0 THEN GOTO Nleft2: REM Left wheel does not
turn¶
      WHEEL%(4) = WHEEL%(4) + 1¶
      IF WHEEL%(4) > ROLL THEN WHEEL%(4) = 1¶
      LOCATE 12, 23¶
      PRINT ROLL$(WHEEL%(4))¶
Nleft2:¶
      IF Right = 0 THEN GOTO Nright2: REM Right wheel does NOT
turn¶
      WHEEL%(5) = WHEEL%(5) + 1¶
      IF WHEEL%(5) > ROLL THEN WHEEL%(5) = 1¶
      LOCATE 12, 33¶
      PRINT ROLL$(WHEEL%(5))¶
Nright2:¶
      TEST$ = INKEY$¶
      IF TEST$ = "" THEN GOTO Continue¶
      IF START = 1 THEN START = 0: Left = 1: GOTO Continue¶
      IF ASTOP = 1 THEN ASTOP = 0: Right = 0¶
Continue:¶
  NEXT SPIN¶
RETURN¶
WIN:¶
  REM Check Winnings¶
  WIN$ = ""¶
  WIN = 0¶
  MAXWIN = 0¶
  R1$ = ROLL$(WHEEL%(1))¶
  R2$ = ROLL$(WHEEL%(2))¶
  R3$ = ROLL$(WHEEL%(3))¶
  R4$ = ROLL$(WHEEL%(4))¶
  R5$ = ROLL$(WHEEL%(5))¶
  IF R1$ = R2$ AND (R1$ = R3$ OR R3$ = WLDCD$) THEN WIN$ =
R1$: GOSUB Calculate¶
```

```
   IF R1$ = R4$ AND (R1$ = R3$ OR R3$ = WLDCD$) THEN WIN$ =
R1$: GOSUB Calculate¶
   IF R4$ = R5$ AND (R4$ = R3$ OR R3$ = WLDCD$) THEN WIN$ =
R4$: GOSUB Calculate¶
   IF R2$ = R5$ AND (R2$ = R3$ OR R3$ = WLDCD$) THEN WIN$ =
R2$: GOSUB Calculate¶
   IF R1$ = R5$ AND (R1$ = R3$ OR R3$ = WLDCD$) THEN WIN$ =
R1$: GOSUB Calculate¶
   IF R2$ = R4$ AND (R2$ = R3$ OR R3$ = WLDCD$) THEN WIN$ =
R2$: GOSUB Calculate¶
   IF MAXWIN <> 0 THEN WIN = MAXWIN: GOSUB Max: GOTO Top¶
   IF R3$ = WLDCD$ THEN MONEY = MONEY + .25
Top:¶
RETURN¶
Calculate:¶
 REM There is a win, calculate it¶
 LOCATE 15, 27¶
 PRINT "WIN" ;¶
 WIN = VAL(WIN$) / 100¶
 IF WIN$ = CHR$(1) THEN WIN = 10¶
 IF MAXWIN < WIN THEN MAXWIN = WIN¶
RETURN¶
Max:¶
 FOR COUNT = MONEY TO MONEY + WIN STEP .1¶
  LOCATE 5, 39¶
  PRINT USING "###.##"; COUNT;¶
  FOR AWAIT% = 1 TO 10000: NEXT AWAIT%¶
 NEXT COUNT¶
 MONEY = MONEY + WIN¶
 LOCATE 5, 39¶
 PRINT USING "###.##"; MONEY¶
 LOCATE 15, 27¶
 PRINT "        ";¶
RETURN¶
```

8. Sequential File Management

In this chapter we want to show you different ways to save data directly from the BASIC program on a diskette or hard drive. This allows us to create programs to find data which are then saved as a separate data file.

QBasic is also capable of reading and processing these data files.

8.1 What Are Sequential Files?

When creating the bar chart program (Chapter 6), we created the data for the individual bars as DATA lines. The READ statement was then used to read the data into the program. Unfortunately, this makes the program permanent and not very versatile.

You can't expect the user of your program to modify the program lines when entering or editing data. Obviously, we must find a different method to manage data.

It's easier to create a BASIC program which obtains the data to be displayed from its own data file. This requires that the program and the data to be stored in separate files.

The most common way to manage the data is to form an independent file on the disk. This file is reserved for data only. These data files are called *sequential files*. Sequential files derive their name from the sequential arrangement of the data, similar to the DATA lines.

In a sequential file, the data records are organized one after the other, separated from each other by the ASCII character CHR$(13). This character corresponds to a carriage return. It is required because the corresponding command to read a record in the sequential file reads up to this character.

A *record* is one single unit in a file.

Examples of Sequential Files

Record #1

S	m	i	t	h	,	J	o	h	n	1

Field 1   Field 2   Field 3

Record #2

A	n	d	e	r	s	o	n	,	A	l	b	e	r	t	4

Field 1   Field 2   Field 3

Record #3

K	e	y	s	,	D	e	l	9

Field 1   Field 2   Field 3

Notice in the above illustration that each record in a sequential file can be a different length. Even the fields can be different lengths. A *field* is data that occurs at the same location for each record, such as name, address, city, etc.

The bar chart program is capable of producing different bar charts from various sequential files. For example, one sequential file can contain data for 1989 and another sequential file can contain data for 1990 and so on.

The program structure must be modified so that the data is read with special commands from one of the media instead of from DATA lines of the program. This makes the main program flexible and capable of handling various applications.

8.2 Working With Sequential Files

You can access BASIC data files that are saved on a diskette or a hard drive. To read data from or write data to a sequential file, the file must first be opened using the OPEN statement.

After the data has been used by the BASIC program and the file is no longer required, it can be closed again using the CLOSE statement, which we'll discuss shortly.

8.2.1 OPEN statement

The OPEN statement must indicate the filename. If the file to be opened is not in the current directory, the path and drive must precede the filename.

The following is an example of using the OPEN statement to open a file called DATA90:

```
OPEN "DATA90" FOR INPUT AS #1
```

and here the same line for writing into a file:

```
OPEN "DATA90" FOR OUTPUT AS #1
```

All additions to the filename, such as drive and path, must be indicated as a string within quotation marks.

8.2.2 Reading from a sequential file

Let's take a closer look at the two previous examples of the OPEN statement. Note the FOR INPUT and FOR OUTPUT statements.

```
FOR INPUT # statement
```

Use this statement if you want to read records from the file, one field at a time.

This statement reads information from the file and assigns them to a program variable (sequential files). It is somewhat similar to the READ statement for reading information from a DATA line.

These statements indicate if this file should be opened for reading (FOR INPUT) or writing (FOR OUTPUT). These two statements only apply to sequential files.

```
LINE INPUT #
```

This statement reads a complete line from a sequential file and saves it in a string variable.

By "complete line" we mean that the text is read exactly as it appears, including commas, periods, etc.

```
INPUT$ function
```

The two previous statements read a line at a time from a sequential file. This function reads a specified number of characters from a sequential file.

Syntax	Application
T$ = INPUT$(50,#1)	Reads 50 characters from file number 1. These characters are then assigned to the T$ variable.
PAYPERIOD$ = INPUT$(5,#3)	Reads 5 characters from file number 3. These characters are then assigned to the PAYPERIOD$ string variable.

We'll use the INPUT$ function in the Vocabulary program later in this chapter.

8.2.3 Writing to a sequential file

If a file was opened for writing, the PRINT # or WRITE # statements are used to write the data into the file.

```
PRINT # statement
```

This statement writes the contents of a variable in a sequential file. The record (or variable) is written to the file exactly as if you were using the PRINT statement to display it on your output screen. Therefore, commas, spaces and semicolons have the same functions as in the PRINT statement.

The file number must match the file number previously used in the OPEN statement.

```
WRITE #
```

This statement also writes data to a sequential file and is similar to the PRINT # statement, except that this statement inserts commas between items when they are written to the sequential file.

8.2.4 Opening several sequential files

You can use the OPEN statement to open several files in one *QBasic* program. Each file in the OPEN statement line is assigned a sequential number with the AS # expression.

The following example:

```
OPEN "DATA90" FOR INPUT AS #1a
```

will open the sequential file called "DATA90" as file number 1.

Therefore, the character "#" following AS represents the file number. This number must be used exclusively for the DATA90 file including the CLOSE statement.

Once the "DATA90" sequential file is closed, you can use #1 to open another sequential file.

8.2.5 Closing a file

You'll need to close the sequential file which you opened with the OPEN statement. To close a file, use the CLOSE statement:

```
CLOSE file_number
```

The CLOSE statement writes the data buffer to disk and closes the file.

The file_number parameter refers to the file number referenced when the file was opened. You can then open the file again using the same file number or use a different file number.

For example, to close the "DATA90" file, type the following:

```
CLOSE #1
```

Remember that we opened the file as file number 1. All open files are closed if you use CLOSE without including a file number.

After you close a file, all attempts to write to the file, read from it or apply a function to it will result in a "Bad file name or number" error message.

8.3 Using A Sequential File

8.3.1 Reading data from a file

In this section we'll show you how data can be read from a file and output on the screen.

We'll use the AUTOEXEC.BAT file from the root directory. Since your AUTOEXEC.BAT file probably contains a different number of lines, we'll use a WHILE loop.

This loop will run until the end of the file has been reached. This can be determined with the EOF (End of File) function.

We assign every line read to the N$ string variable. Then we output this variable using a PRINT statement. The following is the program:

```
REM CH8_3a¶
CLS¶
OPEN "\AUTOEXEC.BAT" FOR INPUT AS #1¶
WHILE NOT EOF(1)¶
INPUT #1, N$¶
PRINT N$¶
WEND¶
PRINT "----- End of the file -----"¶
CLOSE #1¶
```

If you have not installed *QBasic* on the drive from which the computer was started, you must indicate the drive name where AUTOEXEC.BAT is located in the root directory before the backslash.

For example, change the OPEN statement in the above program to the following:

```
OPEN "C:\AUTOEXEC.BAT" FOR INPUT AS #1
```

Notice the following program line:

```
WHILE NOT EOF(1)
```

This line executes the following lines until it reaches the concluding WEND, as long as it did not (NOT) reach the end-of-file (EOF) of the file number 1 (1).

8.3.2 Saving your data

Now that we have discussed using the OPEN and CLOSE statements, the next step is to save data in a file.

The following program opens a file named TEST.DAT for writing (OUTPUT). Then the program writes ten different numerical values from a DATA line before closing the file.

Make certain you do not already have a file named TEST.DAT in the current drive. Otherwise, this program will overwrite it. You can either proceed or change TEST.DAT in the following program lines to another name.

```
REM CH8_3B¶
REM Write ten numeric values into the TEST.DAT file¶
CLS¶¶
OPEN "TEST.DAT" FOR OUTPUT AS #1¶
FOR I = 1 TO 10¶
READ Number¶
PRINT #1, Number¶
NEXT I¶
CLOSE 1¶
DATA 11,22,33,44,55,66,77,88,99,100¶
```

In this case, we do not have to watch for the end of file.

The following program reads the data from the TEST.DAT file:

```
REM CH8_3C¶
REM Read values from TEST.DAT file¶
CLS¶
OPEN "TEST.DAT" FOR INPUT AS #1¶
FOR I = 1 TO 10¶
INPUT #1, number¶
PRINT number¶
NEXT¶
CLOSE #1¶
```

The ten values, which we wrote with the first program into the TEST.DAT file, should now appear on your output screen:

```
11
22
33
44
55
66
77
88
99
100

Press any key to continue
```

We could have omitted the query for the end of the file (EOF) in this example, since we know ten numbers are available.

8.3.3 Modifying sequential files

After learning to read and write files with *QBasic*, you shouldn't have any problems changing the contents of sequential files.

In the following example we want to show you how the contents of the AUTOEXEC.BAT can be changed. For example, you can modify the path (PATH command) by including C:\QB45.

The file must first be read into memory, the contents changed and then saved again.

Remember, that you're working with your AUTOEXEC.BAT in this example. DO NOT save the modified file as AUTOEXEC.BAT. The contents of the original file would be lost and making a mistake or typing error may lead to serious problems.

Therefore, save the file under the name AUTOEXEC.BAK.

Remember, the ¶ character indicates when you are to press the
[Enter] key.

```
REM CH8_3D¶
CLS¶
DIM Lines$(20)¶
Count = 0¶
OPEN "C:\AUTOEXEC.BAT" FOR INPUT AS #1¶
WHILE (NOT EOF(1)) AND (Count < 20)¶
LINE INPUT #1, N$¶
Count = Count + 1¶
Lines$(Count) = N$¶
IF Count = 20 THEN¶
    LOCATE 23, 1¶
    PRINT "The file has more than 20 lines! File was
saved incomplete!"¶
    LOCATE 24, 15¶
    PRINT " - Press any key to continue... -"¶
    WHILE INKEY$ = "": WEND¶
END IF¶
WEND¶
CLOSE #1¶
REM Selection subroutine¶
Selection:¶
CLS¶
FOR I = 1 TO Count¶
PRINT I; " ";¶
PRINT Lines$(I)¶
NEXT I¶
LOCATE 23, 1¶
INPUT "(Number of line=change line, E=Save & End,
Q=Quit): "; Selection$¶
Selection$ = UCASE$(Selection$)¶
IF Selection$ = "E" THEN GOTO Store¶
IF Selection$ = "Q" THEN END¶
Linenr = INT(VAL(Selection$))¶
IF (Linenr > 0) AND (Linenr <= Count) THEN GOTO
Edit¶
BEEP¶
GOTO Selection¶
REM subroutine to save file¶
Store:¶
PRINT "I will save the file as AUTOEXEC.BAK"¶
OPEN "\autoexec.bak" FOR OUTPUT AS #1¶
FOR I = 1 TO (Count)¶
PRINT #1, Lines$(I)¶
NEXT I¶
CLOSE 1¶
```

```
END¶
REM Subroutine to edit file¶
Edit:¶
LOCATE 21, 1¶
PRINT Linenr; "   :";¶
LOCATE 21, 10¶
PRINT Lines$(Linenr)¶
LOCATE 22, 1¶
PRINT Linenr; "   :";¶
LOCATE 22, 10¶
INPUT "", Lines$(Linenr)¶
GOTO selection¶
```

Press the Shift + F5 key combination to start the program. Your output screen should appear similar to the following:

```
1   @ECHO OFF
2   PROMPT $p$g
3   PATH C:\BKTOOLS;C:DOS;c:\C:\WINDOWS
4   SET TREMP=C:\DOS
5   C:\DOS\doskey
6
7




    (Number of line=change line, E=Save & End, Q=Quit): ?
```

How this program works

An AUTOEXEC.BAT file containing more than 20 lines cannot be processed. First the file contents are read line by line through the N$ variable and saved in the Lines$ array. Lines$ was dimensioned to 20 fields at the beginning of the program with the DIM statement.

Note that an AUTOEXEC.BAT file containing more than 20 lines cannot be processed and will be saved as an incomplete file.

Then the content of the file is output on the screen. The program uses a LOCATE statement to display a menu line at the bottom of the screen.

The menu gives you the following options:

- Enter the number of the line which should be changed.

- Save the file and terminate the program.

- Terminate the program without saving the file.

For example, if we wanted to change the @ECHO OFF to @ECHO ON, we would select number for the line with the MS-DOS ECHO command and press the [Enter] key. This is the first line.

The contents of the selected line is displayed so that we can type in the "new" contents of this line:

```
1   @ECHO OFF
2   PROMPT $p$g
3   PATH C:\BKTOOLS:C:DOS;c:\C:\WINDOWS
4   SET TREMP=C:\DOS
5   C:\DOS\doskey
6
7




1  :   @ECHO OFF
1  :   _

(Number of line=change line, E=Save & End, Q=Quit): 1
```

Next we would type the following:

```
@ECHO ON
```

and then press the [Enter] key to insert the changed line into the listing of the AUTOEXEC.BAT file on the screen.

```
1   @ECHO ON
2   PROMPT $p$g
3   PATH C:\BKTOOLS:C:DOS;c:\C:\WINDOWS
4   SET TREMP=C:\DOS
5   C:\DOS\doskey
6
7



    (Number of line=change line, E=Save & End, Q=Quit): 1
```

If you then press the Ⓔ key, the modified file is saved as AUTOEXEC.BAK on the hard drive. If you press the Ⓠ key, the program is ended without saving the file.

In Section 8.5 we'll discuss a more comprehensive example of working with sequential files. It's a vocabulary learning program, which can store any number of words and provides practice sessions for learning a foreign language vocabulary.

This program also uses new *QBasic* statements which we'll explain in the next section.

8.4 String Operations

Character strings are essential for many applications. We have considered only the input of strings (`INPUT input$`), the output on the screen (`PRINT input$`) and simple queries and comparisons (`IF input$ = "Y"`).

QBasic offers powerful statements to use parts of strings. For example, if we were to use the title of this book, *QBasic for Beginners*, we could use only the left part ("*QBasic*"), the right ("*Beginners*") or the middle ("*for*") as a string.

The statements available for this are especially important because they determine whether a character string is present in another string.

The `STRING$` statement saves you a lot of work by letting you quickly create a character string consisting of one character. Instead of:

```
A$ = "----------------------------------------"
```

you can simply write:

```
A$ = STRING$(40,"-")
```

and obtain the same result.

8.4.1 `LEFT$`

QBasic has other functions for manipulating strings. The first function we'll look at is `LEFT$`. This function returns a portion of the designated string.

Type the following program and you'll see how using `LEFT$` can make your programming easier:

```
REM LEFT$.BAS¶
CLS¶
A$="COMPUTER"¶
B$=LEFT$(A$,1)¶
C$=LEFT$(A$,2)¶
D$=LEFT$(A$,3)¶
E$=LEFT$(A$,4)¶
F$=LEFT$(A$,5)¶
G$=LEFT$(A$,6)¶
H$=LEFT$(A$,7)¶
I$=LEFT$(A$,8)¶
PRINT B$:PRINT C$:PRINT D$:PRINT E$¶
PRINT F$:PRINT G$:PRINT H$:PRINT I$¶
END¶
```

Start the program by pressing the (Shift) + (F5) key combination. The result of the program is shown below.

```
C
CO
COM
COMP
COMPU
COMPUT
COMPUTE
COMPUTER




Press any key to continue
```

You should have a good idea how the LEFT$ function works simply by looking at the output screen.

The COMPUTER character string is assigned to the A$ string variable. The next line forms a left partial string of A$ with one character and assigns it to B$. Then in the next line, a string containing the two leftmost characters of A$ and the remaining lines are interpreted in the same manner.

Therefore, LEFT$ (A$, X) generates the leftmost X characters of A$. The PRINT statements in the last lines send the results to the output screen.

8.4.2 RIGHT$

The RIGHT$ function is similar to the LEFT$ function except that it starts the characters starting at the right end of the string.

Let's change all references of LEFT$ in the previous example program to RIGHT$:

```
REM RIGHT$.BAS¶
CLS¶
A$="COMPUTER"¶
B$=RIGHT$(A$,1)¶
C$=RIGHT$(A$,2)¶
D$=RIGHT$(A$,3)¶
E$=RIGHT$(A$,4)¶
F$=RIGHT$(A$,5)¶
G$=RIGHT$(A$,6)¶
H$=RIGHT$(A$,7)¶
I$=RIGHT$(A$,8)¶
PRINT B$:PRINT C$:PRINT D$:PRINT E$¶
PRINT F$:PRINT G$:PRINT H$:PRINT I$¶
END¶
```

Start the program by pressing the (Shift)+ (F5) key combination. The result of the program is shown below.

```
R
ER
TER
UTER
PUTER
MPUTER
OMPUTER
COMPUTER



Press any key to continue
```

8.4.3 `MID$`

One of the more interesting functions used in string processing is MID$.

Type the following program:

```
REM MID$.BAS¶
CLS¶
A$="THIS IS A SAMPLE STRING"¶
B$=MID$(A$,1,4)¶
C$=MID$(A$,6,4)¶
D$=MID$(A$,11,6)¶
E$=MID$(A$,12,6)+MID$(A$,20,4)+MID$(A$,11,1)¶
PRINT A$¶
PRINT B$¶
PRINT C$¶
PRINT D$¶
PRINT E$¶
END¶
```

Start the program and take a close look at the result:

```
THIS IS A SAMPLE STRING
THIS
IS A
SAMPLE
AMPLE RINGS



Press any key to continue
```

Using this function you can isolate one or more characters of a string. These are then placed in a new string. The general syntax is:

```
MID$(M$,X,Y)
```

M$ is the name of the string, X designates the position at which character it will begin and Y determines the number of characters.

```
B$=MID$(A$,1,4)¶
C$=MID$(A$,6,4)¶
D$=MID$(A$,11,6)¶
E$=MID$(A$,12,6)+MID$(A$,20,4)+MID$(A$,11,1)¶
```

The positions are always counted from left to right. So the line B$=MID$(A$,1,4) assigns the substring to B$. A new string is generated from A$ which is to contain four characters and starts with the first character of A$.

The C$ string is formed in the same manner. Here we start with the sixth character so that the string IS A is generated.

Take a look at the following line:

```
E$=MID$(A$,12,6)+MID$(A$,20,4)+MID$(A$,11,1)
```

A linked series of strings is called a *concatenation*, or linked series, to make a string not directly readable from the original string—namely AMPLE RINGS.

You can see that the LEFT$ and RIGHT$ functions can be replaced by the MID$ function. In our examples, the position and number of characters were designated by constants.

You can also specify these through variables and mathematical expressions. In addition, you not only can read characters within a string with MID$, but also change or reassign them. For example, type the following:

```
MID$(A$,3,2)="AT"
```

This changes the third and fourth characters to "A" and "T", creating "THAT IS A SAMPLE STRING".

8.4.4 Using strings

The following small program creates moving text on the screen. You can select any text to output in this display:

```
REM MOVETXT.BAS¶
REM Moving Text¶
Delay = .75¶
CLS¶
PRINT "Please input up to 79 characters of text"¶
INPUT "", N$¶
IF LEN(N$) > 79 THEN N$ = MID$(N$, 1, 79)¶
WHILE LEN(N$) < 40¶
   N$ = N$ + N$¶
WEND¶
N$ = N$ + LEFT$(N$, 79 - LEN(N$))¶

WHILE INKEY$ = ""¶
   time = TIMER¶
   Stay:¶
      IF TIMER - time < Delay THEN GOTO Stay¶
   LOCATE 12, 1¶
   PRINT N$¶
   N$ = MID$(N$, 2, 79) + LEFT$(N$, 1)¶
WEND¶
```

The program multiplies the text you enter so that the text appears to move across the width of the screen. Then the first character is removed from the total string and "attached" again in the back of the string.

You can increase the speed of the moving line by reducing the Delay variable at the beginning of the program.

8.4.5 LEN

You can determine the length of a string by using the LEN (X$) function.

The result is numerical and can be assigned to a corresponding variable. If you use the same example above, type the following:

```
PRINT LEN(A$)
```

and press the (Shift) + (F5) key combination.

The result should be 23. You have determined the number of characters in A$.

When using this function it doesn't matter what characters the string is made up of. All characters in the string are counted, including spaces.

8.4.6 VAL

The VAL(X$) function converts a string X$ into a numerical value. If the string starts with a character that cannot be converted to a number, such as a letter, the result will be zero.

If a letter or other characters which cannot be converted to a number are found within the string, only the first part of the string is converted to a number.

The following examples should clarify this:

Example A

The following program shows what happens when an entire string can be converted.

```
REM VAL$.BAS¶
CLS¶
A$="343.45"¶
A=VAL(A$)¶
PRINT A¶
```

Press the [Shift] + [F5] key combination to display the following on your output screen:

```
343.45


Press any key to continue
```

Example B

This program starts with a character which cannot be converted into a number, and is therefore interpreted as zero.

```
REM VAL$B.BAS¶
CLS¶
B$="D38.47F"¶
B=VAL(B$)¶
PRINT B¶
```

Press the [Shift] + [F5] key combination to display the following on your output screen:

```
0


Press any key to continue
```

Example C

The following program shows a "mixed" string, in which only the first group of digits is converted.

```
REM VAL$C.BAS¶
C$="234FFC54"¶
C=VAL(C$)¶
PRINT C¶
```

Press the [Shift] + [F5] key combination to display the following on your output screen:

```
234


Press any key to continue
```

Example D

This program is intended only to show that the comma is simply seen as a non-convertable character, and only the first group of digits is converted.

```
REM VAL$D.BAS¶
D$="33,221"¶
D=VAL(D$)¶
PRINT D¶
```

Press the (Shift) + (F5) key combination to display the following on your output screen:

```
33


Press any key to continue
```

8.4.7 STR$

The STR$ function is the opposite of VAL$ because it converts a numerical expression into a string.

The string which is produced may start with a space. If the number is positive, the first character will be space. Two examples should clarify this:

Example A

```
REM STR$A.BAS¶
CLS¶
A=1234¶
A$=STR$(A)¶
PRINT A$¶
```

Press the (Shift) + (F5) key combination to display the following on your output screen:

```
1234


Press any key to continue
```

Example B

```
REM STR$B.BAS¶
CLS¶
B=-1234¶
B$=STR$(B)¶
PRINT B$¶
```

Press the [Shift] + [F5] key combination to display the following on your output screen:

```
-1234


Press any key to continue
```

Both of the strings contain five characters each. The values of the numbers themselves could also be converted to strings instead of first assigning them to variables.

We could use STR$(1234) in Example A instead of STR$(A).

8.4.8 INSTR

The INSTR function is another useful function for working with strings. This function lets you search through a string for a desired substring of characters.

The syntax of the function looks like this:

```
INSTR(X,A$,B$)
```

Here the X represents the position at which the string A$ is to be searched. B$ represents the substring to be searched for. The result is the position of the substring within the string. If the substring is not found within the target string, the result is zero.

The following program should clarify the function.

```
REM INSTR$.BAS¶
CLS¶
A$="THIS IS A SAMPLE STRING"¶
B$="IS"¶
C=INSTR(A$,B$)¶
PRINT C¶
END¶
```

Press the ⎙Shift⎚ + ⎙F5⎚ key combination to display the following on your output screen:

```
3


Press any key to continue
```

You may expect to receive 6 as the value for C. However, 3 is returned as the value because *QBasic* found that the word "THIS" contains the B$ search string.

 The INSTR function searches for an exact match of the string. Therefore, in the example program above, a substring containing the word "is" would not have been found since it contains lowercase letters.

8.4.9 STRING$

This function creates a string which contains a sequence of the same character.

Type the following line:

```
A$=STRING$(40,"*"): PRINT A$
```

Press the ⎙Shift⎚ + ⎙F5⎚ key combination to start this program line. This program line outputs a line with 40 asterisks as the output.

```
****************************************

Press any key to continue
```

8.4.10 SPACE$

The SPACE$ function is similar to the STRING$ function.

```
A$=SPACE$(40)
```

For example, the previous program line fills the A$ variable with 40 spaces. This statement can be used for exact positioning of output.

The following example prints 12 spaces followed by the string "HELLO".

```
PRINT SPACE$(12);"HELLO"
```

8.5 A Vocabulary Training Program

The following example program is the longest program we'll discuss in this book. However, it demonstrates the most important BASIC statements, partitioning of a program with subroutines and can be used for learning a foreign language.

The words which are entered can be saved in lessons containing 100 words each. The vocabulary drill can be performed either from English to German or German to English.

The companion diskette available for this book contains the complete program listing and two vocabulary files for the program. The vocabulary files must be contained in the same directory as the program.

Any words which are recognized by the student will not be repeated. A wrong answer causes the program to repeat the drill for the word.

At the end statistical information is displayed on the screen, indicating how many attempts were required for the right answer.

The words can be printed in two ways:

- As an alphabetized list in English/German.

- As an alphabetized list in German/English.

Remember to press the (Enter) key when you see the ¶ character in the following program lines:

```
REM Vocabulary Learning Program¶
REM¶
RANDOMIZE TIMER¶
DIM eng$(128), dt$(128), temp1$(256), temp2$(256),
Count(128)¶
¶
start:¶
CLS¶
PRINT "="; STRING$(78, "="); "=": REM use ASCII code
205¶
```

```
PRINT TAB(28); "   Vocabulary Training   "¶
PRINT "="; STRING$(78, "="); "=": REM use ASCII code
205¶
PRINT¶
PRINT STRING$(80, 196)¶
P R I N T        "V o c a b u l a r y        F i l e:
Vocabulary Count:"¶
LOCATE 6, 18: PRINT File$: LOCATE 6, 75: PRINT USING
"###"; total¶
PRINT STRING$(80, 196)¶
PRINT¶
PRINT "                                    - 1 -   Load
Vocabulary File": PRINT¶
PRINT "                                    - 2 -   Enter
Vocabulary": PRINT¶
PRINT "                                    - 3 -   Save
Vocabulary": PRINT¶
PRINT "                                    - 4 -   Vocabulary
Drill": PRINT¶
PRINT "                                    - 5 -   Print
Vocabulary": PRINT¶
PRINT "                                    - 6 -   End
Vocabulary Program": PRINT¶
PRINT STRING$(80, 196)¶
Menu:¶
LOCATE 23, 30: PRINT SPACE$(20)¶
LOCATE 23, 30: INPUT "Please select "; x$¶
IF VAL(x$) < 1 OR VAL(x$) > 6 THEN GOTO Menu¶
x = VAL(x$)¶
ON x GOTO voc.load, voc.input, voc.store, voc.drill,
voc.print, voc.end¶
END¶
¶
voc.load:¶
¶
CLS¶
PRINT "="; STRING$(78, "="); "=": REM use ASCII code
205¶
PRINT TAB(28); "   Vocabulary Training   "¶
PRINT "="; STRING$(78, "="); "=": REM use ASCII code
205¶
PRINT¶
PRINT STRING$(80, 196)¶
P R I N T        "V o c a b u l a r y        F i l e:
Vocabulary Count:"¶
LOCATE 6, 18: PRINT File$: LOCATE 6, 75: PRINT USING
"###"; total¶
PRINT STRING$(80, 196)¶
PRINT "Vocabulary Files in Current Directory"¶
FILES "*.voc"¶
PRINT " (enter filename without extension) "¶
¶
```

```
LOCATE 6, 18: PRINT "_____                      "¶
LOCATE 6, 18: INPUT "", File$¶
IF LEN(File$) > 8 THEN GOTO voc.load¶
IF File$ = "" THEN GOTO start¶
FOR I = 1 TO LEN(File$)¶


   IF INSTR("+:;.<>/\ ß", MID$(File$, I, 1)) <> 0
THEN BEEP: GOTO voc.load¶
NEXT I¶
¶
I = 1¶
OPEN File$ + ".VOC" FOR INPUT AS #1¶
  DO UNTIL EOF(1)¶
    INPUT #1, eng$(I), dt$(I)¶
    I = I + 1: rec.number = I - 1: total = I - 1¶
      LOCATE 6, 75, 0: PRINT USING "###"; rec.number¶
  LOOP¶
CLOSE #1¶
LOCATE 6, 18: PRINT SPACE$(8)¶
LOCATE 6, 18: PRINT File$¶
save = 0¶
GOTO start¶
¶
¶
voc.input:¶
I = rec.number + 1¶
¶
next.enter:¶
IF rec.number = 100 THEN¶
    LOCATE 12, 20: PRINT "'--------------------------
---------------"¶
      LOCATE 13, 20: COLOR 0, 7: PRINT "      No
additional inputs possible ...   "; : COLOR 7, 0¶
      LOCATE 14, 20: PRINT "'--------------------------
---------------"¶
   x$ = INPUT$(1)¶
   GOTO start¶
END IF¶
¶
CLS¶
PRINT "="; STRING$(78, "="); "=": REM use ASCII code
205¶
PRINT TAB(28); "   Vocabulary Training   "¶
PRINT "="; STRING$(78, "="); "=": REM use ASCII code
205¶
PRINT¶
PRINT STRING$(80, 196)¶
P R I N T        "V o c a b u l a r y        F i l e:
Vocabulary Count:"¶
LOCATE 6, 18: PRINT File$: LOCATE 6, 75: PRINT USING
"###"; total¶
```

```
PRINT STRING$(80, 196)¶
PRINT¶
PRINT "  English word    : "; STRING$(30, "_")¶
PRINT¶
PRINT "  German word     : "; STRING$(30, "_")¶
¶
engl.word:¶
LOCATE 9, 20: PRINT STRING$(30, "_") + SPACE$(20)¶
LOCATE 9, 20: INPUT "", eng$¶
IF LEN(eng$) > 30 THEN GOTO engl.word¶
IF INSTR(eng$, CHR$(34)) <> 0 THEN GOTO engl.word¶
IF eng$ = "" THEN GOTO engl.word¶
¶
dt.word:¶
LOCATE 11, 20: PRINT STRING$(30, "_") + SPACE$(20)¶
LOCATE 11, 20: INPUT "", dt$¶
IF LEN(dt$) > 30 THEN GOTO dt.word¶
IF INSTR(dt$, CHR$(34)) <> 0 THEN GOTO dt.word¶
IF dt$ = "" THEN GOTO dt.word¶
¶
we:¶
LOCATE 15, 25: PRINT "Continue inputs (Y/N) " +
SPACE$(20)¶
LOCATE 15, 48: INPUT ""; x$¶
¶
IF UCASE$(x$) = "Y" OR x$ = "" THEN¶
   eng$(I) = eng$¶
   dt$(I) = dt$¶
   I = I + 1: rec.number = rec.number + 1: total =
total + 1¶
   save = 1: File$ = "UNTITLED"¶
   GOTO next.enter¶
END IF¶
¶
IF UCASE$(x$) = "N" THEN¶
   eng$(I) = eng$¶
   dt$(I) = dt$¶
   I = I + 1: rec.number = rec.number + 1: total =
total + 1¶
   save = 1¶
   GOTO start¶
END IF¶
¶
GOTO we¶
¶
¶
voc.store:¶
file.old$ = File$¶
¶
LOCATE 6, 18: PRINT "_____                    "¶
LOCATE 6, 18: INPUT "", File$¶
IF File$ = "" THEN¶
```

251

```
      IF file.old$ = "" THEN BEEP: GOTO voc.store¶
      File$ = file.old$¶
END IF¶
IF LEN(File$) > 8 THEN GOTO voc.store¶
FOR I = 1 TO LEN(File$)¶
   IF INSTR("+:;.<>/\ ß", MID$(File$, I, 1)) <> 0
THEN BEEP: GOTO voc.store¶
NEXT I¶
¶
OPEN File$ + ".VOC" FOR OUTPUT AS #1¶
   FOR I = 1 TO total¶
      WRITE #1, eng$(I), dt$(I)¶
      LOCATE 6, 75, 0: PRINT USING "###"; total¶
   NEXT I¶
CLOSE #1¶
¶
save = 0¶
¶
LOCATE 6, 18: PRINT SPACE$(8)¶
LOCATE 6, 18: PRINT File$¶
GOTO Menu¶
¶
¶
voc.drill:¶
¶
IF File$ = "" THEN¶
   LOCATE 12, 20: PRINT ""¶
LOCATE 13, 20: COLOR 0, 7: PRINT "  Please load a
Vocabulary File first ...  "; : COLOR 7, 0¶
   LOCATE 14, 20: PRINT ""¶
   x$ = INPUT$(1)¶
   GOTO start¶
END IF¶
¶
¶
CLS¶
PRINT "="; STRING$(78, "="); "=": REM use ASCII code
205¶
PRINT TAB(28); "   Vocabulary Training   "¶
PRINT "="; STRING$(78, "="); "=": REM use ASCII code
205¶
PRINT¶
PRINT STRING$(80, 196)¶
P R I N T         "V o c a b u l a r y        F i l e :
Vocabulary Count:"¶
LOCATE 6, 18: PRINT File$: LOCATE 6, 75: PRINT USING
"###"; total¶
PRINT STRING$(80, 196)¶
PRINT¶
drill:¶
 ¶
   IF flag = 1 THEN¶
```

```
          LOCATE 13, 28: PRINT "Drill : German/English";
SPACE$(20)¶
   ELSEIF flag = 0 THEN¶
          LOCATE 13, 28: PRINT "Drill : English/German";
SPACE$(20)¶
   END IF¶
¶
LOCATE 14, 25: PRINT "SPACE = Change /// ENTER =
Continue"¶
x$ = INPUT$(1)¶
IF x$ = " " THEN¶
   IF flag = 0 THEN flag = 1: GOTO drill¶
   IF flag = 1 THEN flag = 0: GOTO drill¶
END IF¶
IF x$ = CHR$(13) THEN GOTO build.screen¶
GOTO drill¶
¶
build.screen:¶
rec.number = total¶
Count = total¶
FOR I = 1 TO Count¶
   arandom = INT(RND * Count + 1)¶
   IF flag = 1 THEN¶
          temp1$(I)  =  dt$(arandom):  temp2$(I)  =
eng$(arandom)¶
      SWAP dt$(arandom), dt$(Count)¶
      SWAP eng$(arandom), eng$(Count)¶
   END IF¶
   IF flag = 0 THEN¶
          temp1$(I)  =  eng$(arandom):  temp2$(I)  =
dt$(arandom)¶
      SWAP dt$(arandom), dt$(Count)¶
      SWAP eng$(arandom), eng$(Count)¶
   END IF¶
   Count = Count - 1¶
NEXT I¶
CLS¶
PRINT "="; STRING$(78, "="); "=": REM use ASCII code
205¶
PRINT TAB(28); "   Vocabulary Training   "¶
PRINT "="; STRING$(78, "="); "=": REM use ASCII code
205¶
PRINT¶
PRINT STRING$(80, 196)¶
P R I N T         " V o c a b u l a r y        F i l e :
Vocabulary Count:"¶
LOCATE 6, 18: PRINT File$: LOCATE 6, 75: PRINT USING
"###"; total¶
PRINT STRING$(80, 196)¶
PRINT¶
¶
s = 1¶
```

```
next.vocab:¶
   LOCATE 8, 23: PRINT USING "Count of Vocabulary
Drill :###"; rec.number¶
   LOCATE 11¶
   IF flag = 1 THEN¶
      PRINT "  German word    : "; SPACE$(30)¶
      PRINT¶
      PRINT "  English word   : "; STRING$(30, "_")¶
   ELSEIF flag = 0 THEN¶
      PRINT "  English word   : "; SPACE$(30)¶
      PRINT¶
      PRINT "  German word    : "; STRING$(30, "_")¶
   END IF¶
¶
LOCATE 11, 20: PRINT temp1$(s)¶
¶
query:¶
LOCATE 13, 20: PRINT STRING$(30, "_")¶
LOCATE 13, 20: INPUT "", wort$¶
IF LEN(wort$) > 30 THEN GOTO query¶
SELECT CASE flag¶
   CASE 0¶
      IF wort$ = temp2$(s) THEN¶
         PLAY "O2 L40 C L40 D L40 E L40 F L40 G L40 D
L40 E L40 F L40 G"¶
         GOTO right¶
      END IF¶
      PLAY "O2 L40 G L40 F L40 E L40 D L40 G L40 F L40
E L40 D L40 C"¶
      LOCATE 15¶
      COLOR 0, 7: PRINT "Sorry, that is incorrect!":
COLOR 7, 0:¶
      PRINT "The correct answer is: "; temp2$(s)¶
      COLOR 7, 0¶
      x$ = INPUT$(1)¶
      LOCATE 15¶
      PRINT SPACE$(80)¶
      PRINT SPACE$(80)¶
      errors = errors + 1¶
      Count(s) = Count(s) + 1¶
      SWAP temp1$(s), temp1$(rec.number)¶
      SWAP temp2$(s), temp2$(rec.number)¶
      GOTO next.vocab¶
   CASE 1¶
      IF wort$ = temp2$(s) THEN¶
         PLAY "O2 L40 C L40 D L40 E L40 F L40 G L40 D
L40 E L40 F L40 G"¶
         GOTO right¶
      END IF¶
      PLAY "O2 L40 G L40 F L40 E L40 D L40 G L40 F L40
E L40 D L40 C"¶
      LOCATE 15¶
```

```
      COLOR 0, 7¶
       COLOR 0, 7: PRINT "Sorry, that is incorrect!":
COLOR 7, 0:¶
      PRINT "The correct answer is: "; temp2$(s)¶
      COLOR 7, 0¶
      x$ = INPUT$(1)¶
      LOCATE 15¶
      PRINT SPACE$(80)¶
      PRINT SPACE$(80)¶
      errors = errors + 1¶
      Count(s) = Count(s) + 1¶
      SWAP temp1$(s), temp1$(rec.number)¶
      SWAP temp2$(s), temp2$(rec.number)¶
      GOTO next.vocab¶
END SELECT¶
¶
right:¶
¶
FOR k = 1 TO rec.number¶
  temp1$(k) = temp1$(k + 1)¶
  temp2$(k) = temp2$(k + 1)¶
NEXT k¶
¶
rec.number = rec.number - 1¶
IF s <= rec.number THEN GOTO next.vocab¶
¶
finale:¶
CLS¶
COLOR 23, 0: PRINT "Calculating...": COLOR 7, 0¶
FOR s = 1 TO total¶
   IF Count(s) = 0 THEN first.right = first.right +
1¶
   IF Count(s) = 1 THEN second.right = second.right +
1¶
   IF Count(s) = 2 THEN third.right = third.right +
1¶
   IF Count(s) = 3 THEN fourth.right = fourth.right +
1¶
   IF Count(s) = 4 THEN fifth.right = fifth.right +
1¶
     IF  Count(s)  >  4  THEN  worse.than.five  =
worse.than.five + 1¶
NEXT s¶
¶
PLAY "O3 L5 G L30 G L30 F G L15 F E F L18 G L18 G L
15 F E D C"¶
PLAY "O2 L5 G L30 G L30 F G L15 F E F L18 G L18 G L
15 F E D C"¶
PLAY "O1 L5 G L30 G L30 F G L15 F E F L18 G L18 G
L15 F E D L5 C"¶
¶
CLS¶
```

```
PRINT STRING$(80, "*")¶
PRINT "***"; TAB(78); "***"¶
PRINT "***"; TAB(32); "R e s u l t"; TAB(78); "***"¶
PRINT "***"; TAB(78); "***"¶
PRINT STRING$(80, "*")¶
PRINT¶
PRINT "       Count of all words        :"; total¶
PRINT "       Wrong answers             :"; errors¶
PRINT¶
PRINT "           Right  on  first  try           :";
first.right¶
PRINT "           Right  on  second  try          :";
second.right¶
PRINT "           Right  on  third  try           :";
third.right¶
PRINT "           Right  on  fourth  try          :";
fourth.right¶
PRINT "           Right  on  fifth  try           :";
fifth.right¶
PRINT "            Right  after  the  fifth  try  :";
worse.than.five¶
PRINT¶
¶
errors = 0¶
first.right = 0: second.right = 0: third.right = 0¶
fourth.right = 0: fifth.right = 0: worse.than.five =
0¶
¶
PRINT "   Press any key to return to menu..."¶
x$ = INPUT$(1)¶
GOTO start¶
¶
voc.print:¶
CLS¶
¶
printstyle1:¶
¶
  IF still = 1 THEN¶
     LOCATE 13, 28: PRINT "Print : German/English";
SPACE$(20)¶
    ELSEIF still = 0 THEN¶
     LOCATE 13, 28: PRINT "Print : English/German";
SPACE$(20)¶
   END IF¶
¶
LOCATE 14, 25: PRINT "SPACE = Change /// CR =
Continue"¶
x$ = INPUT$(1)¶
IF x$ = " " THEN¶
  IF still = 0 THEN still = 1: GOTO printstyle1¶
  IF still = 1 THEN still = 0: GOTO printstyle1¶
END IF¶
```

```
IF x$ = CHR$(13) THEN GOTO printstyle2¶
GOTO printstyle1¶
¶
printstyle2:¶
¶
   IF stil2 = 1 THEN¶
       LOCATE 13, 28: PRINT "Print : Cheat-Sheet";
SPACE$(20)¶
     ELSEIF stil2 = 0 THEN¶
           LOCATE  13,  28:  PRINT  "Print  :  List";
SPACE$(20)¶
   END IF¶
¶
LOCATE  14,  25:  PRINT  "SPACE  =  Change  ///  CR =
Continue"¶
x$ = INPUT$(1)¶
IF x$ = " " THEN¶
   IF stil2 = 0 THEN stil2 = 1: GOTO printstyle2¶
   IF stil2 = 1 THEN stil2 = 0: GOTO printstyle2¶
END IF¶
IF x$ = CHR$(13) THEN GOTO aPRINT¶
GOTO printstyle2¶
¶
aPRINT:¶
¶
IF stil2 = 1 THEN¶
   LPRINT CHR$(27); "S"; CHR$(1);¶
   LPRINT CHR$(27); "A"; CHR$(3); CHR$(27); "3";¶
   LPRINT CHR$(15)¶
   IF stil1 = 0 THEN¶
     FOR s = 1 TO rec.number¶
       LPRINT eng$(s); " <---> "; dt$(s)¶
     NEXT s¶
     LPRINT CHR$(27); "@"¶
   ELSEIF stil1 = 1 THEN¶
     FOR s = 1 TO rec.number¶
       LPRINT dt$(s); " <---> "; eng$(s)¶
     NEXT s¶
     LPRINT CHR$(27); "@"¶
   END IF¶
END IF¶
¶
IF stil2 = 0 THEN¶
   LPRINT STRING$(75, "*")¶
   LPRINT "***                    Print the Vocabulary
***"¶
   LPRINT STRING$(75, "*")¶
   LPRINT¶
     LPRINT "Vocabulary File: "; File$; USING "
Word Count : ###"; rec.number¶
   LPRINT STRING$(75, "-")¶
   ¶
```

```
        IF still = 0 THEN¶
          FOR s = 1 TO rec.number¶
            LPRINT eng$(s); TAB(35); dt$(s)¶
          NEXT s¶
          LPRINT CHR$(27); "@"¶
        ELSEIF still = 1 THEN¶
          FOR s = 1 TO rec.number¶
            LPRINT dt$(s); TAB(135); eng$(s)¶
          NEXT s¶
          LPRINT CHR$(27); "@"¶
        END IF¶
      END IF¶
      ¶
      ¶
      GOTO start¶
      ¶
      voc.end:¶
      IF save = 1 THEN¶
          LOCATE 12, 20: PRINT "----------------------------
      -------------------"¶
          LOCATE 13, 20: COLOR 0, 7: PRINT " Vocabulary
      File has changed! Please save..."; : COLOR 7, 0¶
          LOCATE 14, 20: PRINT "----------------------------
      -------------------"¶
        x$ = INPUT$(1)¶
        GOTO start¶
      END IF¶
      ¶
      CLS¶
      SYSTEM¶
```

8.5.1 How the program works

After you have typed in the program *QBasic*, save it as
VOCAB.BAS. Then start the program with the [Shift]+[F5] key
combination.

The following display appears on the screen:

```
┌─────────────────────────────────────────────────────┐
│                                                       │
│               Vocabulary Training                     │
├───────────────────────────────────────────────────────┤
│                                                       │
│ Vocabulary File:            Vocabulary Count:     0│
├───────────────────────────────────────────────────────┤
│                                                       │
│          - 1 -    Load Vocabulary File               │
│                                                       │
│          - 2 -    Enter Vocabulary                   │
│                                                       │
│          - 3 -    Save Vocabulary                    │
│                                                       │
│          - 4 -    Vocabulary Drill                   │
│                                                       │
│          - 5 -    Print Vocabulary                   │
│                                                       │
│          - 6 -    End Vocabulary Program             │
├───────────────────────────────────────────────────────┤
│                                                       │
│               Please select ? _                      │
│                                                       │
└─────────────────────────────────────────────────────┘
```

The beginning screen of the Vocabulary training program

Select menu option number 2 (Enter Vocabulary) and press the
[Enter] key.

Type the English word you want to add to the file and press the
[Enter] key. Then add its foreign language equivalent and press the
[Enter] key.

You're prompted to continue adding more words or return to the
main menu. Press either [Y] or the [Enter] key to continue entering
words into the file, or press the [N] key and the [Enter] key to return
to the main menu.

The upper right corner of the screen indicates how many
vocabulary pairs have been entered.

We recommend using only lowercase or only uppercase letters
when typing the vocabulary words. This will prevent potential
problems in the Vocabulary Drill option. The program
differentiates between upper and lowercase spelling.

```
┌─────────────────────────────────────────────────────┐
│                                                       │
│  ┌─────────────────────────────────────────────────┐ │
│  │            Vocabulary Training                    │ │
│  └─────────────────────────────────────────────────┘ │
│  ┌─────────────────────────────────────────────────┐ │
│ Vocabulary File:                 Vocabulary Count:  0│ │
│  └─────────────────────────────────────────────────┘ │
│      English word   : _____           │
│      German word    : _____           │
│                                                       │
│                                                       │
│                                                       │
│                                                       │
│                                                       │
│                                                       │
└─────────────────────────────────────────────────────┘
```

Entering words in the Vocabulary File

Return to the main menu and select menu option 3 (Save Vocabulary). You can use a name of up to eight characters in length for the vocabulary file. The program automatically attaches the .VOC extension to the file to distinguish these files from other files.

Now you can use the vocabulary on a test basis. Select menu option 4 (Vocabulary Drill). Make certain to save the file before selecting the Vocabulary Drill option. Any error may destroy your input before it has been safely saved in the file.

You can switch the sequence of the drill from English to German or German to English by pressing the [Spacebar] key. Press the [Enter] key to start the drill.

The Vocabulary Drill displays how many words were not entered correctly. If you enter a word incorrectly, the program will inform you and display the correct translation.

If all words were entered correctly, the program plays a tune and calculates the results of the drill. It displays the number of words presented and how many were wrongly translated.

```
******************************************************************
***                                                            ***
***                      R e s u l t                           ***
***                                                            ***
******************************************************************

        Count of all  words        : 1
        Wrong answers               : 1

        Right on first try:         : 1
        Right on second try:        : 1
        Right on third try:         : 1
        Right on fourth try:        : 1
        Right on fifth try:         : 1
        Right after the fifth try: : 1

    Press any key to return to menu...
```

Vocabulary Drill evaluation

We have not yet discussed all of the capabilities of the vocabulary program (the printing of vocabulary lists and cheat sheets) but you might want to try these yourself, because the program provides adequate help.

Another Small Suggestion:

You can load these vocabulary files into an editor or word processor program and make changes. It's important that after editing with a word processor, the vocabulary file is saved without formatting (pure ASCII file).

An example vocabulary file:

The following example vocabulary file was created with the program and can be edited using the DOS 5.0 EDIT text editor program. This file is called SHORT.VOC on the companion diskette available for this book.

"apology","abbitte"
"blue","blau"
"cat","katze"
"dentist","zahnarzt"
"evening","abend"
"fat","dick"
"green","grün"
"heart","herz"
"hereupon","hierauf"
"i","ich"
"know","wissen"
"later","später"
"man","mann"
"night","nacht"
"pay","zahlen"
"red","rot"
"sausage","wurst"
"thin","dünn"
"uncover","abdecken"
"white","weiss"
"yellow","gelb"

9. Sound, Graphics and Color

In this chapter we'll discuss the different advanced sound and graphics statements of *QBasic* that allow you to add color and music to your BASIC programs.

A few of these *QBasic* statements may require a knowledge of mathematics and PC hardware. However, a detailed discussion of these subjects is beyond the scope of this book. We can only provide the correct syntax and the effect of the specific statement.

Therefore, do not give up because you cannot understand a statement or function. Also, don't be afraid to experiment. You'll learn much by simply practicing and experimenting.

9.1 Producing Sound

Most PC compatible computers have some form of sound output. For example, some PC compatibles have advanced 3 voice sound chips. *QBasic* offers different statements and functions that are compatible with most of these computers.

Sound can play an important role in many BASIC programs. One of the most obvious reasons to use sound in a program is to warn the user that he or she pressed an incorrect key.

9.1.1 The BEEP statement

This can be handled simply by using the BEEP statement. This statement sends an 800 Hz (cycles per second) signal to the speaker for approximately one quarter of a second.

Type the following program line:

```
BEEP
```

Press the ⌈Shift⌋ + ⌈F5⌋ key combination to hear a quick tone. You may also perform this same function with the following command:

```
PRINT CHR$(7)
```

The ASCII value of seven is called the BEL function. When *QBasic* interprets this function, the "BEEP" tone is sounded.

9.1.2 The SOUND statement

You'll probably find many uses for the simple tone created by the BEEP statement. However, many programs require more sophisticated sounds to play a series of notes or even full songs.

QBasic provides two statements for this type of sound generation. The SOUND statement is the simpler of these to use and requires less programming knowledge.

The SOUND statement has two parameters that you can specify:

```
SOUND frequency, duration
```

The frequency value determines the actual note to be played. The legal range for frequency is from 37 Hz to 32,767 Hz.

The duration value controls how long the note will be played. This value is specified in clock ticks which occur 18.2 times per second. The legal range for duration is .027 to 65,535 in *QBasic*.

The following is an example of using the SOUND statement:

```
FOR I=100 TO 3500 STEP 100:SOUND I,1:NEXT I
```

Press the ⌈Shift⌋ + ⌈F5⌋ key combination to hear the frequency rise quickly from 100 Hz to 3500 Hz in intervals of 100 Hz. Each note will be played for a duration of approximately .054 seconds. You may reverse the effect by using:

```
FOR I=3500 TO 100 STEP -100:SOUND I,1:NEXT I
```

Here is a chart of frequencies for use with the SOUND statement:

NOTE	FREQ	NOTE	FREQ	NOTE	FREQ	NOTE	FREQ
D#$_1$	38.89	B$_2$	123.47	G$_4$	392.00	D#$_6$	1244.51
E$_1$	41.20	C$_3$	130.81	G#$_4$	415.30	E$_6$	1328.51
F$_1$	43.65	C#$_3$	138.59	A$_4$	440.00	F$_6$	1396.91
F#$_1$	46.25	D$_3$	146.83	A#$_4$	466.16	F#$_6$	1479.98
G$_1$	49.00	D#$_3$	155.56	B$_4$	493.88	G$_6$	1567.98
G#$_1$	51.91	E$_3$	164.81	C$_5$	523.25	G#$_6$	1661.22
A$_1$	55.00	F$_3$	174.61	C#$_5$	554.37	A$_6$	1760.00
A#$_1$	58.27	F#$_3$	185.00	D$_5$	587.33	A#$_6$	1864.66
B$_1$	61.74	G$_3$	196.00	D#$_5$	622.25	B$_6$	1975.53
C$_2$	65.41	G#$_3$	207.65	E$_5$	659.26	C$_7$	2093.00
C#$_2$	69.30	A$_3$	220.00	F$_5$	698.46	C#$_7$	2217.46
D$_2$	73.42	A#$_3$	233.08	F#$_5$	739.99	D$_7$	2349.32
D#$_2$	77.78	B$_3$	246.94	G$_5$	783.99	D#$_7$	2489.02
E$_2$	82.41	C$_4$	261.63	G#$_5$	830.61	E$_7$	2637.02
F$_2$	87.31	C#$_4$	277.18	A$_5$	880.00	F$_7$	2793.83
F#$_2$	92.50	D$_4$	293.66	A#$_5$	932.33	F#$_7$	2959.96
G$_2$	98.00	D#$_4$	311.13	B$_5$	987.77	G$_7$	3135.96
G#$_2$	103.83	E$_4$	329.63	C$_6$	1046.50	G#$_7$	3322.44
A$_2$	110.00	F$_4$	349.23	C#$_6$	1108.73	A$_7$	3520.00
A#$_2$	116.54	F#$_4$	369.99	D$_6$	1174.66	A#$_7$	3729.0Q

The following program lets you enter a specific frequency from the keyboard (remember to press the (Enter) key when you see the ¶ character):

```
REM SOUNDDEM.BAS¶
CLS¶
Music:¶
  INPUT "What frequency (37 to 32767) would you like
to hear (99999 to quit)"; FREQUENCY¶
IF FREQUENCY = 99999 then CLS : END¶
SOUND FREQUENCY, 10¶
GOTO Music¶
```

9.1.3 The PLAY statement

The SOUND statement will fill many of your sound effects needs. However, when it comes to actually playing a tune, the PLAY statement is more versatile.

PLAY will allow you to indicate notes and durations in a way that makes converting music to data much easier. It will also allow you to define large amounts of musical information in each line, making your program much more efficient.

The syntax for PLAY is:

```
PLAY "(string)"
```

The (string) used by the PLAY statement may contain any of the parameters listed below. Parameters need not be separated, though you may separate them by semicolons. Extra spaces in the string are ignored.

Here are the available PLAY parameters:

Octave

< n   When you want to increase the octave by 1, precede a note with a greater-than (>) symbol. The highest octave number for an octave is 6.

> n   When you want to decrease the octave by 1, precede a note with a less-than (<) symbol. The lowest limit for an octave is 0.

O n   The O parameter is used to specify the octave. There are 7 octaves in all, numbered from 0 to 6. Middle C (C just below A-440) starts off octave 3. Each octave number starts with C and continues through B. Octave 4 is the default when no octave has been specified.

Tone

A through G
This indicates the value of the note to be played.

Sharps may be indicated by following the note with the number symbol (#) or plus sign (+).

-     Flats are indicated with the minus sign (-). It is important to note that sharps and flats are only legal if they are not equal to some other note value. For example, C flat is not legal since it is equal to B.

.   A period or dot may be used after a note or note value to indicate a dotted note. Dotted notes play for one and a half times the current length. A dotted sixteenth note plays for one sixteenth plus one thirty-second.

N n   This is an alternative means of indicating the note to be played. There are 84 notes in the 7 octaves covered by the PLAY statement. Using the N parameter will allow you to specify the particular note to be played without specifying the octave separately. The legal range is from 0 to 84 with 0 being equal to a rest.

Duration

L n   This parameter is used to indicate the length of the note or notes to follow. The legal range for this parameter is from 1 to 64 and produces a note length of 1/n. Therefore, a length of 1 is equal to a whole note and a length of 64 is equal to a sixty-fourth note.

ML   Each note sounds for the full length of the note length (legato).

MN   Each note sounds seven eighths of the note length (normal).

MS   Each note sounds for three quarters of the note length (staccato).

If none of these are specified in the PLAY statement, the default is MN or Music Normal. The other two parameters useable with M are for setting the mode of the PLAY and SOUND statements. These are:

Tempo

T n   This is used to set the overall tempo (speed) of the notes to be played. The range begins at 32 and extends to 255, with a default value of 120. This value is equal to the number of beats per minute.

P n   The P parameter indicates a pause or rest. The values used with P are the same that are used with the L (length) parameter and will cause the PLAY statement to wait the specified period of time before playing the next note.

Operation

M F   (Music Foreground) All PLAY and SOUND statements are processed by BASIC, which waits for completion of the last note before processing the next note.

M B   (Music Background) Notes from the PLAY and SOUND statements are placed into a buffer and processed by the computers interrupts. This allows program execution to continue while notes are being played.

If no mode is specified in the PLAY statement, MF or Music Foreground is the default. The MB command is best avoided until you become somewhat more proficient at programming. The M commands may not be followed with a semicolon (;) in PLAY strings.

9.1.4 Programs using SOUND and PLAY

The following program will play a small tone sequence:

```
REM PLAYDEM1¶
CLS¶
PRINT "Relax for a moment..."¶
PLAY "o3t190p2L8ABCDDEEEEDEEEEDCCCCBBDDDDAGGGDGGDE¶
```

You can experiment by adding or changing the tones in the PLAY line.

The following program not only uses the PLAY and SOUND statements, but also shows you how to store a song in strings:

```
REM PLAYDEM2¶
REM BUGS PLAYS PIANO¶
PLAY ON¶
A$ = "T200O3L8F#EL4D.L8EDP8L4DF#AGB>D#D#P1"¶
B$ = "T200O3L8F#EL4D.L8EDP8L4DF#AGB>C#C#P2L4D#D#P1"¶
C$ = "T200O3L8F#EL4D.L8EDP8L4DF#AGB>DD"¶
PLAY A$¶
PLAY B$¶
PLAY C$¶
SOUND 37,10¶
END¶
```

9.2 Advanced Graphics

All the programs that we have presented so far have used ASCII characters. These programs can be considered *text mode graphics*. You can run these programs independent of the graphics capabilities of your PC.

However, if you have a graphics adapter installed in your PC, *QBasic* has statements which let you create high resolution programs.

Since lines and circles consist of many points and can only be created slowly from individual points, *QBasic* offers special statements for this task.

You must consider two items when using the graphics capabilities of *QBasic*:

1.   Depending on the available graphics card, the statements for switching on graphics and the maximum number of points that can be displayed (the resolution), differ significantly.

2.   If your PC has a Hercules graphics card, you must start the MSHERC.COM program before starting *QBasic*. Otherwise using these statements and displaying the graphics is not possible.

9.2.1   Important graphic statements

QBasic has so many graphic statements that it would take an entire book to discuss each one. This section will instead explain the principles on which the graphic statements operate, providing some common example programs.

You'll need to practice and experiment with the *QBasic* graphic statements. In this way, you will discover new and more efficient routines for performing graphics.

As we mentioned earlier, if you do not have a CGA (Color Graphics adapter) or EGA (Extended Graphics Adapter) compatible video board installed in your computer, you will not be able to access most screen modes. This is true of the modes used in this section. If you only have a MDA (Monochrome Display Adapter), then you can skip this section.

9.2.2 The SCREEN statement

QBasic helps you handle different displays with *screen modes*. The screen mode controls the video memory, screen clarity and number of available colors.

A SCREEN statement is used to instruct *QBasic* which display or screen mode to use.

This following statement:

```
SCREEN 0,0
```

places the display into text mode and turns off color on color monitors.

The first argument controls the *screen resolution*. Your monitor screen is made up of small dots. These dots are called *pixels* and are displayed in rows and columns on the screen.

Screen resolution is most often referred to in terms of the number of pixels wide by the number of pixels high. Since screen mode 0 is a text only mode, the resolution is measured in characters instead of dots. The resolution of screen mode 0 can be either 80x25 or 40x25, depending on the screen width.

The second argument in the SCREEN statement controls the color signal on a PC compatible that has a CGA (Color Graphics Adapter) installed. This parameter is ignored if there is only a monochrome display adapter (MDA) installed.

There are other parameters available with the SCREEN statement, but the two covered here are the only ones required for most programs.

The following table refers to the CGA screen modes:

Mode	Rows/Col	Colors	Resolution
0	40x25	16	320x200
	80x25	16	640x320
1	40x25	4	320x200
2	80x25	2	640x200

Modes 1 and 2 are probably most important to users with a CGA system. As you can see from the table, the resolution for these modes are 320x200 and 640x200.

The advantages of mode 1 over mode 2 is that mode 1 allows for the use of 4 colors. Although mode 2 offers a much higher resolution, only 2 colors may be used.

9.2.3 The PSET statement

One of the most important commands available for creating graphics in *QBasic* is the PSET statement.

PSET is used to set a starting point on the screen to use with other commands. Here is the syntax for PSET:

```
PSET [STEP] (X, Y) [, drawing color]
```

The STEP part of this statement is optional. If used, the X and Y values will be used as offsets from the current position. This means that if the last pixel accessed by your program was at 200,100 and the program then issued this statement:

```
PSET STEP (20,20)
```

the new pixel position would be located at 220,120.

Using the PSET statement without STEP included would locate the new pixel position at 20,20.

9.2.4 The DRAW statement

DRAW is by far the most extensive graphic statement available in *QBasic*.

The following is the syntax for the DRAW statement:

```
DRAW "string"
```

The "string" expression can be a constant, variable or the result of a string expression. The current position that DRAW starts is either the center of the screen or the last position used by a graphics statement. Any other positions must be set before using DRAW; with a command such as PSET.

The following parameters can be part of the string:

U num	Draws num points up.
D num	Draws num points down.
L num	Draws num points to the left.
R num	Draws num points to the right.
E num	Draws num points diagonally to the upper right.
H num	Draws num points diagonally to the upper left.
F num	Draws num points diagonally to the lower right.
G num	Draws num points diagonally to the lower left.

If the number is not a constant, the numerical value must first be converted to a string. Otherwise, DRAW must be told that a variable is being used with the equal sign (=) in front of the variable and a semicolon after it, as in the PLAY statement.

Cursor movement commands

B *dir* Moves the "pen" one pixel in the given direction without drawing any points. The dir contains the characters U, D, L, R, E, F, G or H.

N *dir* Moves the "pen" one pixel in the given direction, setting that point. The dir contains the characters U, D, L, R, E, F, G or H.

Color, angle and scaling commands

M *X,Y*

If X,Y is specified without a preceding plus or minus sign, then a line is drawn from the current point to the point specified by X,Y (absolute coordinates). If X,Y is preceded by + or -, then X,Y is viewed as the relative coordinates.

V

Draws all subsequent DRAW commands using logical coordinates instead of physical coordinates.

C *color*

Sets the drawing color, based on the available palettes 0 to 3.

P *F,B*

Fills a region enclosed by border color B with a fill color F. The current position must be inside the enclosed area. P does not have default values, so both parameters must be specified. Both values can range from 0 to 3.

A *angle*

Sets the angle of rotation. Possible values: 0 = 0 degrees, 1 = 90 degrees, 2 = 180 degrees, 3 = 270 degrees. This specification takes precedence over the direction of movement. For example, if you specify the command A3, then L goes right instead of left.

TA *angle*

Specifies the angle of the rotation. The difference between TA and A is that you can specify values ranging from -360 to +360 for TA. Enter a positive angle if you want a counter-clockwise rotation or a negative angle for a clockwise rotation.

S *factor*

Determines the scale factor. The scale factor multiplied by the distances in U, D, L, R or relative M provide the true distance travelled. This allows objects to be drawn to scale with one another. Legal values for *factor* range are between 1 and 255.

Substring command

X *string*

Allows often-repeated procedures to be executed from a string. The instructions contained in *string* are inserted at the current position and executed. Remember to include the semicolon following the variable name.

The following is a short example program which uses the PSET and DRAW statements:

```
REM DRAW1.BAS¶
CLS¶
SCREEN 2¶
PSET (160,100),1¶
DRAW "U25R25D25L25E25L25F25BHBLP1,1"¶
```

Press the [Shift] + [F5] key combination. This program draws a small box, divides it into four parts diagonally and fills the bottom quarter.

If you wish to see the same routine in color, make the following changes:

```
CLS¶
SCREEN 1¶
COLOR 7,1¶
PSET (160,100),1¶
DRAW "U25R25D25L25E25L25F25BHBLP2,1"¶
```

9.2.5 The COLOR statement

The COLOR statement lets you select foreground and background display colors. Note that the COLOR statement by itself does not determine the range of colors. The range of colors also depends on the graphics adapter, mode and other statements.

Screen mode 0

The following is the syntax for the COLOR statement in screen mode 0:

```
COLOR [foreground], [background], [border]
```

[foreground]
> Sets the color in which the letters and characters are displayed on the screen. Enter an integer value between 0 and 31.

[background]
> Sets the color of the background on which the text is displayed. Enter an integer value from 0 to 7.

[border]
> This represents the color of the screen border. Enter an integer value from 0 to 7. The following adapters do not support this argument: ICB VGA and MCGA (Multicolor Graphics Array).

Screen mode 1

The following is the syntax for the COLOR statement in screen mode 1:

```
COLOR [background], [palette]
```

[background]
> Sets the color of the background on which the text is displayed. Enter an integer value from 0 to 15 according to the following table:

0	Black	6	Brown	12	Light Red
1	Blue	7	White	13	Light Magenta
2	Green	8	Gray	14	Yellow
3	Cyan	9	Light Blue	15	High Intensity White
4	Red	10	Light Green		
5	Magenta	11	Light Cyan		

[palette]

This argument refers to a group of four colors called *palettes*. In screen mode 1 you can select from two palettes:

Foreground color number	Palette 0 color	Palette 1 color
0	Current background color	Current background color
1	Green	Cyan
2	Red	Magenta
3	Brown	White (or light grey)

9.2.6 COLOR statement with CGA adapter

If you have a CGA, you can only select from two graphics modes: SCREEN 2 or SCREEN 1.

Screen mode 1

```
COLOR [background] [,palette] [,graf_back]
[,graf_fore] [,text_color]
```

This mode sets colors for medium-resolution graphics mode (320x200 pixels). You can select four foreground colors and 16 background colors.

`background`
> Sets the border and background color of the entire screen. Values can range from 0 to 15.

`palette`
> Specifies which of the two palettes are used for drawing colors in graphic commands:

Palette 0	Color 0 = background color
Palette 0	Color 1 = green
Palette 1	Color 0 = background color

`graf_back,graf_fore`
> Specifies the standard values for the drawing colors used in graphic commands, dependent upon the palette previously selected.

`text_color`
> Specifies the text color based on the palette used. Please note that 0 cannot be used for text_color.

The palette is usually specified by 0 or 1. Each of these two palettes contain 3 colors. A palette is actually made up of 4 colors, however, one of the colors is always the background color specified above. Here are the palette colors:

Foreground color number	Palette 0 color	Palette 1 color
0	Current background color	Current background color
1	Green	Cyan
2	Red	Magenta
3	Brown	White (or light grey)

Screen mode 2

This mode sets the colors for high-resolution graphics mode (640x200 pixels). This mode has only one foreground and one background color (also called *monochrome* or one color).

You can use the COLOR statement with the following syntax:

```
COLOR[foreground][,background][,text_color]
```

foreground

Specifies both graphic and text colors. Values range from 0 to 15.

background

Defaults to black in this mode. Graphic statements that give a drawing color as a parameter refer to the foreground and background values set with COLOR. Because high-resolution mode is monochrome and not color, some conversion is necessary. The palette color values are taken and adjusted for the monochrome screen, according to the following table:

Value:	Color:	Value:	Color:
0	Black	2	Black
1	White	3	White

If you have a VGA or EGA installed in your PC, you can use the PALETTE statement (see the following).

9.2.7 The PALETTE statement

The PALETTE statement provides more flexibility in assigning different display colors. The VGA card can display a total of 16 colors. By using the PALETTE statement, you can assign any color from the available palette to any attribute.

It's important to note that the PALETTE statement and the PALETTE USING statement only work with PCs that have an EGA, VGA or MCGA adapter installed. Therefore, the information and programs in this subsection do not work with other adapters (such as the CGA).

As we previously mentioned, the COLOR statement can be used to indicate values between 0 and 15 for the foreground and background colors.

The PALETTE statement has the following syntax:

```
PALETTE [<OldColor>],<NewColor>
```

The following are the descriptions for the arguments:

[<OldColor>]
　　　　Represents the palette attribute you want to change.

<NewColor>
　　　　Represents the display color number to be assigned to the attribute.

9.2.8 The PALETTE USING statement

Although you can assign a new color by using the PALETTE statement, you'll need to include 16 PALETTE statements to assign all 16 colors. This will increase the size of your program and the chances of programming errors.

Therefore, *QBasic* has a statement you can use when assigning colors. This is the PALETTE USING statement. All 16 colors can be assigned by using this statement.

The following program draws 16 boxes in the standard palette and assigns new variables sequentially from the PALAR% array.

```
REM PALUSING.BAS¶
CLS¶
DIM PALAR%(63)¶
SCREEN 9 ' resolution 640*350, 16 colors from 64¶
FOR I = 0 TO 63: PALAR%(I) = I: NEXT I¶
FOR I = 0 TO 15¶
```

```
LINE (I * 15, I * 15)-(I * 30, I * 20), I, BF¶
NEXT I¶
FOR PAL = 0 TO 48¶
PALETTE USING PALAR%(PAL)¶
LOCATE 24, 1¶
PRINT "Press any key to continue or <Esc> to quit";¶
Aloop:¶
   X$ = INKEY$: IF X$ = "" THEN GOTO Aloop¶
   IF X$ = CHR$(27) THEN GOTO Finish:¶
NEXT PAL¶
Finish:¶
   PALETTE ' SET OLD VALUE AGAIN¶
   SCREEN 0 ' BACK TO TEXT MODE¶
```

9.2.9 The `CIRCLE` statement

The CIRCLE statement can be used to draw circles and ellipses (ovals) on the screen. The syntax for this statement is:

```
CIRCLE (X,Y),radius,color,start,end,aspect
```

`(X,Y)`
> The values for *X* and *Y* determine the center of the circle or ellipse to be drawn.

`radius`
> The value for *radius* is specified in pixels.

`color`
> The values allowable for *color* vary with the screen mode. Mode 1 will allow values from 0 to 3, but only 0 and 1 are legal in mode 2.

`start,end`
> The *start* and *end* values determine the beginning and ending points of the circle, allowing this command to be used to draw arcs as well. The values allowable for this parameter must be in the range of -6.28 to +6.28.

`aspect`
> The aspect value can be used to adjust the roundness of the circle. Values less than 1 elongate the circle horizontally. Values greater than 1 elongate the circle vertically.

9.2.10 The PAINT statement

The PAINT statement allows you to fill areas with color and/or patterns. Creating patterns for use with the PAINT statement requires a good working knowledge of binary codes and is beyond the scope of a beginners book. Filling with solid colors, however, is easy to accomplish using the following syntax:

```
PAINT (X,Y),paint color,boundary color
```

(X,Y)
> X and Y must fall within the boundary of the object to be filled.

paint color
> The paint color must be a legal value from the current palette.

boundary color
> The boundary color should be a number which identifies the color of the boundary lines of the object to be painted or filled.

It's often possible to skip specification of the boundary color. This is demonstrated in the following example of using the PAINT and CIRCLE statements:

```
REM PAINT.BAS¶
CLS¶
SCREEN 2¶
CIRCLE (320,100),10¶
CIRCLE (320,100),20¶
CIRCLE (320,100),30¶
CIRCLE (320,100),40¶
CIRCLE (320,100),50¶
PAINT (320,100),1¶
PAINT (320,110),1¶
PAINT (320,120),1¶
```

9.2.11 The LINE statement

The LINE statement can be used to form lines and boxes. It also gives you the option of filling the box. The syntax looks as follows:

```
LINE (X1,Y1)-(X2,Y2),color,BF,style
```

(X1,Y1)

> X1,Y1 signify the starting point, or upper left corner, of the line for the box.

(X2,Y2)

> X2,Y2 gives the ending point, or lower right corner, of the line for the box.

color

> The value for *color* can be any legal value from your color palette.

BF or B

> B is used to inform the program that you wish to form a box. Use BF if you wish to form a box filled with the color specified with *color*.

The value for style is a 16 bit integer used to determine the line pattern to be used. If a filled box is requested in the line, style must be left off or it will cause a syntax error.

This program will draw a large box on the screen filled with the drawing color:

```
REM LINE.BAS¶
CLS¶
SCREEN 2¶
LINE (10,10)-(630,190),1,BF¶
END¶
```

9.3 Creating a Heaven Full of Stars

The following example program functions with EGA and VGA graphic cards with a resolution of 640 * 350 pixels. It draws a colorful "heaven full of stars".

```
REM CH9STARS¶
DEFINT A-Z¶
RANDOMIZE TIMER¶
Mode = 9¶
Height = 350¶
ZWidth = 640¶
SCREEN mode¶
WHILE INKEY$ = ""¶
    ZColor = RND * 15¶
    y = Height * RND¶
    x = ZWidth * RND¶
    PSET (x, y), ZColor¶
WEND¶
SCREEN 0¶
```

The settings for the graphic resolution are determined at the top of the program. They can be easily changed for other graphics resolutions. If you have a Hercules screen and want to try this program, you must change the following three lines:

```
Mode = 3¶
Height = 348¶
ZWidth = 720¶
```

The MSHERC.COM program must have been started before the start of *QBasic*.

The points are placed at random coordinates with a random color (PSET (x, y), Color). The X and Y coordinates are provided in parentheses behind the PSET statement and, if desired, a color. We will discuss the use of random numbers in more detail later.

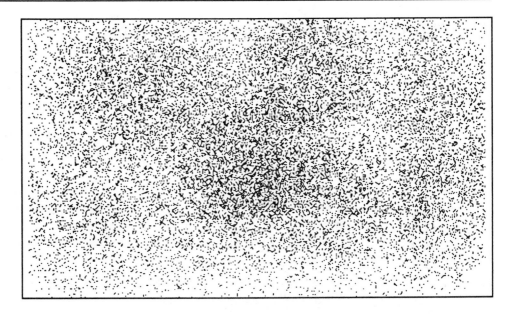

Stars on display

You can end the program at any time by pressing a key. The screen never becomes completely colored because the background color is also used for drawing the dots and this always creates dots in this color and therefore, they seem to disappear.

9.4 High Resolution Random Numbers

There normally should not be anything "random" in a program you create because exact and definitive results are usually required.

However, in certain situations it can be important to let *QBasic* perform something at random to prevent the program execution from always being the same.

A lottery drawing program is an example. Random numbers are important in this type of program because you would really be disappointed if the program always suggested the same numbers.

The following program proposes seven numbers for the lottery drawing:

```
REM LOTTERY.BAS
REM: Random numbers for the lottery
RANDOMIZE TIMER
DIM Lotto(49)
FOR I = 1 TO 49
    Lotto(I) = 0
NEXT I

CLS
FOR I = 1 TO 7
    Ball = INT(RND * 49 + 1)
    WHILE Lotto(Ball) <> 0
        Ball = INT(RND * 49 + 1)
    WEND
    Lotto(Ball) = 1
    PRINT "Ball "; I; " : "; Ball
NEXT I
```

To understand the program, we must first examine the random number generator built into *QBasic*. It uses an initial value (this value must be indicated with the `RANDOMIZE` statement) to determine a random number after every call and to use it for the initial value of the next calculation. The random number generator provides numbers between 0 and 1.

If the same initial value is used every time, the same random number is returned every time. Therefore, the initial value in the first line of the program is determined by the system clock in your PC.

The TIMER function contains the current time and is always updated by *QBasic*. The time is recorded as seconds with two places after the decimal point for hundredth of a second.

The only occasion where the random "random numbers" would be identical is if you were to start the program on two different days at the same hundredth of a second.

In most cases no random numbers between 0 and 1 are required, some calculations are required to obtain numbers in the desired range. In our case we want to obtain random numbers between 1 and 49. Therefore, we multiply the random number (generated by RND) times 49 and add a one to prevent a zero result.

A random number generator must produce random numbers. Under no circumstances can it favor or ignore certain numbers. How can this be tested?

The following example program for a Hercules graphics card calculates random numbers between 1 and 720 (exactly the count of the possible dots on the screen on the horizontal line) and draws a small bar for the frequency of occurrence.

You'll see if certain number ranges were "favored" or "neglected" by watching the screen.

9.4.1 Computer grass

We call this program "Computer grass", and you'll see why when you run it.

```
REM COMPGRAS.BAS¶
REM Random numbers let the "Computer Grass" grow ¶
RANDOMIZE TIMER¶
Mode = 3¶
Height = 338¶
ZWidth = 720¶
```

```
DIM H(Width)¶
CLS¶
Amount = 0¶
SCREEN Mode¶
Continue = 1¶

WHILE Continue = 1¶
    Amount = Amount + 1¶
    IF INKEY$ <> "" THEN Continue = 0¶
    Z = INT(RND * Width) + 1¶
    x = z¶
    y1 = Height¶
    LOCATE 1, 1¶
    PRINT Amount¶
    H(Z) = H(Z) + 1¶
    IF H(Z) > Height - 1 THEN Continue = 0¶
    y2 = Height - H(Z)¶
    LINE (x, y1)-(x, y2), 2¶
    WEND¶
WHILE INKEY$ = "" : WEND¶
SCREEN 0¶
```

This program was designed for a Hercules graphics card. For EGA or VGA graphics cards with a resolution of 640 x 350, change the following lines of the program:

```
Mode = 9¶
Height = 350¶
ZWidth = 640¶
```

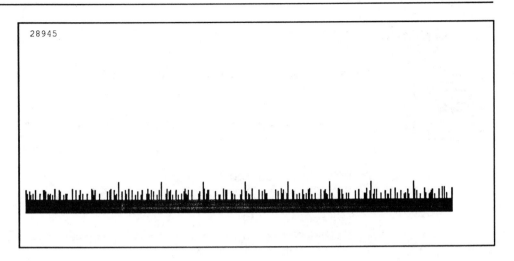

28945

Computer grass grows randomly

9.5 QBasic Displays the Time

Since *QBasic* can use the accurate system clock, we can use *QBasic* as a stopwatch to measure elapsed time.

The following small program demonstrates the use of the TIMER variable:

```
REM STOPWTCH.BAS¶
REM Stopwatch¶
CLS¶
LOCATE 10, 10¶
PRINT "Press any key to start Stopwatch..."¶
WHILE INKEY$ = "": WEND¶

Start = TIMER¶
LOCATE 10, 10¶
PRINT SPACE$(35)¶
WHILE INKEY$ = ""¶
   Stand = TIMER - Start¶
   LOCATE 1, 1¶
   PRINT "Elapsed time: "; USING "#######.##"; Stand¶
WEND¶
```

Press any key to start the clock. The clock then displays the elapsed seconds and hundredth seconds. Press any key to stop the clock and view the elapsed time.

The USING statement in the second to the last line is used to format the output of the time. The "#" character represents any numbers and the period determines the position of the decimal point.

9.6 Advanced Math Operations

The math operations we discussed earlier only dealt with the basic math functions. However, *QBasic* is capable of performing the trigonometric functions: sine, cosine, tangent and cotangent (including the root and exponential functions).

It's very simple to represent a trigonometric function using ASCII characters. The following example displays a sine wave on the output screen:

```
REM SINE.BAS
REM Display a sine wave
CLS
FOR I = 1 TO 80
Y = I * 3.14 * 2 / 80
Y = INT(SIN(Y) * 12) + 13
LOCATE Y, I
PRINT CHR$(249);
NEXT I
WHILE INKEY$ = "": WEND
```

The most difficult problem in the program is the "scaling", which is the conversion to screen coordinates.

Since the sine repeats after 2*π, we distribute this numeric range exactly to the 80 columns of the screen. However, this makes the result appear square and inaccurate.

Therefore, we want to display the same sine with the graphics capabilities of *QBasic*. Here is an example for the sine on a Hercules graphics card:

```
REM Mode = 3
Height = 348
ZWidth = 720

SCREEN Mode
CLS
FOR I = 1 TO ZWidth
Y = I * 3.14 * 2 / ZWidth
Y = INT(SIN(Y) * Height / 2 + Height / 2)
PSET (I, Y), 15
```

```
NEXT I¶
WHILE INKEY$ = "": WEND¶
```

For EGA/VGA, with a resolution of 640 x 350, we can change the following lines:

```
Mode = 9¶
Height = 350¶
ZWidth = 640¶
```

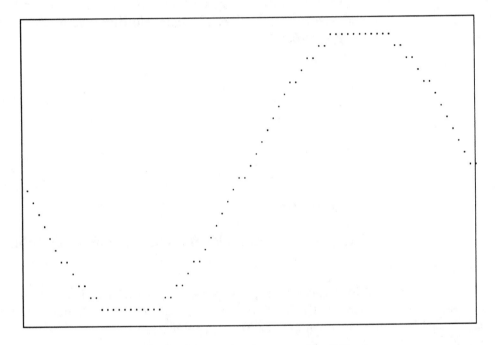

Displaying a sine wave with QBasic

In the previous section, we created a stopwatch program using TIMER. If you do not like the digital display, try using an analog display instead.

We'll need to use a few math operations in this program. It displays a clock (including a second hand) which moves according to the elapsed time.

To avoid making the program longer and more complicated, we omitted displaying the minutes and seconds. Instead, we're including the digital time display at the top, left corner of the screen:

Remember to press the ⌊Enter⌋ key when you see the ¶ character in this program listing.

```
REM Analog-clock: Second pointer¶
Mode = 9¶
Height = 350¶
ZWidth = 640¶
DispFactor=1.4¶
X1 = ZWidth / 2¶
Y1 = Height / 2¶
Length = 100¶
PI = 3.14159¶
PI2 = PI * 2¶
Scale = 60 / PI2¶
¶
SCREEN Mode¶
CIRCLE (X1, Y1), Length¶
¶
WHILE INKEY$ = ""¶
    LOCATE 1, 1¶
    Time = INT(TIMER)¶
    Hours = INT(Time / 3600)¶
    Minutes = INT((Time - Hours * 3600) / 60)¶
    Seconds = INT(Time - (Hours * 3600) - (Minutes *
60))¶
    PRINT Hours; ":"; Minutes; ":"; Seconds¶
¶
    SekX2 = (SIN(Seconds / Scale) * Length) + X1¶
    SekY2 = Y1 - (COS(Seconds / Scale) * Length /
DispFactor)¶
    LINE (X1, Y1)-(SekX2, SekY2), Length¶
    WHILE TIMER - Time < 1: WEND¶
    LINE (X1, Y1)-(SekX2, SekY2), 0¶
WEND¶
SCREEN 0¶
```

Each position of a point on the circle can be calculated with sine and cosine. Several calculations are required to make the pointer turn and at the same time make it correspond exactly to the current second.

The display factor (here 1.4) is required because the screen points are not exactly round, but are slightly distorted in height, which requires a correction. If no compensation was provided, the pointer would extend beyond the clock, in the top and bottom position.

You can test this for yourself by deleting this line:

```
DispFactor=1.4
```

and changing this line:

```
    SekY2 = Y1 - (COS(Seconds / Scale) * Length /
DispFactor)
```

to:

```
    SekY2 = Y1 - (COS(Seconds / Scale) * Length)
```

Then start the program. You'll see the second hand now "sweeps" beyond the circle.

For Hercules graphics cards change the following lines of the program:

```
Mode = 3¶
Height = 348¶
ZWidth = 720¶
DispFactor=1.6¶
```

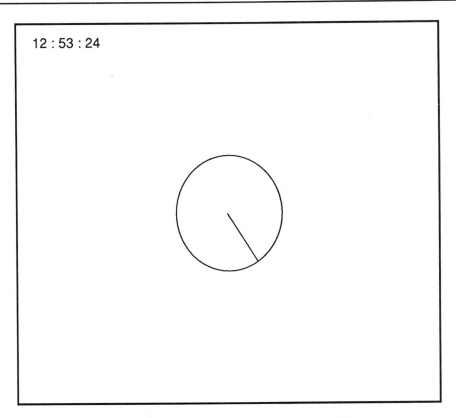

12 : 53 : 24

Using QBasic to display a second hand

As we mentioned at the beginning of this chapter, *QBasic* has so many graphic statements and functions that we cannot discuss each one in detail.

This section will help you better understand some of the more advanced statements and functions in *QBasic*. Most importantly, you should never be afraid to experiment and try new things.

Remember, as long as you keep backups of important programs and data, there is nothing for you to damage.

10. Debugging Features of QBasic

The **Debug** menu contains the *QBasic* commands you'll use in *debugging* (finding errors) your BASIC programs.

To open the commands of the **Debug** menu, press the [Alt] + [D] key combination:

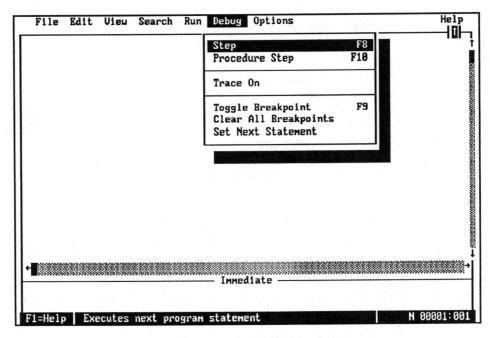

The QBasic Debug menu

10.1 Tracing Your Program's Execution

The term *tracing* refers to the ability of *QBasic* to follow the steps of your program's execution to find programming errors. We'll discuss the different tracing possibilities of *QBasic* in this section.

10.1.1 Single step tracing

The single step tracing commands will execute and check your program one line at a time.

QBasic Step command

Select this command if you want *QBasic* to execute the current statement (line where the cursor is located) of your program.

The **Step** command lets you move through a program one statement at a time while checking for program logic errors.

If the statement is supposed to print data to the output screen, the output window will appear only briefly before *QBasic* returns to the View window. If necessary, press the (F4) key to switch to the output screen.

Note the shortcut key for the **Step** command is the (F8) key.

Procedure Step command

This command is similar to the **Step** command because it single steps through a program. However, the **Procedure Step** command executes procedure calls as a single statement.

Note the shortcut key for the **Procedure Step** command is the (F10) key.

10.1.2 Animated tracing

QBasic can check your entire program, line-by-line, and highlight (or animate) the line that it is currently checking.

Trace On command

This command highlights each statement in a program as it is executed. This command lets you view the flow of a program.

Notice that the **Trace On** command has a marker next to it in the Debug menu to show that it has been selected:

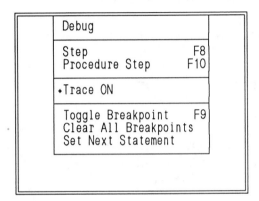

The **Trace On** command executes the program in "slow-motion animation" so you are able to follow the progress of the debugging feature.

10.1.3   Breakpoints

A *breakpoint* is a point that you can specify in your program where the execution is to stop. This lets you test only certain parts of the program.

Toggle Breakpoint command

Use the **Toggle Breakpoint** command to turn breakpoints on and off. To turn on a breakpoint, move the cursor to highlight the line where you want the breakpoint, then press F9 or choose this command.

The program line will appear in red or reverse video. Your program will run until it reaches this line, then it will stop, permitting printing variables in the Immediate window or single stepping from this point forward.

Disable breakpoints

To disable a specific breakpoint line, move the cursor to the desired line and press the F9 or select the **Toggle Breakpoint** command.

If you want to disable or clear all breakpoints, then select the **Clear All Breakpoints** command. Make certain you want to clear all breakpoints before selecting this command. A dialog box asking for confirmation will not appear on the screen.

10.1.4 Controlling program execution

Set Next Statement

Select this command when you want to change the program execution sequence so that the next line executed is where the cursor is currently located.

Since the **Set Next Statement** command has a similar effect as the GOTO statement, you should follow the same rules as those for the GOTO statement.

Continue execution

If you want to continue a program that has been suspended, press the F5 key. This is the shortcut key for the **Continue** command in the **Run** menu.

You can use this command in combination with the **Toggle On** command.

One of the most common uses of **Continue** is to restart a program following a breakpoint. For example, you can check the syntax of a suspended program, make any necessary corrections and then press F5 to continue executing the program to the next breakpoint or end of the program.

After pressing the F5 key, the program continues executing from the line immediately following the breakpoint.

Executing to the cursor

Press the ⬚F7⬚ key to execute the program to the current location of the cursor.

The program line where the cursor is located must be in the "flow" of the program. Otherwise, pressing the ⬚F7⬚ key has the same affect as pressing the ⬚F5⬚ key.

Resetting variables to zero

Since **Continue** cannot clear variables, you'll need to use another command to reset variables to zero. Select the **Restart** command in the **Run** menu.

This command clears all variables in preparation for single-stepping through a program while debugging. The first executable statement in the program is highlighted.

One of the most common uses of **Restart** is to restart a program from the beginning and check program lines that occur before a breakpoint.

Appendix A: QBasic Math Functions

Addition

Addition is indicated with the plus sign (+):

```
RESULT = expression_1 + expression_2
```

Subtraction

Subtraction is indicated with the minus sign (–):

```
RESULT = expression_1 - expression_2
```

Multiplication

Multiplication is indicated with the asterisk (*):

```
RESULT = expression_1 * expression_2
```

Division

Division is indicated with the slash (/):

```
RESULT = expression_1 / expression_2
```

A backslash (\) is used for integer division:

```
RESULT = expression_1 \ expression_2
```

Exponentiation

Exponentiation is indicated with the caret (^):

```
RESULT = expression_1 ^ expression_2
```

Extended math functions

ABS (expression)

Returns the absolute value of expression. The degree of precision corresponds to the type declaration for the variables used in the expression.

ATN (expression)

The angle of the arctangent is calculated and returned (in radians) in single-precision. If *QBasic* was called with the [/D] parameter, the calculation is performed in double-precision.

COS (expression)

The cosine of expression is calculated and returned in radians in single-precision. If *QBasic* was called with the [/D] parameter, the calculation is performed in double-precision.

CVSMBF *and* CVSMBF

Converts data that was compressed with MKD$, MKI$ or MKS$ to normal numerical format.

This function is only effective when you use it on strings preprocessed using the MKD$, MKI$ or MKS$ functions. If other strings are used, their contents are viewed as compressed numerical data and are improperly converted.

CVDMBF returns a double-precision (8-bytes) result.

CVSMBF returns a single-precision (4-bytes) result.

EXP (expression)

The constant e is raised to the power of expression and the value is returned in single-precision. If *QuickBASIC* was called with the [/D] parameter, the calculation is performed in double-precision.

LOG (expression)

Returns the natural logarithm of the expression in single-precision. If *QBasic* was called with the [/D] parameter, the calculation is performed in double-precision. The expression must be greater than zero.

MKSMBF$ *and* MKDMBF$

Converts a numerical expression into a string for compressed storage in random access files.

MKDMBF$ converts a double-precision value into an 8-byte string.

MKSMBF$ converts a single-precision value into a 4-byte string.

 The data you compress using MKSMBF$ or MKDMBF$ cannot be stored in sequential files because the bit pattern of a byte could correspond to a separator or the EOF marker.

SIN (expression)

The sine of expression in radians is calculated and returned (in radians) in single-precision. If *QBasic* was called with the [/D] parameter, the calculation is performed in double-precision.

SQR (expression)

Returns the square root of expression in single-precision. If *QBasic* was called with the [/D] parameter, the calculation is performed in double-precision. The expression must be greater than or equal to zero.

TAN (expression)

The tangent of expression in radians is calculated and returned in single-precision. If *QBasic* was called with the [/D] parameter, the calculation is performed in double-precision.

Appendix B: Programming Errors

The following are examples of common errors and their solutions:

Error 1

You want to write a word on the screen using the `PRINT` statement. However, `PRINT` outputs a 0 instead of the desired word.

Solution

You forgot the quotation marks. If you want to output something unchanged and without any calculations on the screen, it must be placed between quotation marks.

Error 2

The `PRINT` statement does not output the value of the variable, but the variable names.

Solution

You accidentally included quotation marks. *QBasic* outputs what follows without any change on the screen. Remove the quotation marks.

Error 3

You wrote a program which obtains input with the `INPUT` statement. However, when you type something at the prompt, *QBasic* displays a "Redo from start?" error message.

Solution

When you use the INPUT statement, a variable must be indicated to accept this entry. In your case, this is a numeric variable that can only store numbers. You enter a string (character string) instead of a number. Either you forgot the $ character on the variable name or your entry contains letters and special characters.

Error 4

You want to use a variable but *QBasic* responds with a "Expected: Expression" error message, although the line appears to be correct.

Solution

You accidentally used a statement or a reserved word as a variable name. Use another variable name. Refer to Appendix D for a list of *QBasic* statements and reserved keywords.

Error 5

You receive a "Type mismatch" error message.

Solution

This error occurs if you confuse or equate the numeric variables with string variables. Numeric variables can only store values from other numeric variables or the results of calculations. String variables can only accept character strings (in quotation marks) or the contents of other string variables.

For example, the following assignments are not allowed:

```
Input = "Hello" (Left numeric, right string)
Input$ = 4 (Left string, right numeric)
Input$ = Myinput (Left string, right numeric)
```

However, *QBasic* has statements to convert string variables into numeric variables and visa versa. The VAL statement converts a string into a number and STR$ converts a number into a string. The following example lines show the various possibilities:

```
Text$ = "12345"
Number = VAL(Text$)
PRINT number
Text$ = STR$(number)
PRINT Text$
```

Error 6

You wrote a program which starts and executes successfully but cannot stop.

Solution

Press the [Ctrl] + [Pause] keys for *QBasic* to stop the program. The last line executed is highlighted.

Before starting this type of program, make the necessary changes so that it ends in the normal way.

Error 7

You receive a "NEXT without FOR" error message.

Solution

This error message is the result of several errors. One common error is a mistyped variable name. For example, FOR I = 1 TO 100 requires a NEXT I and not a NEXT J.

If you used a FOR...NEXT statement in a nested loop, make certain that the loop started last is the first to end. The following nested loop is not correct:

```
FOR I = 1 TO 10
FOR J = 1 TO 10
PRINT I,J
NEXT I : REM NEXT J is correct for this line
NEXT J : REM NEXT I is correct for this line
```

Error 8

You receive a "RETURN without GOSUB" error message.

Solution

When *QBasic* encounters the RETURN statement, it wants to return to the line where the corresponding GOSUB was located. In this example *QBasic* has encountered a RETURN without a corresponding GOSUB statement. Most likely you forgot the GOSUB.

Another possibility is if you have a main program which calls a subroutine, however the main program does not end with the END statement and *QBasic* mistakenly encounters the subroutine somewhere. This error occurs in the following program:

```
REM This is the main-program
FOR I = 1 TO 100
GOSUB Subroutine
NEXT I
Subroutine:
REM Subroutine
PRINT I
RETURN
```

Insert the following line behind NEXT I and before the beginning of the subroutine:

```
END
```

Error 9

You try starting one of the graphic programs from Chapter 8 but *QBasic* always displays an "Illegal Function Call" error message.

Solution

This error message has two common sources. The most likely is that you did not indicate the correct information corresponding to your graphics adapter.

The second possibility is that your PC has a Hercules graphics card and you did not run the necessary utility program. You must exit *QBasic*, start the MSHERC.COM utility program and reload *QBasic*. Then you can start your graphics program.

These are some of the most common errors that beginning users encounter in *QBasic*. In the next section we'll list and discuss the *QBasic* error messages.

Invalid Statements and Functions

If you have been using another version of BASIC, such as GW-BASIC or PC-BASIC, you may have tried using certain statements and functions that *QBasic* cannot accept. These statements and functions include the following:

AUTO	CONT	DEF USR	DELETE	EDIT
LIST	LLIST	LOAD	MERGE	USR
MOTOR	NEW	RENUM	SAVE	

You'll receive a "Syntax error" error message when you use these statements and functions in your programs.

Appendix C: QBasic Error Messages

Array already dimensioned

In most cases this error is the result of using more than one DIM statement for the same array.

Bad file mode

You tried to use a file in a way that does not correspond with its mode. In other words, you tried to use PUT # or GET # on a sequential file or to read something from the printer.

Bad file name

The filename used has illegal characters or has too many characters. See the MS-DOS manual for valid characters or shorten the name.

Bad file name or number

You tried to access a file that was not opened with OPEN, the file number lies outside the range specified at initialization or the maximum number of files is already open.

Bad record number

The specified record number is either zero or negative.

Block IF without END IF

You did not include a corresponding END IF in a block construction.

Communication-buffer overflow

The receive buffer for the COM interface has exceeded its capacity. Either set a larger buffer with /C: buffer when calling *QBasic*, select a lower baud rate if the data cannot be processed fast enough or use ON ERROR GOTO.

Device fault

The addressed device does not exist. Check the call.

Device I/O error

An error occurred during output to the diskette or printer. It is possible that the floppy diskette is not formatted, is write-protected or cannot be written to for some other reason.

If this error occurs with a hard drive, there can be a problem with the drive itself.

For a printer, either the printer device is not turned on (is not online) or sent an error code that cannot be interpreted. Check the printer device.

Device timeout

The expected answer was not received from a peripheral device within the specified time. Make certain that the device is present and switched on. For COM operations you can specify longer delay times for CS time, DS time and CD time.

You can also trap the error with ON ERROR GOTO and IF ERR=24 THEN RESUME. This generates an infinite loop at worst.

Device unavailable

An attempt was made to access a nonexistent device with OPEN.

Direct statement in file

A statement without a line number was discovered while loading a file. The loading process is terminated. Check the program and insert line numbers as needed.

Disk full

Your disk is full. Insert a new disk or delete unneeded files.

Disk not ready

You did not close the disk drive door or did not insert a floppy diskette into the drive.

Disk-media error

The disk controller has discovered irregularities during data transfer. There can be several reasons for this:

- There is something physically wrong with the diskette.

- The read/write head cannot be positioned correctly.

- The diskette contains defective sectors.

- The read/write head is dirty.

Check the disk with CHKDSK.COM and copy the files to another disk. If you can't find the reason for the problem, see your dealer to have the drive(s) checked.

Division by zero

You attempted to divide a value by 0. Check the value before the division to see if it is zero.

Duplicate definition

An array was redefined with DIM or an array being used with default dimensioning was redimensioned with DIM.

It's also possible that OPTION BASE was used after arrays were referenced. To redimension an array, it must first be deleted with ERASE.

OPTION BASE must be used at the beginning of the program before all DIMs.

Duplicate label

You assigned the same label in two program lines. You cannot use the same label more than once in a module.

FIELD overflow

You tried to make the field larger than the record length specified in OPEN. Check the specified variable lengths or the LEN=rec_len parameter.

File already exists

When you change the name of a file with NAME, you gave the specification of an existing file as new_filespec. Choose a different name.

File already open

You tried to use a file number that is currently in use in another OPEN command. Choose a different file number or close the other file. The same error is printed if you try to KILL an open file or change its name with NAME. In these cases the file must first be closed.

File not found

The file addressed cannot be found. Check the drive, path, filename and extension.

FOR without NEXT

There is no NEXT for the FOR to be executed or loops are not nested correctly. (For more information read Error 7 in the Programming Errors section.)

Illegal function call

This error has many potential sources:

- The record number for GET#/PUT# for a random access file is 0 or negative.

- USR command without previous DEF USR.

- The value of a mathematical operation was illegal.

- An illegal parameter was passed to a function.

- • You tried to index an array with a negative number.

For more information read Error 9 in the Programming Errors section.

Illegal in direct mode

You tried to execute a statement in the Immediate window that can only be used in a program.

Input past end of file

You tried to read past the end of a sequential file. Use EOF to check for the end of the file.

Internal error

An error occurred within the interpreter that was the fault of the interpreter.

Label not defined

You did not include a label line in your program, although you did reference one in a GOSUB or GOTO.

NEXT without FOR

During program execution a NEXT is discovered that was not preceded by a FOR. This error usually occurs in nested FOR...NEXT loops from which FOR was deleted. (For more information read Error 7 in the Programming Errors section.)

No RESUME

After an ON ERROR GOTO, the interpreter discovered your error-handling routine did not contain a RESUME.

Out of DATA

READ attempted to read more data than was available in DATA statements. Check the DATA lines. Also, RESTORE could have been specified with an incorrect line.

Out of memory

The program is so large that there is not enough memory for the variables and stack.

A second possibility is that the instructions could be nested too deeply or are too complex. This usually is a sign that you have too many `FOR...NEXT` statements, `WHILE...WEND` statements or `GOSUB...RETURN` statements open at one time.

Make certain that subroutines are not exited using `GOTO`, that `FOR...NEXT` and `WHILE...WEND` loops are terminated and the calculations and expressions are as simple as possible.

Out of paper

The printer sent an "out of paper" error code.

Out of string space

String memory will overflow if too many string operations and not enough *garbage collections* are used. Garbage collection is a routine that searches memory for unnecessary `DATA` lines or program segments.

Keep string operations to a minimum and execute garbage collections often with `FRE ("")`.

Overflow

The result of a calculation is too large. Check the arguments.

Path not found

The path specified for a file access is not correct.

Path/File access error

The given path/file specification contains an error.

Permission denied

It was found during file output that the diskette is write-protected. Remove the write-protect tab or use another diskette.

Redo from start

You used the wrong type of data when answering an INPUT statement. Retype the answer in the correct format.

Rename across disks

You specified different drives in the file specifications for renaming.

RESUME without ERROR

A RESUME was encountered in the program but an error did not occur. Check the routine.

RETURN without GOSUB

The interpreter encountered a RETURN without first having executed a GOSUB. This error usually occurs in nested GOSUB/RETURN sequences. (For more information read Error 8 in the Programming Errors section.)

Statement unrecognizable

This error usually occurs when you incorrectly type a *QBasic* statement.

String formula too complex

The string operation you tried to perform is too complex for the interpreter. Divide the operation into several smaller operations.

String variable required

You did not include an argument when using a string variable.

Subscript out of range

You attempted to address an array element that is either beyond the dimension set with `DIM` or less than the lower index boundary set by `OPTION BASE`. Check the indices.

Syntax error

The interpreter cannot identify the statement or function that it is supposed to execute. You either entered the keyword incorrectly, entered an illegal parameter, forgot special characters like parentheses, commas or semicolons or entered too many characters in a program line.

Too many files

There is not enough room in the directory on the disk to store the entry for the file. Use a different diskette or subdirectory.

Type mismatch

The variable types used in a string or mathematical operation do not match. Check the variable types. (For more information read Error 5 in the Programming Errors section.)

WEND without WHILE

A `WEND` was encountered without a `WHILE` having been executed.

WHILE without WEND

A `WHILE` occurred in the program without a corresponding `WEND`.

Appendix D: Customizing The Screen

One of the *QBasic* menus we haven't discussed yet in great detail is the **Options** menu. Press the [Alt] + [O] key combination to open the **Options** menu.

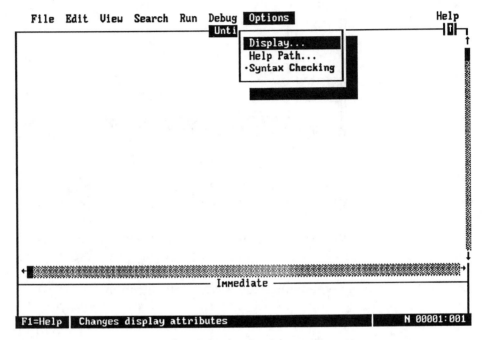

The QBasic Options menu

Display... command

Selecting the **Display...** command lets you choose foreground (font) and background color (screen).

You can also switch the scroll bar on and off and to set the distance between the tabs.

Press the [D] key to open the **Display...** command dialog box:

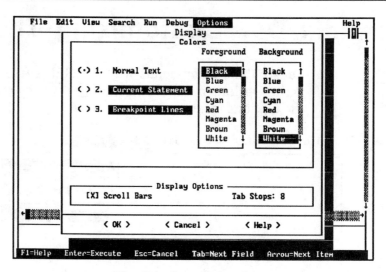

The Display dialog box

For example, if you want to change the foreground, press the [Tab] key until the cursor is blinking in the **Foreground** selection box.

Then use the [↑] and [↓] direction keys to select the desired color. Notice that the color of the Normal Text radio button changes as you scroll through the **Foreground** selection box. Press the [Enter] key when you have made your selection.

Follow these same steps if you want to change the color of the View window. Press the [Tab] key to move the cursor to the **Background** selection box. Use the [↑] and [↓] direction keys to select the desired color. Press the [Enter] key when you have made your selection.

You can also change the color of the breakpoint lines in the **Display...** command dialog box.

Press the [Tab] key to move the cursor to the **Breakpoint Lines** radio button. Then press [Tab] again to move the cursor to the **Foreground** or **Background** selection box.

If you're not using a mouse, you can remove the scroll bars from the View window by moving the cursor to the **Display Options** check box and **Scroll Bars**:

```
┌─────────────────────────────────────────────────────┐
│ ┌────────────────────Display Options───────────────┐ │
│ │   [X] Scroll Bars         Tab Stops:  8           │ │
│ │                                                   │ │
│ └───────────────────────────────────────────────────┘ │
└─────────────────────────────────────────────────────┘
```

Press the ⊥ direction key to toggle the **Scroll Bars** option off:

```
┌─────────────────────────────────────────────────────┐
│ ┌────────────────────Display Options───────────────┐ │
│ │   [ ] Scroll Bars         Tab Stops:  8           │ │
│ │                                                   │ │
│ └───────────────────────────────────────────────────┘ │
└─────────────────────────────────────────────────────┘
```

Changing tab settings

You'll usually use the (Spacebar) to indent a few spaces in a program line. However, you may also need to use the (Tab) key; especially in longer programs.

The normal tab setting in *QBasic* is 8 spaces. You can change the tab setting in the **Display...** command of the **Options** menu.

Press the (Tab) key to move the cursor to the **Tab Stops:** option in **Display Options** check box. Type in the new number for the tab setting and press the (Enter) key.

Specifying a path for Help

Use the **Help Path...** command to specify the path for the directory containing the QBASIC.HLP file.

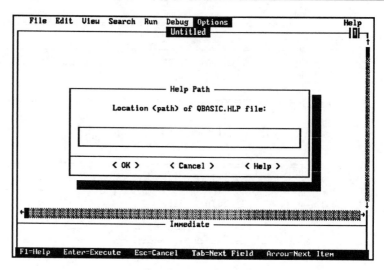

The Help Path dialog box

You do not need to change this setting if you entered the information with the DOS PATH environment variable in DOS or if QBASIC.HLP is in the current directory.

Appendix E: QBasic Keywords

The following is a list of the *QBasic* keywords. These are names reserved for statements and functions used by *QBasic*.

Therefore, you cannot use these words for variable names or other names when writing your BASIC program.

ACCESS	CLS	DRAW	GOTO
ALIAS	COLOR	ELSE	HEX$
AND	COM	ELSEIF	IF
ANY	COMMAND$	END	IMP
APPEND	COMMON	ENDIF	INKEY$
AS	CONST	ENVIRON	INP
ASC	COS	ENVIRON$	INPUT
ATN	CSNG	EOF	INPUT$
BASE	CSRLIN	EQV	INSTR
BEEP	CVD	ERASE	INT
BINARY	CVDMBF	ERDEV	INTEGER
BLOAD	CVI	ERDEV$	IOCTL
BSAVE	CVL	ERL	IOCTL$
BYVAL	CVS	ERR	IS
CALL	CVSMBF	ERROR	KEY
CALLS	DATA	EXIT	KILL
CASE	DATE$	EXP	LBOUND
CDBL	DECLARE	FIELD	LCASE$
CDECL	DEF	FILEATTR	LEFT$
CHAIN	DEFDBL	FILES	LEN
CHDIR	DEFINT	FIX	LET
CHR$	DEFLNG	FOR	LINE
CINT	DEFSNG	FRE	LIST
CIRCLE	DEFSTR	FREEFILE	LOC
CLEAR	DIM	FUNCTION	LOCAL
CLNG	DO	GET	LOCATE
CLOSE	DOUBLE	GOSUB	LOCK

LOF	PMAP	SLEEP	VARSEG
LOG	POINT	SOUND	VIEW
LONG	POKE	SPACE$	WAIT
LOOP	POS	SPC	WEND
LPOS	PRESET	SQR	WHILE
LPRINT	PRINT	STATIC	WIDTH
LSET	PSET	STEP	WINDOW
LTRIM$	PUT	STICK	WRITE
MID$	RANDOM	STOP	XOR
MKD$	RANDOMIZE	STR$	
MKDIR	READ	STRIG	
MKDMBF$	READIM	STRING	
MKI$	REM	STRING$	
MKL$	RESET	SUB	
MKS$	RESTORE	SWAP	
MKSMBF$	RESUME	SYSTEM	
MOD	RETURN	TAB	
NAME	RIGHT$	TAN	
NEW	RMDIR	THEN	
NEXT	RND	TIME$	
NOT	RSET	TIMER	
OCT$	RTRIM$	TO	
OFF	RUN	TROFF	
ON	SADD	TRON	
OPEN	SCREEN	TYPE	
OPTION	SEEK	UBOUND	
OR	SEG	UCASE$	
OUT	SELECT	UNLOCK	
OUTPUT	SETMEM	UNTIL	
PAINT	SGN	USING	
PALETTE	SHARED	USING	
PCOPY	SHELL	USR	
PEEK	SIGNAL	VAL	
PEN	SIN	VARPTR	
PLAY	SINGLE	VARPTR$	

Appendix F: The ASCII Table

Dec	Hex	Char	Dec	Hex	Char	Dec	Hex	Char	Dec	Hex	Char
0	00		32	20		64	40	@	96	60	`
1	01	☻	33	21	!	65	41	A	97	61	a
2	02	●	34	22	"	66	42	B	98	62	b
3	03	♥	35	23	#	67	43	C	99	63	c
4	04	♦	36	24	$	68	44	D	100	64	d
5	05	♣	37	25	%	69	45	E	101	65	e
6	06	¬	38	26	&	70	46	F	102	66	f
7	07	•	39	27	'	71	47	G	103	67	g
8	08	▫	40	28	(	72	48	H	104	68	h
9	09	o	41	29	)	73	49	I	105	69	i
10	0A	j	42	2A	*	74	4A	J	106	6A	j
11	0B	k	43	2B	+	75	4B	K	107	6B	k
12	0C	l	44	2C	,	76	4C	L	108	6C	l
13	0D	m	45	2D	–	77	4D	M	109	6D	m
14	0E	♫	46	2E	.	78	4E	N	110	6E	n
15	0F	☼	47	2F	/	79	4F	O	111	6F	o
16	10	►	48	30	0	80	50	P	112	70	p
17	11	◄	49	31	1	81	51	Q	113	71	q
18	12	↕	50	32	2	82	52	R	114	72	r
19	13	‼	51	33	3	83	53	S	115	73	s
20	14	¶	52	34	4	84	54	T	116	74	t
21	15	§	53	35	5	85	55	U	117	75	u
22	16	▬	54	36	6	86	56	V	118	76	v
23	17	↨	55	37	7	87	57	W	119	77	w
24	18	↑	56	38	8	88	58	X	120	78	x
25	19	↓	57	39	9	89	59	Y	121	79	y
26	1A	→	58	3A	:	90	5A	Z	122	7A	z
27	1B	←	59	3B	;	91	5B	[	123	7B	{
28	1C	∟	60	3C	<	92	5C	\	124	7C		
29	1D	↔	61	3D	=	93	5D	]	125	7D	}
30	1E	▲	62	3E	>	94	5E	^	126	7E	~
31	1F	▼	63	3F	?	95	5F	_	127	7F	⌂

Dec	Hex	Char	Dec	Hex	Char	Dec	Hex	Char	Dec	Hex	Char
128	80	Ç	160	A0	á	192	C0	└	224	E0	α
129	81	ü	161	A1	í	193	C1	┴	225	E1	β
130	82	é	162	A2	ó	194	C2	┬	226	E2	Γ
131	83	â	163	A3	ú	195	C3	├	227	E3	π
132	84	ä	164	A4	ñ	196	C4	─	228	E4	Σ
133	85	à	165	A5	Ñ	197	C5	┼	229	E5	σ
134	86	å	166	A6	ª	198	C6	╞	230	E6	μ
135	87	ç	167	A7	º	199	C7	╟	231	E7	τ
136	88	ê	168	A8	¿	200	C8	╚	232	E8	Φ
137	89	ë	169	A9	⌐	201	C9	╔	233	E9	Θ
138	8A	è	170	AA	¬	202	CA	╩	234	EA	Ω
139	8B	ï	171	AB	½	203	CB	╦	235	EB	δ
140	8C	î	172	AC	¼	204	CC	╠	236	EC	∞
141	8D	ì	173	AD	¡	205	CD	=	237	ED	Ø
142	8E	Ä	174	AE	«	206	CE	╬	238	EE	∈
143	8F	Å	175	AF	»	207	CF	╧	239	EF	∩
144	90	É	176	B0	░	208	D0	╨	240	F0	≡
145	91	æ	177	B1	▒	209	D1	╤	241	F1	±
146	92	Æ	178	B2	▓	210	D2	╥	242	F2	≥
147	93	ô	179	B3	│	211	D3	╙	243	F3	≤
148	94	ö	180	B4	┤	212	D4	╘	244	F4	⌠
149	95	ò	181	B5	╡	213	D5	╒	245	F5	⌡
150	96	û	182	B6	╢	214	D6	╓	246	F6	÷
151	97	ù	183	B7	╖	215	D7	╫	247	F7	≈
152	98	ÿ	184	B8	╕	216	D8	╪	248	F8	°
153	99	Ö	185	B9	╣	217	D9	┘	249	F9	•
154	9A	Ü	186	BA	║	218	DA	┌	250	FA	·
155	9B	¢	187	BB	╗	219	DB	█	251	FB	√
156	9C	£	188	BC	╝	220	DC	▄	252	FC	ⁿ
157	9D	¥	189	BD	╜	221	DD	▌	253	FD	²
158	9E	₧	190	BE	╛	222	DE	▐	254	FE	■
159	9F	ƒ	191	BF	┐	223	DF	▀	255	FF	

Index

Companion Disk

For your convenience, the source codes and data files described in this book are available on a 3-1/2" or 5-1/4" IBM format floppy diskette. You should order the companion diskette if you want the programs, but don't want to type them in from the listings in the book.

All programs on the diskette has been fully tested. You can change the programs to suit your particular needs. The companion diskette is available for $14.95 + $2.00 for postage and handling within the U.S.A. ($5.00 for foreign orders).

When ordering, please give diskette preference, your name and shipping address. Enclose a check, money order or credit card information. Mail your order to:

5370 52nd Street S.E.,
Grand Rapids, MI 49512

Or for fast service, call **616/698-0330**

Order Toll Free 1-800-451-4319

5370 52nd Street SE • Grand Rapids, MI 49512
Phone: (616) 698-0330 • Fax: (616) 698-0325

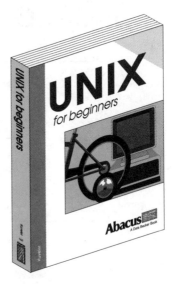

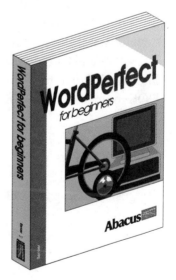

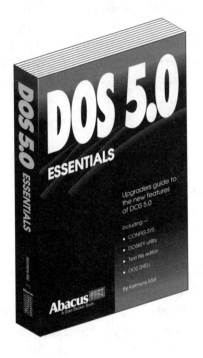

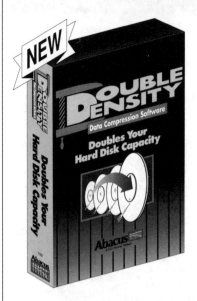

Double Density

Doubles your hard disk storage space!

DoubleDensity is a hard disk doubler for DOS. **DoubleDensity** increases the storage capacity of any hard drive. For example increasing a 40 meg hard drive to 80 meg, or a 200 meg hard drive to a 400 meg hard drive. At the same time, **DoubleDensity** increases the speed of read accesses on faster computers.

DoubleDensity does not require any additional hardware purchases. Thanks to the fully automatic installation program anyone can install **DoubleDensity** quickly and easily. You don't even need to open the PC.

DoubleDensity:

- Increases the storage capacity of your hard drive up to twice its original capacity
- Increase the speed of read accesses of 386's and higher
- Is easy to install because installation is fully automatic
- Offers continued availability of all DOS commands such as DIR or UNDELETE
- Works with system programs such as SpeedDisk, Compress, DiskDoctor and many cache programs
- Is fully compatible with Windows 3.0 AND 3.1
- Takes up no space in main memory with MS-DOS 5.0
- Provides you with the option of protecting your data with passwords
- Uses approximately 47K and can be loaded into high memory

System requirements:
IBM 100% compatible XT, AT, 386 or 486 (recommend minimum AT 12 MHZ).
Microsoft DOS 3.1 or higher.

Order Item #S152. ISBN 1-55755-152-0. Suggested retail price $79.95.